ST. THOMAS AQUINAS

Philosophical Texts

SELECTED AND TRANSLATED
WITH NOTES
AND AN INTRODUCTION
BY
THOMAS GILBY

THE LABYRINTH PRESS
Durham, North Carolina

ST. THOMAS AQUINAS

Born, Castle of Rocca Secca, Kingdom of Sicily
about 1225
Died, Abbey of Fossa Nova, States of the Church
7 March 1274

First Labyrinth Press Edition 1982

Library of Congress Cataloging in Publication Data

Thomas, Aquinas, Saint, 1225?-1274.
    Philosophical Texts

    Reprint. Originally published: London; New York:
Oxford University Press, 1951.
    Includes index.
    1. Philosophy—Collected works. I. Gilby, Thomas,
1902-   . II. Title.
B765.T52E5   1982   189'.4   82-12638
ISBN 0-939464-06-3

Printed in the United States of America

Preface

ST. THOMAS AQUINAS left nearly one hundred works behind him, some of great size: nine of biblical exegesis, twelve commentaries, some incomplete, on the Aristotelean corpus, eight large systematic works of his own, apart from the long expositions included among the forty-five *opuscula,* numbered in this collection according to the arrangement of Pierre Mandonnet. By their circumstances of composition they may be divided into his prepared lectures, thus his commentary on the *Sentences;* his debates, thus the *Quaestiones Disputatae* or ordinary discussions that were weekly features of his lecturing and the *Quaestiones Quodlibetales* which are the record of his disputations on special occasions; and his own free compositions, which are either systematic studies, such as the *Summa Theologica,* or monographs in response to a demand, such as most of the *opuscula.* Some he wrote down himself, others he dictated, others we owe to a reporter.

As the text references will show, the philosophy of St. Thomas should be sought even in his mystical and biblical works. The major sources can be grouped under five headings. First, the early commentaries on Boethius and the Pseudo-Dionysius composed between 1257 and 1261, namely the *Expositio in librum Boethii de Hebdomadibus, Expositio super librum Boethii de Trinitate,* and *Expositio in Dionysium de Divinis Nominibus.* Secondly, the commentaries on Aristotle composed between 1266 and 1272, notably *in libros de Anima, lectura in librum I* (written up by his secretary), and *expositio in libros II et III; in XII libros Metaphysicorum expositio; in VII libros Physicorum expositio;*

in X libros Ethicorum expositio; *in libros Peri Hermeneias
expositio* (completed to Book II, *lect.* 2 inclusively);
in libros Posteriorum Analyticorum expositio; *in libros
Politicorum expositio* (completed to Book III, *lect.* 6
inclusively). To these may be added *in Librum de
Causis expositio,* a commentary on an extract from the
Elementary Theological Instructions of Proclus, credited
before St. Thomas's days to Aristotle.

In the third place come the three great systematic
treatises, the *Scriptum in IV libros Sententiarum magistri
Petri Lombardi,* written about 1255; the *Summa contra
Gentes* (Book I, 1259; Books III–IV, 1261–3); and
the *Summa Theologica,* started in 1266 and completed
as far as the Third Part, question XC inclusively, in
1273. Fourth come the disputations which often
offer St. Thomas's most developed treatment of a
subject: *de Veritate* (1256–9), *de Potentia* (1265–7),
*de Malo, de Spiritualibus Creaturis, de Anima, de
Virtutibus in communi, de Virtutibus cardinalibus* (all
after 1266 and before 1272). Mandonnet reckons
1259–63 for *de Potentia,* and 1263–8 for *de Malo.*
The twelve groups of *Quaestiones Quodlibetales*
were probably reported at various dates between 1265
and 1272.

The fifth heading covers the *opuscula*; the authenticity
of thirty-one of these is generally accepted, including
the *Compendium Theologiae ad fratrem Reginaldum
socium suum carissimum, de Unitate Intellectus contra
Averroistas Parisienses, de Perfectione Vitae Spiritualis,
de Regimine Judaeorum ad ducissam Brabantiae, de
Aeternitate Mundi contra murmurantes,* and *de Ente et
Essentia ad fratres socios.* The authenticity of the *de
Regimine ad regem Cypri* has been questioned on
internal evidence; Ptolemy of Lucca is certainly the
author from Book II, chap. 5.

The translation is a compromise between a paraphrase and an exact and literal rendering such as will be found in the versions of the *Summa Theologica*, the *Summa contra Gentes*, and the *de Potentia* made by Laurence Shapcote and published by the English Dominicans. Sometimes sentences have been transposed, at other times clauses have been omitted to avoid repetition. St. Thomas is his own best interpreter; consequently cross-references have been preferred to footnotes,[1] and even to parentheses in the original. Terms have been inflected from their sense in parallel passages and occasionally according to the living tradition of his school. Many of the texts are taken from works not yet critically edited.

I gratefully acknowledge the help of David Slattery, Elizabeth Gully, Drostan Maclaren, and Stanislaus Parker in preparing this collection. To Henry St. John and Richard Kehoe it is inscribed with affection.

T. G.

BLACKFRIARS, CAMBRIDGE

1950

---

[1] Cross-references, to other sections of this book by number, are given immediately below the text at the left. Biblical references (in the footnotes) are to the Vulgate: this should be noted particularly with the Psalms, where the numbering from Psalms 10 to 146 in the Vulgate is one less than in the Authorized and other English versions, and 1–4 Kings, which are called 1 and 2 Samuel and 1 and 2 Kings in the English versions.

Contents

Introduction

FEW voluminous writers have been less autobiographical than St. Thomas. An impersonal and self-effacing disposition is suggested but not much more of his character, except that he was singularly free from bad temper in controversy, took an interest in everything, found nothing incongruous in the works of nature, and combined an immense reverence for his predecessors with an originality eased, and perhaps sometimes disguised, by the traditional phrases he adopted. He was, however, a famous figure among his contemporaries and greatly loved, seemingly more by the arts students than the divinity professors. A giant of a man, with a complexion compared to corn, large regular features and a steady gaze, he was lordly yet gentle of bearing; frightened only of thunderstorms. The tales of his absent-mindedness testify to his powers of abstraction: that he was remote and ineffectual is not confirmed by the consultative demands made on him by rulers of Church and State, nor by his interests when he lay dying—a treatise on aqueducts, a commentary on the *Song of Songs*, and a dish of herrings.

He was born in the castle near Aquino commanding the Liri Valley. His family, probably of Lombard origin, was related by service, and probably by marriage, to the Hohenstaufens. His mother, it has been said, was of Norman stock. The influence of his people, though considerable, was uneasy in those marches between the Patrimony of Peter and the Kingdom of Sicily; its allegiance was not to be easily settled in the imbroglios of Papalists, Suabians, and Angevins. He was sent to the neighbouring Abbey of Monte Cassino for his early education. The Benedictine peace seems rarely to have deserted him, though after leaving the monastery for the university his life was to be lived trudging the roads of Europe and busied in the throng of lecture-rooms and courts. He was not to know this cloistral calm again until he returned to die, thirty-four years later, among the monks of an abbey in the hills south-east of the beaches of Anzio.

The University of Naples was about as old as the young undergraduate. Founded in 1224 by the Emperor Frederick II at the meeting-place of Greek, Latin, Saracen, and Norman cultures, and Suabian customs, it was to shine perhaps more with the glint of a State service than with the glow of passion for science, jurisprudence excepted. Yet nearly four centuries later another Dominican Thomas was to come from Naples to startle the conventions in the name of a fresh and candid study of nature. Thomas Campanella, however, was more careless and erratic than his master, and his works were not to become part of the canon.

Though by temper Thomas Aquinas was to be a man of Paris rather than of Naples, or even of Bologna, a philosopher and theologian rather than a lawyer or official; already as an undergraduate he studied scientific method under Martin of Dacia and natural science under Peter of Ireland. Then to the energetic displeasure of his powerful family he joined the Order of Preachers, an association of wandering scholars, Guelph by sympathy, urban-minded, not at all feudal in temper, clerical in status, disinclined to dance attendance on magnates. Neither violence nor allurements from *curia* and courtesan could shift him from his purpose, and after various adventures the Dominicans kept their prize, but sent him out of reach beyond the Alps, first to Paris, probably, and then to Cologne for his professional studies under Albert the Great, a wizard in legend but a dogged experimentalist in fact, whom he was to surpass in power of synthesis, though not in learning.

His teaching career, which began in 1252, falls into four periods—Paris, Rome, Paris again, Naples. Academic politics were factious and suspicious, and papal pressure had to be applied before he was admitted as a Master of Theology by the Faculty of Paris, jealous for its privileges and hostile to the new religious orders. Yet his intellectual work began quietly enough with a commentary in the approved manner on the *Sentences* of Peter Lombard, expositions of Scripture, and of traditional texts of Boethius and the Pseudo-Dionysius. Moreover, he was much occupied with the general organization of studies for his Order. Nevertheless three works of the period presage the change that was to come, the tractate *de Ente et Essentia*, the disputations *de Veritate*, and the start of the *Summa contra Gentes*, addressed to the Muslim and Jewish world.

In 1259 he was called to the papal court, and the ten years that followed were the period of his most massive work, challenging alike the current Platonism of the schools and the new Latin Averroism. He was presently joined by his old master, Albert, and by his friend the Flemish Hellenist William of Moerbeke, who provided him with revised and fresh versions of the texts of Aristotle. His scientific philosophy grew at once more adventurous and confident with the commentaries on the *de Anima*, the *Metaphysics*, and the *Physics*, the disputations *de Anima, de Potentia*, and *de Spiritualibus Creaturis*, the completion of the *Summa contra Gentes*, and the beginning of the *Summa Theologica*. The legacy of credit left by the great Innocent was still unspent, and Thomas enjoyed the confidence of Rome: from this centre he was always to receive understanding and unwavering support, whatever might be the condemnations of provincial authorities for his profanity, novelty, and materialism.

The third period opens with his return to the Priory of the Jacobins at Paris. The current controversies had come to a head. The attack on the friars may be neglected: it was the flood of Averroism that was the threat, the spread of the doctrine that the light of intelligence was not personal to men and that matter lay outside creation and providence, of the suggestion that we could hold by divine faith what is unfounded in reason. Yet Thomas was fighting on two fronts, for behind him the cautious theologians objected to his readiness to engage the Averroists without privilege on their own ground and to his thoroughgoing conclusions that the spiritual soul is primarily the substantial form of the human body, and that creation does not involve a beginning in time. Their objections were to culminate in his censure by the Bishop of Paris three years after his death, a ban afterwards lifted. The two spirited treatises *de Unitate Intellectus contra Averroistas Parisienses* and the *de Aeternitate Mundi contra Murmurantes* are typical of this period, but throughout these controversies he was pushing on with the *Summa Theologica*, conducting the disputations *de Malo*, composing his commentaries on the *Nicomachean Ethics* and the logical works of Aristotle.

Three years later he was back in Italy, directing the studies of his own provincial group, dictating the *Compendium Theologiae* to his secretary, Reginald of Piperno, preaching in the Neapolitan vernacular, treating his students to a gaudy, busied with the troubles of his hot-blooded and tragic family. Then towards the end of 1273 he fell into a trance, and on coming to declared that his writings now seemed to him like so much chaff compared with what he had experienced. Courteous but rather remote, he still continued to work. Early in the following year, on his way to assist at the Council of Lyons, he fell sick and died, not many miles from his birthplace: in the words of an early biographer, *ut cantando moreretur et moriendo cantaret rogatu monachorum Fossae Novae cantica canticorum exponens majoris vi amoris quam morbi ad caelum raptus.*

Hellenism had re-entered the West, bearing with it the stranger learning of Arab schools from Baghdad to Cordova. Aristotle was the Philosopher, Averroes the Commentator, Maimonides a revered guide in divinity. From Avicenna, high and clear, came the first notes of the metaphysical reality of many things and the transcendence of their Creator. In the sudden mingling of wilder strains with patristic theology, Neo-platonic philosophy, Stoic morals, and Roman jurisprudence, one fact was certain. The frontiers were open.

Christian thought henceforth was never to lose the temper of science, nor science the sensibility of matter. Nature was recovered from pledge, invective was replaced by irony, devotion was to be matched with irreverence. What Thomas had done seems to have been appreciated more keenly by his opponents than by many of the orthodox. Whatever its reputation some centuries later Aristoteleanism stood in the thirteenth century for a free and impenitent spirit of rationalism and unfettered investigation, a strong sense of the truth here and now, a dialectic of control, not of escape from the present world: all this had been practised by religious men before, but in future it was to be defended as well. To the great prelates who had administered a world they did not believe in and the lawyers who had run the machinery of a Rome salvaged from the scrapheap of the Caesars were added the clerks of the new universities, humanists more convinced, if less graceful, than the men of the Renaissance.

In the lifetime of St. Thomas his great antagonist, Siger of Brabant, became one of his admirers; after some hesitation the English Dominicans swung over to his side, and Oxford bred some of the greatest of his followers in the generation after his death. Nevertheless, it may appear to the historian of philosophy that his friends have recognized his true stature only within the last few decades. He was canonized, true, declared a Doctor of the Church, and by the sixteenth century his *Summa Theologica* had displaced the *Sentences* as the classical work for scholastic commentary. But while he was now the major authority among Latin theologians, his philosophical thought had become, as it were, tamed. Most of his followers expounded it rabbinically, or treated it as a utility for something else. It was not until after the revival inaugurated by Leo XIII that the grand whiggery was recovered; a system that might be recommended, but not demonstrated, by official reception; the spirit of a patrician, not of a functionary. Many of his present admirers, incidentally, would not claim that they had a system, still less that they belonged to a school, since the sectarianism suggested does not accord with the *philosophia perennis* for which they follow him.

Without distorting their proper natures, St. Thomas sees parts steadily in the whole. The entire universe is all of a piece, the most fugitive phenomenon is not a metaphysical outcast; there are tensions, but not contradictions, in the order of being. This is the background to the universal method of analogy he uses with such effect in his approach to the meaning of the world and its maker. Contrasts are struck for the harmony of extremes in a higher principle, not as a prelude to the rejection of one or the blurring of both. Synthesis, rather than compromise, is the result from such issues as that of the One and the Many in metaphysics, deduction and experiment in scientific method, nature and grace in theology, pleasure and duty in moral philosophy, law and liberty in social philosophy, body and spirit in psychology. Though the refinements and complications of sensibility and empiricism had not then reached their present pitch, and his world was simpler than ours, his vast work is a feat of coherence: there are so many and such various parts, yet all are quickened by the same reasons and values and compose interlacing societies of the sciences free alike from eclecticism and totalitarianism.

The systematic exploration of different branches of knowledge is called science, their arrangement into a unity is the work of wisdom, the knowledge of things by their ultimate causes. There are two wisdoms, he held, natural and supernatural; the acquired knowledge of things in their highest rational causes, and the infused knowledge of things in the revelation of the divine mysteries. The texts that follow are selected to illustrate the former; it is hoped that they may be succeeded by an anthology of his Christian theology, or *sacra doctrina*. The supernatural he preaches is gracious in the ordinary sense of the term; morbidities, violences, and many miracles he would relegate to the preternatural. His theology starts with an examination of the truly scientific status of argument from the premises of revelation, and then successively considers the intimate life of the three blessed persons in the Trinity, the primitive production of man aright in a state of integrity, the lapse into original sin, and the new birth into grace; the activity of the supernatural virtues, with particular reference to the assent of faith, obedience to Church authority, the adultness and heroism of charity; finally the Incarnation and the sacramental economy.

But it is impossible to understand his theology without appreciating the rational foundation on which he built. The distinction of nature and grace is a question that calls for the greatest delicacy of treatment. Certainly the corresponding conditions cannot be separated like different phases of history. Man has always lain under the law of grace, and though this may not require a clearly articulated awareness of the Christian covenant, his state has always been one either of acceptance or rejection of the revelation of God. There never was a purely natural man for St. Thomas; though scientific generalization demands reference to pure types, his abstract and concrete terms, the philosophical deductions, and the statements of a theology based on the *gesta Dei* are often as textually intermingled as men and women in a crowd.

Moreover, he possessed a ranging and communicative mind; ideas in one department are shot through with likenesses from another. Analogy is used, not merely as rhetorical comparison or as a logical method of sampling from particulars in order to frame a general law, but as standing for a complexion of being itself, revealing the kinship in difference of all things and calling for a sympathy rather than a technique. Consequently natural philosophy is written in the theological scene, and humdrum facts are not awkwardly taken along with the highest mystical contemplation. He has no special tone of solemnity, no consciousness of bathos. His teaching on a point is not always best consulted by turning to the appropriate section-heading: biology is likely to appear under law, and the analysis of knowledge under spiritual substances. And for a connected reason he is an

intractable author for an anthologist; he rarely goes in
for passages of fine writing, epigrams are few, and often
these are echoes of Aristotle or Augustine; his mind
works laconically at a level and sustained speed, not in
a series of spurts; the unit of thought is the treatise,
not the phrase; the style is sober, expository, and repeti-
tive; the ideas more exciting than the images and richer
than the vocabulary. Extracts cannot show the close
backing of the whole to every part; they should be
taken more as manifestoes than as complete proofs in
themselves.

Nevertheless, it is possible to perform an excision of
the purely rational organs incorporated in the living
unity, and find oneself then faced with a prospectus of
pure philosophy, coherent, consistent, and as complete
as can be expected; an independent prologomenon to
belief which may be of special, and even urgent, interest
to those who find themselves alien to the official
organization of Christianity. Here also may be associated, if not for agreement then at least for conversation,
not only Christians of different loyalties, but also those
with no religious convictions but who would accept the
reasonable life and are not insensitive to hints that there
may be something more generous beyond it. A philosophical attitude may not be enough for health and happiness or for complete adaptation to reality, but it is
a sound beginning.

This selection is offered in the hope that it will not
be scanned as a set of archaeological fragments, but that
the crabbed words will not be allowed to hide the
ardour and generosity of a mind marked by the dis-
interested curiosity of the Greeks and the practical
good sense of the Romans, and uttering convictions that
may be heard echoing through wider regions and more
lasting periods. Perhaps St. Thomas himself had little

sense of history, at least as we understand the word; certainly he treats his great forerunners as though they were speaking to him then and there. His own writing attempts, not a personal proclamation, but a tracing of the perennial patterns of reality; his debates expose the permanent crises for the human spirit.

The texts themselves are arranged according to the order of subjects in his final systematic work, the *Summa Theologica,* though many are from other places, and have not hitherto been translated into English. The plan begins by broaching the possibility of a rational science, or sciences, able to deal authentically with our environment, and then proceeds to the question of the existence of God, who is the ground of reasonableness, and to the examination of his being and activity. The world itself is seen streaming out of God, wholly dependent by creation and contrived by him in all its distinctions, though the fissures of good and evil running throughout set up a special problem. We are on the frontier between matter and spirit; the treatment of human nature constitutes the philosophical psychology of the *Summa Theologica,* and contains the thesis on the psycho-physical unity of man which was St. Thomas's most dramatic entrance into the play of religious philosophy. In this part may also be placed his analysis of the problem of knowledge and of the limits of human freedom. Then man is seen returning to God as to his home; the moral theory that is developed is founded on scientific humanism. Right activity is considered first in general terms, and afterwards in the details of the four cardinal virtues and their auxiliaries. The good life does not lie in conformity to an artificial scheme however august; the essential rational measures are not civilized mannerisms; friendship is the climax of the code.

The translator's task is to keep the meaning while changing the turn of speech. A
word-for-word version is unsuitable when
putting Latin into the vulgar tongue.

Opusc. xxvii, *Contra Errores Graecorum*, Introduction

I

Science and Wisdom[1]

1. *First run to thy house, and there withdraw thyself, take thy pastime, and do what that hast a mind.*[2] The more pursued the more self-contained it shows itself, that is the prerogative of wisdom. In external works a man relies on assistance from many others, but with contemplation he operates more expertly by dwelling alone. Therefore the text recalls a man to himself, bidding him *first run* to his house and be set on avoiding outside worries before he can be caught up by them. Therefore it is said, *when I go into my house I shall repose with her,*[3] that is with wisdom. The whole mind should be bent on her presence and not wander; consequently the text adds, *there withdraw thyself,* that is having desire concentrated entire. The house being still and the man intent and eager, what next must be done is then set out; *there take thy pastime.*

Notice how aptly contemplating is compared with playing, and because of two characteristics. First, play

---

[1] Distinguish in order to unite. Throughout the analyses runs a singleness of purpose to possess existents in simplicity and richness. The distinction of the various abilities and sciences according to their special abstractions and interests is corrected by the sense of concrete wholes. Analogies penetrate all things and many different notes are combined in the strong and gentle rule of wisdom. There is no hint of violence or of suppression. St. Thomas's most spirited polemic is directed against those of his contemporaries who taught that a religious value could be scientifically improbable, and his chief offence in the eyes of some divines is his insistence on the dignity of what to them are 'profane vanities and secular novelties'.

[2] Ecclus. xxxii. 15.   [3] Wisd. viii. 16.

is delightful, and the contemplation of wisdom brings the greatest joy; *my spirit is sweet above honey*.[1] Second, sports are not means to ends but are sought for their own sake, so also are the delights of wisdom. When a man takes pleasure in thinking about an object he desires and for which he proposes to act, his pleasure is conditional on what in fact may fail or be delayed. Then to the joy supervenes no less a grief, according to the proverb, *laughter shall be mingled with sorrow*.[2] But wisdom holds the cause of its own delight and suffers no anxiety, for there is no waiting for something to arrive; *her conversation hath no bitterness nor her company any tediousness*.[3] Divine wisdom compares its joy with play; *I was delighted every day, playing before him at all times*;[4] and suggests many gazings on a variety of truths.

16, 516, 731, 1003   Opusc. IX, Exposition *de Hebdomadibus*, Prologue

2. Doctrinal instruction is nobler than chant as a method of rousing men to devotion.

94   *Summa Theologica*, 2a–2ae. xci. 2, *ad* 3

3. Song is the leap of mind in the eternal breaking out into sound.

287, 602   Exposition *in Psalmos*, Prologue

4. As dawn is the opening and dusk the close of the ordinary day, so the knowledge of the original being of things in the Word is described as the morning light, while the knowledge of them as they stand in their own natures is described as the evening light.[5] The Word is the source, as it were, from which realities stream,

[1] Ecclus. xxiv. 27.   [2] Prov. iv. 13.
[3] Wisd. viii. 16.   [4] Prov. viii. 30.
[5] St. Augustine, *de Genesi ad litteram*, ii. 8.

flowing into the very being things have within themselves.

65, 312, 516 *Summa Theologica*, 1a. lviii. 6

I. THEORY AND PRACTICE

5. The theoretical and practical casts of mind are not
diverse faculties. For faculties are not diversified by
conditions extraneous to their essential objects; one and
the same faculty of sight apprehends coloured surfaces
whether these be large or small, or human or not.
Whether or not a truth can be directed to a job of work
is quite incidental to purely intellectual apprehension.
The practical reason parts from the theoretical when
what is apprehended is turned to account: the two
differ in their ends,[1] the former is executive, the latter
contemplative.

575, 1080 *Summa Theologica*, 1a. lxxix. 11

6. When findings are desired for their own sake then
the sciences engaged are theoretical, not practical.

41, 612 Commentary, *I Metaphysics, lect.* 3

7. The theoretical sciences are present in their own
right whereas the practical sciences are expected to be
useful. The former are fine and honourable, the latter
merely laudable.

215, 854, 1080 Commentary, *I de Anima, lect.* 1

8. The theoretical sciences are ranked by their certitude, also by the dignity of their subject-matter. Of the
practical sciences, the most valuable is the one that
serves the most far-reaching purpose: hence political
science is set over military science, for the efficiency of
an army is subordinate to the good of the State.

61, 1078 *Summa Theologica*, 1a. i. 5

[1] *de Anima*, 433ᵃ14.

9. Better to build a house than to make a bed.

Commentary, I de Anima, lect. 1

10. The more detailed its application the more successful a practical science will be.

Summa Theologica, 1a. xxii. 3, *ad* 1

11. Practical sciences proceed by building up; theoretical sciences by resolving into components.

106, 1078   *Commentary, I Ethics, lect.* 3

12. For God the whole fullness of intellectual knowledge is contained in one object, namely the divine essence, in which he knows all things. Rational creatures achieve a lower and less simple completeness. What he knows in single simplicity they know in many forms. How a less exalted mind needs more ideas is partly illustrated by the fact that people of lower intelligence need to have things explained to them point by point in detail, while those of stronger mind can grasp more from a few hints.

280   *Summa Theologica,* 1a. lv. 3

13. In contemplation the mind is not at pause but fully active.[1]

136   *Summa Theologica,* 1a. lviii. 1, *sed contra*

14. Yet speculative science awakens the mind to some degree of actuality; not however to its ultimate and complete actuality.

190, 652   *Summa Theologica,* 1a–2ae. iii. 6, *ad* 3

15. Speculation, as the Gloss of Augustine remarks, comes from *speculum,* looking-glass, not from *specula,*

---

[1] *Active* and *productive* are not equivalent terms.

watch-tower.[1] Seeing a thing in a mirror is like seeing cause through effect.

744 *Summa Theologica*, 2a–2ae. clxxx. 3, *ad* 2

16. Contemplation can be delightful both as a function and for its content. The activity itself is congenial to human nature and instinct, and especially when a man thereby holds a thing he loves. Thus seeing is enjoyable itself, and more so when it gazes on the form of the beloved.

1, 374 *Summa Theologica*, 2a–2ae. clxxx. 7

17. Better to light up than merely to shine, to deliver to others contemplated truths than merely to contemplate.[2]

516, 1083 *Summa Theologica*, 2a–2ae. clxxxviii. 6

18. Primarily and directly a science is directed on the general types that are the foundations of its inquiry; secondarily and reflexively, aided by the application of humbler senses which deal with fact, it applies itself to the things in which these formal reasons are embodied. Consequently a scientist employs the concept of a general nature both as an article and as a medium of knowledge.

647, 967 Opusc. xvi, Exposition, *de Trinitate*, v. 2, *ad* 4

19. Contingent events cannot be resolved into pure meanings which are the proper affair of theoretical understanding; they are known in some other way.

308, 659, 1068 Disputations, xv *de Veritate*, 2, *ad* 3

20. The sufficient cause of any particular being cannot

---

[1] St. Thomas's etymologies, often taken from Isidore of Seville, are usually of greater metaphorical than linguistic interest.

[2] From the argument that the perfect life is neither exclusively contemplative nor exclusively active.

be deduced from the common principles of being as being.

307, 969   Commentary, *IV Metaphysics, lect.* 2

21. A singular truth is never produced no matter how many generalities are assembled.[1]

658, 661   Disputations, *de Anima,* 20

22. To appreciate existing human nature we must reckon with the particular physique and mentality of Peter and Martin.

533   *Summa Theologica,* 1a. cxix. 1

23. The intellectual virtues are mental habits through which the soul expresses what is true. They are five in number; the understanding of principles, the science of conclusions, the wisdom of judging by the highest causes involved in a given situation, the prudence of right doing, and the art of right making. Suspicion, which guesses at particular facts, is not included, nor is opinion, which reaches general judgements by conjecture.

548, 852   Commentary, *VI Ethics, lect.* 3

24. A truth may be accepted as evident either in itself or through another truth. What is self-evident is like a first principle; the quality of mind perfecting knowledge at this stage is termed understanding, or sense of principle. What is evident through another truth is not perceived immediately but arrived at by inference. The conclusion may be confined to one department or it may embrace all human learning; in the former case the appropriate habit is termed science, in the latter case wisdom. Scientific habits differ according to the various branches of inquiry, whereas wisdom is single.

106   *Summa Theologica,* 1a–2ae. lvii. 2

[1] A particular, e.g. *a man*; a singular, e.g. *Paul of Tarsus, Peter Abelard.*

25. In the field of human science the argument from authority is weakest.

936, 1096 *Summa Theologica*, 1a. i. 8, *ad* 2

26. What a pity if philosophers, who are expected to be the chief seekers and lovers of truth and to see as much of it as can be seen by man, should decide after all that truth cannot be discovered. How they should then grieve that their studies have been all in vain.

585, 604 Commentary, *IV Metaphysics, lect.* 12

27. Theoretical habits of mind can be called virtues inasmuch as they render a man prompt to consider truth, the right and proper function of mind. But they do not ensure that either they or the mind will be used aright. Just because a man has a scientific training he is not necessarily bent on making good use of it. He is equipped to consider a special province of truth, but when goodwill is absent he may fail to turn his science to human betterment. The right use of speculation is decided by some virtue perfecting the will, such as justice or friendship.

859, 964 *Summa Theologica*, 1a–2ae. lvii. 1

II. DIVISION OF THE SCIENCES

28. A theoretical interest is properly distinguished from a practical interest in that it is bent on a truth considered in itself, not as directed to the doing of something. The purpose of the former is truth which we do not produce; the purpose of the latter is action about something in our capacity to do or to make. The preoccupation of theory is not with driving a trade or with contriving means to ends. Accordingly, the distinction of the theoretical sciences should leave their usefulness out of account.

Keep in mind that not any sort of distinction in objects serves to differentiate the abilities or habits dealing with them, but only those distinctions that are essential to the objects as objects: for instance, a sense-object may happen to be a plant or an animal, but this does not multiply the senses engaged. It is otherwise with the difference between colour and sound. The theoretical sciences therefore should be divided by the different pitch of truths in the very medium of theory.

Now there are two notes in a theoretical truth, its spirituality responding to a non-material faculty, and its necessity responding to a scientific habit. Any object of theory, precisely as such, is free from matter and mutability, and consequently the theoretical sciences are divided according to the degree of their abstraction from matter and motion.

Some objects of theory, however, depend on matter for their existence. These are subdivided into two groups. Some depend on matter both for their being and for their being understood, for they include sensible material in their definition and cannot be understood apart from it, thus the definition of man involves flesh and bones: with such objects natural science is concerned. But others, though dependent on matter for their existence, can be defined and grasped without reference to sensible matter, thus lines and numbers: with such objects mathematical science is concerned.

There are furthermore some objects of theory independent of matter in their being, for either they always exist without matter, thus God and spiritual substances, or they are sometimes in matter and sometimes not, thus substance, quality, ability, actuality, plurality, unity, and so forth. Such objects are engaged by the divine science[1] which by another title is called metaphysics, that is beyond physics, for we who perforce must work from sensible to suprasensible objects must tackle it after physics. It is also described as prime philosophy, for all the other sciences suppose it.

55, 56, 77, 806   Opusc. XVI, Exposition, *de Trinitate*, v. 1[2]

29. Different kinds of evidence in a common object induce diversity of sciences. The same conclusion, for example that the earth is round, may be demonstrated by astronomer and physicist alike; the former, however, uses a mathematical medium abstract from matter, while the latter uses the medium of material processes.

Summa Theologica, 1a. i. 1, *ad* 2

30. Each science has its own appropriate questions, replies, and arguments; and correspondingly its own snares and ignorances.

Commentary, *I Posterior Analytics, lect.* 21

31. The same sort of certitude is not to be expected in all fields of scientific inquiry. The well-disciplined mind will not demand greater certitude than the subject will offer, nor be content with less. To accept mathematical truth on rhetorical persuasions is almost a crime; so also to exact mathematical demonstrations from an orator.

69   Commentary, *I Ethics, lect.* 3

32. Decision about what is possible and what impossible is settled by two calculations, one working from the character of the science concerned, the other from the character of the object under review.

[1] Metaphysics and natural theology, not to be confused with *sacra doctrina*, or the theology of revelation.
[2] Based on Boethius, *Liber quomodo Trinitas unus Deus ac non tres dii.*

As regards the first, bear in mind that when two sciences are engaged, of which one takes the wider and the other a narrower view, their respective conclusions are not counterbalancing but should be rated according to their own systems of reference. Observe one difference between astrophysics and medical science, the former treats decay in terms of distant cosmic conditions, the latter sticks to the pathology of organisms. A similar difference lies between secular wisdom or philosophy which considers and judges by caused causes, and sacred wisdom or theology in which higher and divine causes are the criteria. Also bear in mind that the effects of higher causes cannot be measured by the estimated power of lower causes. When broaching the problem about the possible effects of secondary causes we should allow for the influence both of higher and lower causes. In deciding what is feasible the theologian refers to the former, the philosopher to the latter.

When the judgement is based on the nature of the event under review, then emphatically the reference should be to the proximate causes, which stamp their likeness and modify the remote causes at work. The point may be illustrated from raw material: we do not say with propriety that a subject can be made into something when its matter is remote, for instance that earth can be made into a goblet; but we require the material to be disposed and ready to be formed by one cause, thus gold is potentially the goblet into which it can be fashioned by the processes of a single art.

360   Disputations, 1 *de Potentia*, 4

33. The appropriate course of education will be as follows: the instruction of the young in logical topics to begin with, for logic teaches method for all scientific inquiry; then a training in mathematics, which neither

need experiment nor lie beyond the range of the imagination; thirdly, in physics, where much experimentation is demanded though sensation is not surpassed; fourthly, in moral science, which requires experience and a mind free from passion; finally, in wisdom or theology, which transcends imagination and demands robust understanding.[1]

1091   Commentary, *VI Ethics, lect.* 7

[1] The distribution of the scholastic sciences may be outlined as follows. Since all are directed at real objects, logic stands apart as the study of scientific method and the ordered reflection on purely mental constructions as such, though its activity runs through the other sciences. The first division is between

    { theoretical science and
      practical science (*cf.* 5–27).

By its predominant function a theoretical science may be either

    { particular and experimental or
      general and explanatory.

The former, which may be mingled with the practical sciences, frames laws from facts sufficiently observed and tested, and imposes hypotheses to rationalize the findings and to discover fresh facts and laws. Starting with inductions it ends with provisional deductions, and so verges on the condition of a general and explanatory science, *scientia* in the strict scholastic sense, which demonstrates the particular from the general, and explains details in the light of a universal meaning. This type of science is divided according to the three degrees of abstraction (cf. 28, 55, 56) into

    { natural philosophy,
    { mathematics,
    { metaphysics.

The part of natural philosophy that studies inanimate things is currently termed cosmology, the part that studies animate things is termed psychology and is restricted usually to human animals. Metaphysics has three sections, epistemology or the criticism of knowledge, the general philosophy of being, and natural theology.

The chief practical science is moral philosophy, of which political philosophy is the final part. Yet its premises are theoretical and derived from psychology and metaphysics. Here also may be added the technical sciences and the dialectics of argument.

III. LOGIC AND NATURAL SCIENCE

34. A student should address himself to logic before the other sciences, because it deals with their common procedure.

Commentary, II Metaphysics, lect. 5

35. Mistakes are made on two counts: an argument is either based on error or incorrectly developed.

Disputations, XVII de Veritate, 2

36. Logical theory takes mental categories and establishes the modes of inference; as such it has the status of a strict and demonstrative science. Practical dialectic applies the rules of working with probabilities in various fields of knowledge, and therefore falls short of this status.

Commentary, IV Metaphysics, lect. 4

37. The logician considers, not the existing of things, but the manner of attributing predicates to them.[1]

589, 594, 600   *Commentary, VII Metaphysics, lect.* 17

38. The term *being* can be employed in two senses. It can signify either what is divided into the ten categories of reality[2] or what denotes the truth of propositions.[3] There is this difference between them: in the latter sense anything about which affirmative propositions can be formulated can be regarded as being, even though nothing thereby is posited in reality, thus in

[1] Logical being, *ens rationis*, is what can exist only in the reason, e.g. the negativeness of a proposition, or its implication in premisses. Figures of fiction or fantasy are not examples.

[2] Substance and the nine types of accident, the ten predicaments of Aristotle.

[3] The copula *is* uniting subject and predicate.

the case of negative and privative terms,[1] as when we say, *negation is* the opposite of affirmation, or, *blindness is* in the eye: but in the first sense of the term, that only can be called being which declares an existent; in this sense blindness and so forth are not things.

109, 589   *Opusc.* VIII, *de Ente et Essentia*, 1

39. In every true affirmative proposition subject and predicate, though diverse as thoughts, signify in some way the same thing in reality. This is verified in contingent judgements as well as in necessary judgements. Subject and predicate answer to the diversity of notes; the affirmation states the thing's identity.

606   *Summa Theologica*, 1a. xiii. 12

40. Distinctions drawn by the mind are not necessarily equivalent to distinctions in reality.

190   *Summa Theologica*, 1a. l. 2

41. Theoretical science is about things we desire to know for their own sake. Logical entities are not such objects: they are more like props. Therefore logic is not a major interest in philosophy, though it must be brought in to provide the instruments of speculative thought. Boethius thought logic was rather the method of science than a science itself.

295   *Opusc.* XVI, Exposition, *de Trinitate*, v. 1, *ad* 2

42. To the query whether the little hands of the new-born Christ created the stars, I reply that it is not properly couched, for they are human hands without the power of creation. Nevertheless, because one and the same person dwells in divine and human nature, we

---

[1] Privation, the absence of a note that should be present, or of a due form, e.g. blind man, not mere absence or negation, e.g. featherless man.

do not have to strain the sense to make the sentence mean that he who is this baby with hands is also he who created the stars. The phrase can be paralleled by others used by theologians and liturgies, for example, that the hands that formed us were pierced by nails. Such expressions, however, are better not enlarged on and broadcast. When they are traditional I do not think they need be retracted, unless they be the occasion of scandal or error, in which case their sound sense should be explained. As far as possible in such matters the unsophisticated should not be upset.

Opusc. xxiv, *Declaratio sex Quaestionum ad lectorem Bisuntinum*[1]

43. As a friend[2] you have sought my opinion concerning physical phenomena which appear natural enough though their factors are beyond our apprehension. Some effects result from the dominant elements, for example the gravitation of bodies and the temper of metals, and their origins present little problem. Other physical actions, however, are inexplicable by the theory of elements, for example magnetic attraction and the special therapeutic properties of certain drugs; these, it seems, must be referred to higher principles.

Remember at the outset that a lower active principle may act under the influence of a higher in one of two ways: either the action may proceed from an inherent form impressed on the lower by the higher, as when the moon is lit by the sun; or the action may proceed from the lower, which though set in motion by the higher, is endowed with no form thereby, as when a carpenter uses a saw: he is the principal cause and the saw is merely the instrumental cause in virtue of the motion

[1] Gerard of Besançon.
[2] The soldier to whom the letter is addressed.

he imparts; the skill does not reside in any form or power remaining in the tool after it is laid aside.[1]

Well then, if material elements do share in the actions of higher principles, this must come about in one of these two ways.

The heavenly bodies[2] and purely spiritual substances are the principles of observed phenomena resulting, not from any settled active form in the material bodies concerned, but from the motions these receive from above; the ebb and flow of tides is from the moon's influence, not from the inherent properties of water; similarly enchantments may be produced by demons, and sometimes, I believe, by good spirits. That the shadow of the apostle Peter or the touch of holy relics should heal sickness is through no inherent virtue, but by the application of divine power turning these bodily influences to such an effect.

Clearly every mysterious operation of nature is not preternatural after this fashion. Many are regular and constant, whereas not every saintly relic is endowed with healing power, but only some and then only on occasion; nor are all fetishes harmful, nor does all water ebb and flow. Some mysterious forces seem to belong to all bodies of the same kind, thus every magnet attracts iron. Consequently we are left to suppose that they must result from some intrinsic principle common to all things of that kind. Moreover, preternatural phenomena are not uniform, an evident sign that they

---

[1] Efficient causes are divided into the first cause—which transcends the classification—and secondary causes. Secondary causes are divided into principal causes, which are active by their own proper and stable forms, and instrumental causes, which are active by a transient motion communicated to them.

[2] The argument depends on no special theory of medieval astronomy. These substances may be taken as physical factors outside our immediate environment.

do not derive from an inborn and permanent quality, but from the activation of a superior power; a saw cuts wood on which it is placed only when it is moved by the carpenter. Yet there are some rather mysterious actions of lower bodies that produce constant effects, rhubarb always purges certain humours, for instance; and therefore the inference is that they are elicited by stable powers intrinsic to those bodies.

Such powers are the natural result of forms embodied in such and such matter. The reading of the Platonists is that the principles engaged are bodiless substances, which they call species or ideas, natural forms being the images of these impressed on matter. This, however, fails to meet the situation at two points. First, maker and made are like one another; a physical reality is not merely a form but a compound of form and matter; and so likewise its immediate producer. Secondly, a form existing apart from matter would be unchanging and would regularly act to produce an unvarying form, not a bodily thing that comes to be and afterwards dies away.

117, 359, 516   Opusc. 1, *de Operationibus occultis Naturae ad quemdam militem ultramontanum*

44. On account of the difficulty of fixing any certainty in the flow of phenomena, Plato was driven to postulate that ideas, or substances apart from sensible things, are the objects we can know scientifically and define. Here also other shrewd judges were deceived from not discerning between what is essential and what is incidental. For in our immediate environment there is a contrast between integral things which are compounds, and pure meanings which are forms. The processes of generation and corruption directly attack the former, while the latter are affected only indirectly because of mutations in their subjects: you build this particular house, not house as such.

Now anything can be examined free from non-essential involvements, and therefore the forms and meanings of things, though committed to a changing reality, can be considered as invariable in themselves and ascertainable by scientific definition. Yet natural science is not thereby based on the knowledge of substances existing apart from sensible reality.

When significant forms are considered apart from movement they are also isolated from the conditions of time and place, which are the corollaries of reality individuated by matter having determinate dimensions. It follows that these objects of our scientific knowledge about a changing reality should be studied without reference to determinate matter and its consequences; not, however, without reference to matter in general, for the very notion of substantial form entails the appropriation of matter. What *man* means, the definition from which any anthropological science must start, may be taken without reference to this flesh and these bones, but not without reference to flesh and blood in general. A singular term implies determinate matter, a universal term merely vague matter. The scientific process of natural science abstracts universal from particular, not form from matter.

The resulting abstract meanings can be considered consequently in two ways. First, in themselves, leaving motion and individual matter out of the picture; as such they exist only in the human mind. Secondly, in relation to the changing and material things of which they are the meaning and the principle of evidence, for things are known by their forms. Through unvarying reasons studied in isolation from particular matter, natural science may know changing and material existents outside the mind.

112, 520, 659   Opusc. xvi, Exposition, *de Trinitate*, v. 2

45. Natural things lie midway between God's knowledge and ours. Human science derives from them, and they derive from God's own vision.

Summa Theologica, ia. xiv. 8, *ad* 3

46. What is false to nature is false from every point of view.

604   Disputations, i *de Potentia*, 3, *ad* 4, *i*

IV. NATURAL PHILOSOPHY, MATHEMATICS, AND METAPHYSICS

47. Explanation is of two kinds. One goes to the root of the matter, as in natural science when a sufficient proof is advanced to show that the velocity of astronomical motion is constant. The other is less radical, but lays down an hypothesis and shows that the observed effects are in accord with the supposition, as when astronomy employs a system of eccentrics and epicycles to justify our observations about the motions of the heavenly bodies. It does not carry complete conviction, because another hypothesis might also serve.

77   *Summa Theologica*, ia. xxxii. i, *ad* 2

48. Because we are unacquainted with the inner natures of things we have to make use of their accidental differences to designate their substance; to be two-legged, though not essential, may serve to describe what man is. The situation is not straightforward, for we should previously know what the soul is in itself if we are to discover without trouble what its derived properties are—thus in mathematical theorems the

advantage of previously understanding lines and surfaces. Yet conversely, accidents are a present help in
providing postulates for the definition of essential
natures. If anybody advances a definition that does not
lead him to the properties of a thing, his definition is
fanciful, off the subject, merely a debating point.

107, 517   Commentary, *I de Anima, lect.* 1

49. Though mathematical truths are verified in natural
objects, these latter have about them something outside
mathematics, namely sensible matter. Here physical
science can indicate reasons that mathematics cannot
touch.

647   Opusc. xvi, Exposition, *de Trinitate*, iv. 3

50. The difference between snub-nosed and curvature
is a good example of the difference between physical
and mathematical objects. For an uptilted nose exists
in sensible matter, as do all the objects of natural
science, from men to stones. But the meaning of curvature prescinds from the investing sensible matter; so
does the meaning of mathematical objects, such as
numbers, magnitudes, and figures.

653, 654   Commentary, *I Physics, lect.* 1

51. A blacksmith should be a metallurgist, and a natural
scientist should study the natures of stones and horses as
pure meanings appearing in sensation. Nevertheless,
a blacksmith who does not know how a ploughshare is
used will be incompetent, and a natural scientist without feel for sensible qualities will not do justice to
physical things.

Summa Theologica, 1a. lxxxiv. 8

52. A definition that concentrates on pure form belongs
rather to logic than to natural science. A definition

about material conditions without reference to form could come only from physics, for it takes a physicist to deal with matter like that. Nevertheless a definition covering what is from both, namely matter and form, has a more authentic ring of natural science.

511, 647   Commentary, *I de Anima, lect.* 2

53. Some sciences are intermediate between physics and mathematics. They accept purely mathematical propositions and apply them to sensible matter. In musical theory, for instance, arithmetical reflections on numerical proportions are turned to sound.

423   Commentary, *II Physics, lect.* 3

54. Accidents arrive in the following sequence.[1] First quantity, afterwards quality, then transmutation and change. Hence, quantity can be conceived as investing substance without implying sensible qualities. Its meaning does not depend on sensible but on intelligible matter. When accidents are removed, the naked substance can be grasped only by the mind. The senses cannot reach it. The mathematician deals with such abstractions as quantities and their consequences, namely figures and so forth.

Opusc. xvi, Exposition, *de Trinitate*, v. 3

55. Mathematical demonstrations are analytic and explicate the formal cause, but when, as in the natural sciences, the proof proceeds by outside causes, a peculiarly rational measure is set, namely the discursive process from one object to another. Hence it has been remarked how the ratiocinative process is appropriate to natural science, not exclusively, but as being most strongly emphasized there. In much the same way the didactic process is appropriate to mathematics, for we

[1] Not necessarily chronological.

are said to proceed didactically when our argument is purely deductive.

Mathematics comes midway between physics and metaphysics, and is more certain than either of them. It is more certain than natural science because its reflections are above matter and motion. Natural science should take into account many material factors and physical dispositions, and therefore its reckonings are the more difficult; it must envisage as well things that are moving and inconstant, and therefore its findings are the less fixed. Often it should attempt the proof of things that could be otherwise. The closer it gets to singular cases, as in practical sciences such as medicine, chemistry, and morals, the less certain it becomes owing to the variety and number of the elements that must be allowed for; if one be left out error will creep in.

Mathematical processes also enjoy more certainty than do the processes of metaphysical science, for metaphysical objects are more withdrawn from sensation whence our knowledge starts. Spiritual substances are imperfectly known from sense-evidence; moreover, the general conceptions of being are highly universal and remote from particular events registered by the senses. Mathematical objects, on the other hand, fall under the senses and imagination; therefore the human mind, which takes its knowledges from sense-images, has greater facility in working with them than with substantial essence, potentiality, actuality, and so on. We find mathematical knowledge clearer and more assured than the findings of physical or metaphysical science, indeed even more so than those of practical science.

The processes of metaphysical science are said to be marked with insight, for there most of all is found the fullest understanding. Reasoning differs from understanding as multitude from unity, as time from eternity,

as a circumference from a centre. Reasoning is charac-
teristically busied about many things, but understanding
rests on one simple truth and there covers all the sections.

28, 497, 1053   Opusc. xvi, Exposition, *de Trinitate*, vi. 1,
                  i & ii

56. Let us pause at two periods in knowing, one at the
start and the other at the finish, corresponding respectively with the apprehending and the judging. The
beginning or principle of every scientific inquiry lies
in the senses, and all our intellectual apprehension is
abstracted from their data. The boundary or term,
however, is not so invariable, for sometimes it is reached
in the senses, sometimes in the imagination, sometimes
in the pure reason.

When the properties disclosed in sensibility adequately express the nature of a thing then the judgement of the mind should subscribe to the witness of the
senses. The natural sciences operate at this stage, for
they deal with truths whose existence and meaning
involve sensible matter. Therefore their findings should
be checked by sense-observation and experiment, and
they lapse into error when this empiricism is neglected.

Secondly comes the class of mathematical truths.
Their meaning is independent of sensible matter,
though they exist in it, and judgement about them does
not depend on sense-perception to the same extent. Yet
their definitive meaning does not abstract from matter,
but merely from sensible matter. When sensible conditions are set aside an imaginable residue still remains
and, consequently, mathematical judgements arising at
this stage should square with the data of the imagination.

Lastly there are objects transcending sense and
imagination alike, wholly independent of matter as
regards both their being and their being understood,
and the relevant judgement stays neither in the

senses nor in the imagination. Since we reach metaphysical truths through sensible and imaginable entities
we can say that their origins and principles rise from
them. On the other hand, we should neither deal with
the results according to the appreciation of the senses
and imagination nor mistake their images for the terms
of metaphysical thinking.

627, 630, 647   Opusc. XVI, Exposition, *de Trinitate*, vi. 2

57. The accomplishments of wholly spiritual substances are beyond all the compositions of sense our
minds are able to master. Theoretical research can tell
us that such things exist, but not what are their inner
natures. It is idle to urge that we may yet establish a
theory properly devoted to them though hitherto it has
not been discovered. For so long as we work with the
scientific principles accessible to us, all of which depend
on knowledge acquired from material phenomena, complete spiritual understanding is bound to escape us.

105, 504   III *Contra Gentes*, 41

58. To strive for an end that cannot be secured is
futile, and the hope of satisfaction there is illusory.

III *Contra Gentes*, 44

59. Gradually, and as it were step by step, the old
philosophers advanced to the knowledge of truth. They
floundered at first and mistook bodily things for entire
reality. Those who allowed for movement allowed for
no more than accidental changes, such as rarefaction
and condensation, commingling and separation. On the
supposition that bodily substance is uncaused they
attempted to assign various causes for these accidental
changes—attraction and repulsion, or perhaps a Mind
regulating brute matter.[1]

[1] The reference is to Empedocles and Anaxagoras.

A further advance was made when they discerned between substantial form and matter. They recognized that essential changes take place in bodies with regard to essential forms though they still held that matter was uncreated. These transmutations they attributed to more universal causes, such as geometrical forms or bodiless ideas. But taking into account that matter is limited by form to a special type of being, just as substance is modified by a supervening accident to one determinate mode of existence—man, for instance, by whiteness—we can tell that these opinions were restricted to a sectional reality, namely to this or that kind of thing, and so did not go beyond the departmental efficient causes.

Finally others climbed higher and recognized *being* as such. They considered the cause of things simply speaking, not just the cause of this or that. Whatever is the cause of things considered as beings must be the cause of things with respect to everything that belongs to them in their entirety, not merely with respect to characteristics resulting from their accidental forms, or with respect to their essential types as determined by their substantial forms.

387, 936   *Summa Theologica,* 1a. xliv. 2

60. In meditating on the universal truth of beings, primary philosophy must also scrutinize the general setting of truth.

585, 604   Commentary, *II Metaphysics, lect.* 2

61. Among the arts we observe that one governs another whose end it controls. Medical art rules and commands the technique of applying medicaments and surgical dressings, because health, which is the proper concern of medicine, is the end of the subordinate arts engaged; similarly with regard to the art of politics in

relation to naval construction, or military art in relation
to the cavalry arm and ordnance. Such ruling arts are
termed architectonic; those who work at them are
termed masters and deserve the title of wise. When
they are occupied with special sections that do not
touch human destiny in the main they are called wise
in a qualified sense. The title without qualification
should be reserved to him who envisages the end,
which also is the principle, of the whole universe.

1 *Contra Gentes*, 1

62. One science may be subordinate to another in two
ways. First, as a part, when its special subject is contained in a more general field: plants are included
among natural bodies, and therefore botany is a species
of natural science. Second, as subaltern, when the
higher science provides the postulates of the lower
science yet not its special subject: for instance, the
human body as curable by art, not by nature, is the
special interest of medical science. Thus arithmetic
rules musical theory, and natural science rules medicine,
chemistry, and agricultural science.

Though, in a sense, all scientific subjects are parts of
general reality, which is the proper study of metaphysics, it does not follow that all the sciences are
departments of metaphysics. For they employ their
special methods and examine a part of being in a style
quite their own and different from that of metaphysics.

302, 307, 396   Opusc. xvi, Exposition, *de Trinitate*, v. 1,
ad 5, 6

63. Since the wise man's office is to set things in order
and pass judgement on them, and since lesser affairs
should be measured by greater, he is called wise in any
sphere who studies there the highest causes, like the
architect in comparison with the builder's men who

hew the timber and trim the stones. In the human scene prudence becomes wisdom when all conduct is controlled by the proper end of human living. He then who considers the highest cause of the whole universe, namely God, deserves the title of wise man with least reservation.

1067   *Summa Theologica*, 1a. i. 6

64. What is regulated by the human reason is regulated also by the divine law, but not conversely.

1094   *Summa Theologica*, 1a–2ae. lxiii. 2

65. The higher reason and the lower reason, of which Augustine speaks,[1] are in no wise distinct faculties. For he says that by the former a man is intent on things eternal, contemplating them in themselves and consulting them for his rule of conduct, while by the latter he is intent on things temporal. Now these two, namely eternity and time, are so related that one is the medium in which the other is known. For in the order of discovery, we come to the knowledge of things eternal through things temporal, according to the words of St. Paul, *the things of God are clearly seen, being understood by the things that are made.*[2] On the other hand, in the order of interpretation, we judge of temporal things in the light of eternity and dispose of temporal matters according to eternal laws. The higher and the lower reason, then, are one and the same faculty, distinguished only by different habits and active functions. Wisdom is attributed to the higher reason, scientific knowledge to the lower.

4, 238   *Summa Theologica*, 1a. lxxix. 9

66. Because philosophy arises from awe a philosopher is bound in his way to be a lover of myths and poetic

[1] *de Trinitate*, xii. 4.   [2] Rom. i. 20.

fables. Poets and philosophers are alike in being big with wonder.

632   Commentary, *I Metaphysics, lect.* 3

67. The final joy of man consists in the superlative activity of his supreme power, namely the activity of mind engaged with incomparable truth. Since effect is known through cause, obviously cause in itself is more lucid than effect, though sometimes effects appear more manifest to us. We draw our knowledge of universal and intelligible causes from particular events registered in our sensations. Absolutely speaking, the first causes of things should possess the most and noblest meanings, for they are superlatively real and consequently the truest. Though these first causes of all other realities and truths may appear less evident to us, the most complete happiness open to us in our present life really consists in considering them. The glimpse we catch is lovelier and more sublime than any understanding of lesser things.

99   Opusc. x, *de Causis, lect.* 1

68. When asked what he professed himself to be, Pythagoras was unlike his predecessors and would lay no claim to be a wise man, for to him that appeared presumptuous; he professed to be a philosopher, that is a lover of wisdom.

Commentary, *I Metaphysics, lect.* 3

69. There were wise students among the Greeks who brought in gods in order to hide the truths of divinity under the guise of fables. So also Plato clothed philosophy in mathematics.

256, 496, 648   Commentary, *III Metaphysics, lect.* 11

70. The literal sense is what words stand for, and this

significance may come either from the proper force of
the words themselves, as when I say *a smiling man,* or
from likeness or metaphor, as when I say *a smiling
meadow.* The mystical sense is engaged with the things
signified by the things signified by the words.

287   Commentary, *Galatians, iv, lect.* 7

71. When we assert that the Passover was a sign of
delivery from the land of Egypt, or that circumcision
was a sign of God's covenant with Abraham, we assign
the literal cause.

Summa Theologica, 1a–2ae. cii. 2, *ad* 1

72. The original meaning whereby a word stands for
a thing is its historical or literal sense. The meaning
whereby one thing symbolizes another belongs to the
spiritual sense; it presupposes and is based on the
literal sense.

Summa Theologica, 1a. i. 10

73. History, aetiology, and analogy are grouped under
the literal sense: for history, as Augustine says,[1] simply
relates what happened; aetiology assigns the cause of the
facts; analogy combines different truths; and allegory
alone comes under the spiritual sense.

Summa Theologica, 1a. i. 10, *ad* 2

74. The parabolic sense is contained under the literal.
Words may signify something properly or something
figuratively. The literal sense of a parable is not the
figure itself but the object figured. When the Bible
speaks of God's arm the literal sense is not that he has
such a physical member, but what is signified by it,
namely the might of action.

270   *Summa Theologica,* 1a. i. 10, *ad* 3

[1] *de Utilitate Credendi,* 3.

V. THEOLOGY

75. Some hold that our views about creatures are irrelevant to the truth of faith so long as our religious attitude is correct. They have adopted a thoroughly unsound position.

374, 633   11 *Contra Gentes*, 3

76. A man should remind himself that an object of faith is not scientifically demonstrable lest, presuming to demonstrate what is of faith, he should produce inconclusive reasons and offer occasion for unbelievers to scoff at a faith based on such grounds.

Summa Theologica, 1a. xlvi. 2

77. There are two methods of argument, demonstrative and persuasive. Demonstrative, cogent, and intellectually convincing argument cannot lay hold of the truths of faith, though it may neutralize destructive criticism that would render faith untenable. Persuasive reasoning drawn from probabilities, however, does not weaken the merit of faith, for it implies no attempt to convert faith into sight by resolving what is believed into evident first principles.

47, 105   Opusc. XVI, *de Trinitate*, ii. 1, *ad* 5

78. There is a double canon for the theological truths we profess. Some surpass the ingenuity of the human reason, for instance the Trinity. But others can be attained by the human reason, for instance the existence and unity of God, also similar truths demonstrated in the light of the philosophical reason.

1 *Contra Gentes*, 3

79. I say a double truth about divine things, double, not on the side of God who is single and simple truth,

but on the side of our knowledge which variously responds to the truths of divinity.

1 Contra Gentes, 9

80. Christian theology issues from the light of faith,
philosophy from the natural light of reason. Philosophical truths cannot be opposed to the truths of
faith, they fall short indeed, yet they also admit common analogies; and some moreover are foreshadowings,
for nature is the preface to grace.

Opusc. xvi, Exposition, de Trinitate, ii. 3

81. From bare acquaintance with the commentary of
Averroes it is strange how some have presumed to pro-
nounce that his sentiments are shared by all philosophers,
the western Christian philosophers excepted. It is an
occasion of greater surprise, indeed of indignation, how
any professing Christian can talk so irresponsibly about
his faith as to contend that these westerners do not
accept the doctrine of an unique intelligence because
their religious belief happens to be against it.

Here two mischiefs are at work. First, that the
repugnance of religious faith to such teachings should
be left in doubt. Second, that their irrelevance to the
creed should be alleged. Nor is another assertion less
rash, namely that God himself could not produce a
multitude of intelligences, for that implies a contradiction. More serious is a later statement, 'Rationally
I infer of necessity that intelligence must be numerically
one, but by faith I firmly hold the opposite.' This is
tantamount to holding that belief can be about things
whose contrary can be demonstrated. Since what can
be so demonstrated is bound to be a necessary truth
and its opposite false and impossible, the upshot would
be that faith avows what is false and impossible. This

is intolerable to our ears, for not even God could contrive such a situation.

427, 559   Opusc. VI, *de Unitate Intellectus contra Averroistas*[1]

82. What is natural cannot wholly perish.

441   *Summa Theologica*, 2a–2ae. cxxvi. 1

83. Nature is to blessedness as first to second. Blessedness is grounded on nature. The groundwork is safeguarded in the achievement, and therefore nature is preserved in blessedness, likewise the activity of nature in the act of bliss.

744   *Summa Theologica*, 1a. lxii. 7

84. The divine rights of grace do not abolish the human rights of natural reason.

1047   *Summa Theologica*, 2a–2ae. x. 10

85. Grace and virtue copy the order of nature instituted by divine wisdom.

          Summa Theologica, 2a–2ae. xxxi. 3

86. There are two classes of science: some enlarge on principles evident to the natural light of the reason while others develop principles taken from elsewhere. In this last way Christian theology proceeds from the principles of the high knowledge enjoyed by the blessed. As musical theory accepts principles delivered by mathematics so Christian theology believes principles divinely revealed.

928   *Summa Theologica*, 1a. i. 2

87. From doctrines held by faith the knowledge of other truths can be developed by discourse from principles to conclusion. The truths of faith are the

[1] This pamphlet, directed against the double-truth theory of the Latin Averroists of Paris University—that true in religion can be false in science—is written with unusual temper.

first principles, as it were, of the science of Christian theology, the others are like conclusions. Christian theology is nobler than divine metaphysics for it derives from higher principles.

1033   Opusc. xvi, Exposition, *de Trinitate*, ii. 2

88. I think our hesitation over some of the sayings of the old Greek Fathers comes from two causes. When errors against faith crop up theologians are then put on their guard and write more warily: the ante-Nicene Fathers did not expound the unity of the divine nature so accurately as did the later Fathers; and we may also recall the case of Augustine, an eminent authority, who proceeds more circumspectly about freewill in the books he composed after the rise of Pelagianism than beforehand when he was attacking the Manichees. Moreover, some expressions ring well in Greek but are not so happy in Latin.

Opusc. xxvii, *Contra Errores Graecorum*, Introduction[1]

89. It would scarcely accord with the character of divine goodness were God to keep his knowledge to himself without intimately disclosing himself to others, since to be generous is of the nature of good.

208   Opusc. xiv, Exposition, *de Divinis Nominibus*, i, *lect.* 1

90. Instruction by divine revelation was necessary even concerning truths about God accessible to rational investigation, for otherwise they would have been arrived at only by few, and after a long period, and then mixed with errors; more especially when we consider that man's entire salvation, which is God, depends on such knowledge.

516   *Summa Theologica*, 1a. i. 1

[1] Addressed to Pope Urban IV.

91. Alexander[1] and Averroes alike recognized that man's ultimate happiness does not lie in knowledge acquired by scientific means, but in continuous conjunction with an unearthly substance. Yet, as Aristotle was aware, there seems no other way open at present save the scientific, and so the happiness in our power is qualified and not complete. This goes to show how great minds have been hemmed in. We shall be free of these straits, however, if we suppose that the human soul is immortal and that men can reach perfect happiness after this life, when their understanding will be like that of spirits.

527, 744   III *Contra Gentes*, 48

92. Not merely learning about divine things but also experiencing them—that does not come from mere intellectual acquaintance with the terms of scientific theology, but from loving the things of God and cleaving to them by affection. Fellow-feeling comes from fondness rather than from cognizance, for things understood are in the mind in the mind's own fashion, whereas desire goes out to things as they are in themselves; love would transform us into the very condition of their being. Thus, by the settled bent of his affections, a virtuous man is well apt to judge straightway the affairs of virtue; so also the lover of divine matters divinely catches their gist.

916, 957   Opusc. xiv, Exposition, *de Divinis Nominibus,* ii, *lect.* 4

93. There is a twofold wisdom, according to the two modes of judgement. A man may judge from sympathy, because by virtue he is already inclined that way, or he may proceed by theoretical reasoning, as when a man

[1] Alexander of Aphrodisias.

well instructed in moral science may judge of the virtue
he lacks.

863, 919, 954 *Summa Theologica*, 1a. i. 6, *ad* 3

94. He learns who takes a meaning in the spirit of its
utterance. The Word of God the Father breathes love.
A loving welcome is a condition of learning. *It moves
into holy souls and makes saints and friends of God.*[1]

4, 286, 314 Commentary, *in Joannem, vi, lect.* 5

95. The main effort is directed to yield knowledge
about God, not exclusively as he is in himself but also
as the alpha and omega of things, especially of rational
beings. Consequently this exposition will treat:

first, of God;
second, of the motion of rational creatures into him;[2]
(third, of Christ, who as man is the way of our going
to God).
The first part will be divided into three:
one, the divine nature;
(two, the trinity of persons;)
three, the coming forth of creatures from God.
The first section will be taken under three
headings:
first, whether God exists at all;
second, how he exists, or rather in what
manner he does not exist;
third, his active characteristics, namely his
knowledge, will, and power.
The third section will be taken under three
headings:

[1] Wisd. vii. 27.
[2] The *Prima Pars* and the *Secunda Pars* of the *Summa Theologica*,
corresponding respectively to Chapters II–XI and Chapters XII–
XX of this anthology. Phrases bracketed represent theological
sections omitted.

first, the production and first cause of things;
second, their distinction in general and in
    detail;
third, their preservation and government.
The second part will study:
  first, the destiny and blessedness of man;
  second, morality in human acts, or how man
  can succeed or fail in arriving at this end.

Summa Theologica, 1a. ii & xliv: 1a–2ae. i & vi. Prologues

II

Existence of God[1]

96. Truth is a divine thing, a friend more excellent than any human friend.

Commentary, I Ethics, lect. 6

97. Nobody is blamed for lacking happiness; on the contrary those who lack it and seek it are commended. Yet seemingly a man who has reached no general theological conclusions should be gravely censured for his dullness in failing to perceive the evident signs of God's existence—similarly if from his experience of men he fails to allow for the existence of the soul. Hence the verse in the psalm, *the fool hath said in his heart, there is no God.*[2] One conclusion, however, that can be drawn is that final happiness does not consist in merely rational knowledge about God.

744   III *Contra Gentes*, 38

[1] St. Thomas decides that, for the religious philosopher, the existence of God is neither axiomatic nor a postulate. It is a conclusion to be rigorously proved, though *a priori* demonstration is not to be expected. The arguments are summarized in the famous *quinque viae* which combine in their premisses a judgement of necessity with a judgement of fact. The first approach presupposes the fact of change, which is elucidated by the concepts of potentiality and actuality backed by the principle of contradiction; the others enter more fully and freely into the metaphysical medium of causality. These five ways lead immediately to five different truths under the same name of *God*, but they are drawn together in a subsequent argument when the revelation *I am who am* is set in the philosophy of Pure Act.

[2] Ps. liii. 1 (Vulgate).

I. UNREASONED THEISM

98. The attempt to demonstrate the existence of God seems superfluous to some people, who assert that there can be no debate about a self-evident and indemonstrable truth, the contrary of which is unthinkable.

They are persuaded partly by tradition. From infancy men are accustomed to hear and invoke the name of God. Now custom becomes second nature, especially when its influence has been at work on us from a tender age; doctrines instilled then come to be taken for granted. In addition some confusion between what is evident in itself and what is evident to us should be allowed for.

Others also profess that the attempt to prove the existence of God is useless, but for very different reasons. Impressed by the weakness of the arguments sometimes adduced, they hold that this truth cannot be discovered by the reason. What is needed, they say, is an act of faith in divine revelation.

1 *Contra Gentes*, 10–12

99. Whether God's existence[1] is self-evident. . . . We advance on this point as follows.[2]

[1] *Deum esse*, that God is. The usual sense of *existing* as meaning being established *extra causas*, or as we might say, past undoing, does not apply to God who has no cause. Yet it is easier to speak of his existence than of his is-ness. So *esse* when it stands for ultimate substantial actuality has been translated as *existence* or *existing*. Even in the case of creatures, these terms are too meagre and adventitious to stand for what St. Thomas meant by *esse*; yet they seem preferable to the vaguer *being* or even *actual being*, and to the more pedantic *is-ness*.

[2] An article of the *Summa Theologica* is here set out in full. It shows the typical structure of 1. *Title*, which advances an open question ('Whether, &c.'); 2. *Objections* ('It appears, &c.'); 3. *Sed Contra* ('But on the contrary, &c.'); 4. *Body of the Article* ('I give judgement that, &c.'); 5. *Replies to the objections* ('To the first, &c.').

It appears to be self-evident that God exists. For those truths are self-evident about which our knowledge is innate. Now, as Damascene says,[1] the knowledge that God exists is implanted naturally in all men.

Moreover, those truths are called self-evident which are at once assented to when the meaning of their terms is recognized. When we know the meaning of *whole* and *part* we instantly agree that every whole is greater than any one of its parts. Well then, as soon as we grasp the meaning of this term *God* we are bound to see immediately that his existence is implied. For it signifies that than which nothing greater can be conceived. Now what exists really as well as mentally is greater than what exists merely in our mind. When the term *God* is understood, an object with mental existence is present which must also be credited with existence in reality. Therefore that God exists is a self-evident proposition.[2]

Moreover, the existence of truth is self-evident. The denial that truth exists is an assertion that truth does not exist, and this, if well-founded, is itself a true proposition. If anything be true, then truth must exist. But God is truth. Therefore his existence is self-evident.

But on the contrary: nobody can conceive the opposite of what is self-evident. The denial of God's existence can, however, be entertained by the mind. Therefore his existence is not self-evident.

I give judgement by saying: a truth can be self-evident in two manners, in itself but not to us, or in itself and to us as well. A proposition is self-evident when the predicate is contained in the very notion of the subject. If, therefore, the meaning of both subject and predicate be well recognized the proposition will

[1] *de Fide orthodoxa*, i. 1.
[2] The famous Anselmic argument from the *Proslogion*.

be unanimously admitted, as in the case of the first principles of thought where the terms, such as being, non-being, whole, part, and the like, express hackneyed notions with which everybody is familiar. But to those who are unacquainted with the meaning of its subject and predicate, a proposition, though indeed evident in itself, may not so appear; as Boethius says, some notions are commonplaces and self-evident only to experts, for instance that incorporeal things do not occupy place. I declare then that this proposition, *God exists*, though of itself self-evident—since subject and predicate are identical, for God is his existence, as will be shown hereafter—is nevertheless not self-evident to us, because we do not know what the essence of God is; it requires to be demonstrated by truths more evident to us though less evident in themselves, namely by his effects.

To the first objection: an undifferentiated knowledge that God exists is implanted by nature, for he is the health we instinctively desire, and what we naturally, desire that also we somehow know. But this does not amount to a knowledge of God's existing as such, any more than to know that somebody is approaching is to know Peter, though in fact it is Peter. For there are many who imagine that man's perfect good, or bliss, lies in riches or pleasures or something of the sort.

To the second objection: he who hears this term *God* perchance may not understand it to signify that than which nothing greater can be conceived. Some have thought that God was a body. But granting that everybody accepts the term in this sense, it still does not follow that something existing in reality is entailed, or anything more than an object of mind. Nor can we urge that it must exist in reality, unless we concede that there is in reality a being than which nothing greater can be thought of, and this is not assumed by those who deny the existence of God.

To the third objection: the existence of abstract truth in general is self-evident, but the existence of a primary true thing is not self-evident as far as we are concerned.

179   *Summa Theologica*, 1a. ii. 1

100. Though God is at the spring of natural desire and is the last end in achievement, it does not follow that he comes first in the content of consciousness.

589, 744   Opusc. xvi, Exposition, *de Trinitate*, i. 3, *ad* 4

101. The sun shines from outside us, but the sun of the mind, which is God, lights from within.

Summa Theologica, 1a–2ae. cix. 1, *ad* 2

102. Some have taught that the first object of knowledge even in this life is God himself who is the first truth, and that through him everything else is known.[1] Others have professed what is less obviously unwarranted, that the divine essence, though not in itself the original object of consciousness, is yet the light in which everything is seen. Yet they cannot be supported. To begin with, the light divinely shed within us is the natural light of our intelligence, which is not the first object of knowledge, either as regards its nature, for elaborate analysis is required to know the nature of mind, or as regards its existence, for we do not perceive that we have an intelligence except when we perceive that we are understanding something else. Nobody knows that he is knowing save in knowing something else, and consequently the knowledge of an intelligible object precedes intellectual self-consciousness.

48, 662   Opusc. xvi, *de Trinitate*, i. 3

[1] A doctrine commonly called ontologism.

103. In the light of the first truth we see and discern all things because the light of our mind, whether innate or infused, is naught but the reflection of that truth. The light of our intelligence is not the first object of our understanding but its medium: with still less justification can we claim that God is the first object we know.

650   *Summa Theologica*, 1a. lxxxviii. 3, *ad* 1

104. In replying to the inquiry whether the human spirit knows all things in the eternal exemplars, a distinction should be drawn between the two ways along which one thing may be known in another. First, as in an object which is itself known, as when we see a mirror and also the objects reflected therein. At present our spirit cannot see all things in the divine exemplars in this manner. Secondly, as in the principle of knowledge, as when we say we see things in the rays of the sun. In this manner we must needs grant that the human spirit knows things in the eternal exemplars from which they derive and that our light of intelligence is lit by the uncreated light holding the eternal exemplars.

111, 160, 192, 203   *Summa Theologica*, 1a. lxxxiv. 5

II. DEMONSTRATION AND CAUSALITY

105. There can be two procedures in demonstration: one is through the cause, and is termed a proof for-the-reason-that; this type of argument works from what is prior in reality. The other is through an effect, and is termed a proof inasmuch-as; and this type of argument works from what strikes us first.[1] When an effect is

---

[1] These two procedures are known as demonstration *propter quid* (διότι) and demonstration *quia* (ὅτι).
The modes of proof are divided into
{ induction and
{ deduction.
The former is an argument from the particular to the general,

better known to us than its cause then we proceed through the effect to the knowledge of the cause. From any effect we can demonstrate the proper cause[1] of its being, so long as the effect is more palpable; because if the effect exists the cause must pre-exist, since every effect depends upon its cause. Hence the existence of God in so far as it is not self-evident to us is open to demonstration from those of his effects which are known to us.

55, 181 *Summa Theologica*, 1a. ii. 2

106. In the building up of scientific knowledge the elements and principles are not always present from the beginning. Sometimes we have to reach to principles and intelligible causes from sensible effects. In the completed construction of science, however, the knowledge of effects depends on the knowledge of principles and elements.

666 *Summa Theologica*, 1a. lxxxv. 8, *ad* 1

107. Effect supplies the place of the cause's definition when a cause is demonstrated by an effect. This is noteworthy when we would address ourselves to the existence of God, for in order to prove that something exists, what has to be assumed as the middle term of the proof is the nominal definition, not the real definition, of the thing. The question, what kind of thing is it?

the latter conversely is from the general to the particular. Deduction may be either
{ *a priori* or
{ *a posteriori*.
The former is from cause to effect, the latter from effect to cause. Though not precisely the same, the distinction may be taken here as corresponding to that between *demonstratio propter quid* and *demonstratio quia*.
    [1] i.e. the direct and immediate sustaining antecedent.

follows the question, does it exist? Now the names ascribed to God are drawn from his effects, as will be shown later,[1] and therefore a nominal definition must be used as a middle term in demonstrating his existence.

180, 605 *Summa Theologica*, 1a. ii. 2, *ad* 2

108. Reasoning cannot stretch to a simple form as though to grasp its essence, but only to touch its existence.

199 *Summa Theologica*, 1a. xii. 12, *ad* 1

109. Existence is taken in two senses, signifying either the actuality of being or the propositional affirmation effected by the mind in joining subject and predicate. In the first sense the existence of God can no more be known than his essence; but in the second sense we might be able to know that the statement we formulate, namely that he exists, is true.

38 *Summa Theologica*, 1a. iii. 4, *ad* 2

110. The existence of God and similar truths about him attainable by strict rationalism are not articles of faith, but preambles to them. Faith presupposes natural knowledge, even as grace presupposes nature, and perfection the capacity for it. Nevertheless there is nothing to prevent a man from accepting as an article of belief something that can be scientifically known and demonstrated, though perchance not by him.

929 *Summa Theologica*, 1a. ii. 2, *ad* 1

111. Aristotle enumerates the varieties of causes and reduces them to four kinds.[2]

He observes first that cause means the immanent

---

[1] 264–88.

[2] These four types, with their sub-headings, may be set out as shown overleaf:

material in which a thing comes into being, that is existing within it. He says this in order to stress its difference from a contrary state or a privation, from which something is said to come about but which does not remain in the event, as when something white is produced from something black or non-white. But when a statue is made from bronze, or a cruet from silver, these materials are intrinsic to the product, for statue does not abolish bronze nor cruet silver. Such are causes after the manner of matter.

Intrinsic cause
  material cause
    materia prima, the potential and partial substantial principle in all bodily substances;
    materia secunda, an existing body as a subject of change. Here also may be added causal dispositions and conditions.
  formal cause
    substantial form, the primary actuality of a physical thing;
    accidental form, its supervening determinants.
Extrinsic cause
  efficient cause
    first cause
    secondary cause, or causal cause
      principal cause, causative by its form
      instrumental cause, causative by the motion of a principal cause. Here for convenience may be added such incidental factors as occasions and opportunities
  final cause
    end
      ultimate
      non-ultimate. This distinction corresponds to the distinction above between first and secondary principal causes.
    means

The exemplar cause is the idea or formal cause of the effect in the mind of the maker; as such it is an extrinsic cause.

Secondly, cause means the form or pattern or type of a thing. This is the formal cause, and it effects a thing in two ways; either as its intrinsic form, and this is called its species, or as the extrinsic form to whose likeness it is made, thus the exemplar of a thing is termed its form, which is why Plato said that ideas were forms. The genus and kind of a thing, stated by the definition of its nature, is settled by the form. Therefore the form, which is the meaning of the Aristotelean 'what it was for it to be',[1] is the determinant of what a thing is. For though definition includes the material parts its emphasis is on form.

Thirdly, cause means the first principle of change and rest, and this is the moving or efficient cause.[2] Aristotle speaks of change and rest in the same breath, for natural motion and rest must be resolved into the same cause, as also violent movement and forced repose. He gives two examples, of the counsellor whose advice is the cause of a line of policy, and of the father who is the cause of his child; these touch the two principles of efficient motion, namely, will and natural determinism. In general every maker is the cause of the thing made, and every change-producer the cause of the thing changed. Anything which makes something in any kind of way whatsoever, whether as to substance or accidents, should be classed as an efficient cause. So therefore Aristotle couples maker and changer; the former is the cause of a thing, the latter of its variations.

Fourthly, cause means the end, that for the sake of which something is. For example, health is the cause of going for a walk. The question, why? seeks a cause.

[1] The formula of the essence, ὁ λόγος τοῦ τί ἦν εἶναι, literally translated in medieval Latin, *ratio ipsius quod quid erat esse.*

[2] Unless otherwise qualified, the term *cause* means the efficient cause.

And this includes not only the last end for which the efficient cause acts but also all the means that interpose.

    212, 360, 487, 689   Commentary, *V Metaphysics, lect.* 2

112. There are three kinds of definition. One allots the species and its meaning; this is purely formal, as when a house is explained as a shelter against rain, wind, and sun. Another allots the matter, as when a house is described as a shelter made of brick, stone, and beams. The third includes both form and matter, saying that it is such a shape in such material and also assigning its purpose. The natural philosopher requires all these three notes for a good definition.

    52, 55   Commentary, *I de Anima, lect.* 2

113. Action comes from the efficient cause; longing and desire from the final cause.

        Disputations, xxii *de Veritate,*

114. Every composite thing has an efficient cause, for realities of themselves diverse cannot unite to constitute one single thing save by some cause binding them together.[1]

        Summa Theologica, 1a. iii. 7

115. Whatever belongs to a thing otherwise than of its very nature belongs to it through some efficient cause.

    What is essentially so is the efficient cause of things that are so by sharing.

    181, 435, 1091   ii *Contra Gentes,* 15

116. A proper cause sustains its dependent effect.

    1901   *Summa Theologica,* 1a. civ. 2, *ad* 2

[1] The argument is dealing with partial principles in the depth of being rather than about parts displayed dimensively—though these are not excluded: it is concerned with things not utterly simple rather than with constructions in quantity.

117. An effect depends on its cause just in so far as that is its cause. Note that a cause may be the cause of the coming to be of the effect, yet not directly of its existing. Examples can be taken from artificial and natural processes alike. A builder causes the constructing of a house, but not the enduring construction; that depends on the consistence of the components. Any efficient principle that is not the cause of a natural form as such is the cause of a becoming; it is not the direct cause of the being that results. It stands to reason that with two things of the same species one cannot be the direct cause of the specific form of the other; this would be equivalent to causing its own specific form, for on that head they are identical. Yet one may be the cause of the other's coming to exist in this or that determinate matter, as when one man begets another. In other words, it is the cause of a becoming.

But when an effect derives from a cause of a different nature then the latter may be the cause of the form as such and not merely of its arriving in such material. It will then be the cause of a being and not merely of a becoming. The becoming of a thing must stop when the action of its cause is over, similarly the being of a thing cannot persist when the action of its cause has ceased.

406, 427   *Summa Theologica*, 1a. civ. 1

118. Though the first cause flows more strongly into an effect than does the secondary cause, the effect is not completed without the latter's operation.

324, 359   Disputations, II *de Veritate*, 14, *ad* 5

119. The thesis that natural things are not causes, but that God effects everything by himself alone, is clearly contrary to experience.

360   Disputations, III *de Potentia*, 7

120. Three points of comparison of the first cause with secondary causes: its influence arrives sooner to the effect, goes deeper, and lasts longer.

388   Opusc. x, Exposition, *de Causis, lect.* I

121. It may be argued that God does not exist. For if one of two contraries is unbounded its opposite is altogether ousted. But the word *God* means that he is existing infinite goodness. Were he to exist no evil could remain. But we come across evil in the world. Therefore he does not exist.

Moreover, explanations should be economical.[1] It seems that everything that appears in the world can be accounted for on the supposition that God does not exist. Natural processes can be resolved solely into physical determinism, and design can be resolved solely into the factors of human reason or will. There is no need then to postulate the existence of God.

But on the contrary, God said in person, *I am who am.*[2]

I explain by saying that the existence of God can be proved in five ways. . . .

475   *Summa Theologica,* ia. ii. 3

III. PRIMA VIA, THE ARGUMENT FROM CHANGE

122. The first and most open way is presented by change or motion.[3] It is evident to our senses and certain that in the world some things are in motion.

Whatever is in motion is set in motion by another. For nothing is in motion unless it be potential to that to which it is in motion; whereas a thing sets in motion

---

[1] Ockam's Razor was a truism long before the fourteenth century.

[2] Exod. iii. 14.

[3] Motion, movement, change, *motus,* are synonymous throughout. Note, the argument is not restricted to local motion.

inasmuch as it is actual, because to set in motion is naught else than to bring a thing from potentiality to actuality, and from potentiality a subject cannot be brought except by a being that is actual; actually hot makes potentially hot become actually hot, as when fire changes and alters wood. Now for the same thing to be simultaneously and identically actual and potential is not possible, though it is possible under different respects; what is actually hot cannot simultaneously be potentially hot, though it may be potentially cold. It is impossible, therefore, for a thing both to exert and to suffer motion in the same respect and according to the same motion.

If that which sets in motion is itself in motion then it also must be set in motion by another, and that in its turn by another again. But here we cannot proceed to infinity,[1] otherwise there would be no first mover, and consequently no other mover, seeing that subsequent movers do not initiate motion unless they be moved by a former mover, as stick by hand.[2]

Therefore we are bound to arrive at the first mover set in motion by no other, and this everyone understands to be God.

Summa Theologica, 1a. ii. 3

123. Having indicated that the attempt to prove God's existence is not hopeless from the outset, we proceed now to fix on the arguments of philosophers and theologians alike, beginning with Aristotle who sets off from the concept of change. His argument takes two directions,[3] of which the first is as follows.

Everything in a process of change is set in motion by another. Our senses tell us that things are in motion, the

[1] Cf. 145, 423. [2] *Physics*, 256ᵃ6.
[3] Cf. *Physics*, 241ᵇ24, 257ᵃ33.

sun for instance. Therefore they are set in motion by another. Now this setter-in-motion is either itself in motion or it is not. If not, then we have our conclusion, namely the necessity of inferring a motionless mover which we term God. But if it is itself in motion then it must be set in motion by another. Either we have an infinite series or we arrive at a changeless mover. But we cannot go back infinitely. Therefore we must infer a first changeless mover.

There are two propositions to be proved; first, that everything in motion is set in motion by another; second, that an infinite series of things setting and set in motion is impossible.

1 *Contra Gentes*, 13

124. Since anything set in motion by another is a kind of instrument, all things in motion would be instruments were there no first mover. Furthermore if there were an infinite series of movers and things in motion and no first mover all these infinite movers and things moved would be instruments. Even without expert information one can see something ridiculous in the notion of an instrument that is not moved by a principal: it would be like saying that a saw or axe had been at work in the making of a bunk or chest, but workman none.

145   Opusc. xiii, *Compendium Theologiae*, 3

125. A thing must exist before it can set another in motion. Motioning presupposes being. If that thing in its turn is subject to motion, well then, some principle that sets it in motion must then be presupposed, and so again and again until we arrive at a being that is motionless in itself though the mover of all others.[1]

239, 252   Opusc. x, Exposition, *de Causis, lect.* 18

[1] Not inert, but so actual as to be still.

126. Were a thing in motion to move itself this would come about in one of two ways. Either because it was actively initiating motion and passively receiving motion at the same point, or because it was active at one point and passive at another. The former hypothesis is out of the question since it involves being identically actual and potential. Neither will the second hypothesis meet the situation, for given something actively moving by one part and passively set in motion by another part, it would not be singly and wholly the first active mover. What is wholly and essentially so, is prior to what is partially and indirectly so. Consequently a thing that is an active mover through one of its parts cannot be the first mover, for this must be wholly unmotioned.

245 Opusc. xiii, *Compendium Theologiae*, 4

127. A thing is not subject to motion because it is an agent of motion.

Commentary, *III Physics*, lect. 4

128. The healer has not necessarily been healed himself. What ultimately initiates motion is itself motionless.

Commentary, *VIII Physics*, lect. 9

129. Enduring steadfast, yet changing all things.

Exposition, *in Psalmos*, xxxii. 1

130. All mutables bring us back to a first immutable.

Disputations, xvi *de Veritate*, 2

131. Those who define change as the process from potentiality to actuality without suddenness anticipate too much. For any process is a kind of change and what happens suddenly is temporal, for it is what happens in a moment of time. Time itself is defined in terms of change.

411 Commentary, *III Physics*, lect. 2

132. Note that Plato, who says that movers are in motion,[1] takes the term *motion* in a wider sense than does Aristotle who keeps to its narrowest sense, meaning the actuality still potential of a subject in potentiality, which applies only to quantified and corporeal reality.[2] Whenever Plato speaks of a thing that moves itself not being a body he includes in motion such operations as understanding and thinking. In other contexts Aristotle also adopts this usage, as when he speaks of the first mover moving itself by understanding and willing and loving itself.[3] There is no embarrassment here, for it amounts to the same whether with Plato we arrive at the first thing that moves itself or with Aristotle at the first thing that is altogether motionless.

241, 519   1 *Contra Gentes*, 13

133. The Platonists held that material things do not move themselves, but that spiritual substances alone are self-moving because they can understand and love themselves. They treat all operations as motions. So also does Aristotle in the *de Anima* when he names sensation and understanding as motions.[4] In that context motion means achieved activity. But in the present proof it means the activity of a thing still in a process of becoming, that is not yet out of potentiality. This does not apply to simple realities. The two doctrines do not disagree in sense, but only in phraseology.

Commentary, *VII Physics, lect.* 1

134. Movement received from another is termed passion; its origin, as implying a beginning from one and a terminating in another, is termed action. Take

---

[1] *Phaedrus*, 245ᶜ; *Laws*, 893ᵇ–896ᵇ.   [2] *Physics*, 201ᵃ10.
[3] *De Anima*, 433ᵇ15.   [4] 408ᵇ8.

away the process of motion, and action will still retain the sense of origin.

Summa Theologica, 1a. xli. 1, *ad* 2

135. As meaning the actuality of a thing not yet out of potentiality, motion carries a note of imperfection; as meaning the application of power, motion carries a note of perfection.

344   *Summa Theologica,* 1a. liii. 1, *ad* 2

136. Rest should be contrasted with the start of motion, not with the climax.

13, 252, 747, 821   Commentary, *V Physics, lect.* 9

137. Aristotle was convinced that motion was everlasting, and time likewise. But his arguments [in the eighth book of the *Physics*] are probable and not cogent, except perhaps as disproofs of some early physical theories about the inception of motion.

Commentary, *XII Metaphysics, lect.* 5

138. The most effective proof for God's existence will even allow for the eternity of the world, despite the apparent handicap. For the argument would undoubtedly run more easily on the supposition that there is a start to the world of change. For then there would obviously be a producing cause, for what is new must be made by something else.

411   1 *Contra Gentes,* 13

139. Perfect immortality implies complete immutability: as Augustine says, every change is a kind of death.[1]

Summa Theologica, 1a. l. 5, *ad* 1

[1] *Contra Maximinum,* ii. 12.

140. Immutability is the strength of God.

Summa Theologica, 1a–2ae. lxi. 5

141. Stability is a necessary condition of happiness—as Aristotle remarks, we do not look upon the happy man as a kind of chameleon.[1]

244   III *Contra Gentes*, 48

142. God wakens and causes the motions of things. Therefore is he love and the creator of love in others.

Opusc. xiv, Exposition, *de Divinis Nominibus*, iv, *lect.* 11

IV. SECUNDA VIA, THE ARGUMENT FROM EFFICIENT CAUSALITY

143. The second approach starts from the nature of efficient causality.[2] Among phenomena we discover an order of efficient causes. But we never come across, nor ever shall, anything that is an efficient cause of itself; such a thing would be prior to itself, which is impossible. It is also impossible to go on to infinity with efficient causes, for in an ordered series[3] the first is the cause of the intermediate and the intermediate is the cause of the last. Whether or not the intermediate causes be one or many is irrelevant. Take away the cause and the effect also goes. Therefore if there were not a first among efficient causes—which would be the case in an infinite series—there would be no intermediate causes nor an ultimate effect. This plainly is not the case. A

[1] *Ethics*, 1101ª9. Cf. Commentary, *I Ethic. lect.* 15.

[2] The argument follows the plan of the *prima via*, but deepens to include the being as well as the becoming of the realities about us.

[3] That is a series in essential subordination, or causes depending on another for their causality. The argument abstracts from whether or not a series in accidental subordination, or of events in succession, need ever be closed.

first cause, generally termed God, must therefore be inferred.

117, 394, 425   *Summa Theologica*, 1a. ii. 3

144. The intervening causes may be one or many, but the conclusion is not affected. If they be many, then they are all classed together as possessing the character of being intermediaries. Similarly it makes no difference whether they be limited in number or infinite, for so long as they are intermediate causes they never possess the character of a first cause.

If efficient causes were imagined as stretching to infinity it would follow that all causes would be intermediate. For in general one is bound to say that all parts in any infinite system of magnitude or causality must be middle parts, otherwise one part would be first and another part last; both notions are irreconcilable with the infinite, which excludes every limit, either of beginning or of end.[1]

162, 418   Commentary, *III Metaphysics, lect.* 3

145. An infinite series of efficient causes in essential subordination is impossible. Causes essentially required for the production of a determinate effect cannot consequently be infinitely multiplied, as if a block could be shifted by a crowbar, which in turn is levered by a hand, and so on to infinity.

But an infinite series of causes in accidental subordination is not reputed impossible, so long as all the causes thus multiplied are grouped as one cause and their multiplication is incidental to the causality at work. For instance a blacksmith may work with many hammers because one after another breaks in his hand, but that one particular hammer is used after another

[1] *Metaphysics*, 994^{a}1–^{b}31.

particular one is incidental. Similarly that in begetting a child a man was himself begotten by another man; for he is father as man, not as son. In a genealogy of efficient causes all men have the same status of particular generator. Hence, for such a line to stretch back to infinity is not unthinkable.

419, 423, 492   *Summa Theologica*, 1a. xlvi. 2, *ad* 7

146. Man's natural reason tells him that he is under a higher power because of the deficiencies he feels in himself crying out for care and comfort. Whatever that higher may be, it is what all men term God.

332   *Summa Theologica*, 2a–2ae. lxxxv. 1

V. TERTIA VIA, THE ARGUMENT FROM THE GROUND OF NECESSITY

147. We observe in our environment how things are born and die away; they may or may not exist; to be or not to be—they are open to either alternative. All things cannot be so contingent, for what is able not to be may be reckoned as once a non-being, and were everything like that once there would have been nothing at all. Now were this true, nothing would ever have begun, for what is does not begin to be except because of something which is, and so there would be nothing even now. This is clearly hollow. Therefore all things cannot be might-not-have-beens; among them must be being whose existence is necessary.[1]

Summa Theologica, 1a. ii. 3

148. Necessary reality is always actual; it is never poised between existence and non-existence. It is primary, and were it to disappear nothing would remain.

Commentary, *IX Metaphysics, lect.* 9

[1] The argument derives from Avicenna, *Metaphysics*, II. i. 2, 3.

149. Everything that is a possible-to-be has a cause, since its essence as such is equally uncommitted to the alternatives of existing and not existing. If it be credited with existence, then this must be from some cause. Causality, however, is not an infinite process. Therefore a necessary being is the conclusion. The principle of its necessity is either from outside or not. If not, then the being is inwardly necessary. If necessity comes from without, we must still propose a first being necessary of itself, since we cannot have an endless series of derivatively necessary beings.

1 Contra Gentes, 15

150. Substances are the primary realities. Destroy what is primary and everything else goes as well. Were all substances mortal and none of them everlasting, nothing would be permanent and everything would be transient. This is inconceivable.

Commentary, *XII Metaphysics, lect.* 5

VI. QUARTA VIA, THE ARGUMENT FROM THE DEGREES OF BEING

151. Imaginable objects are congenial to our minds. The notion of growth, like other notions born of quantity and bodies, can be accommodated to spiritual and intellectual things. In bodily quantities greatness is proportionate to seemly perfection; a quantity great in a man would be small in an elephant. Forms are called great when they are perfect. As Augustine remarks, the terms *greater* and *better* amount to the same in things not great by weight.[1]

497   *Summa Theologica*, 1a–2ae. lii. 1

152. Quantity is twofold, dimensive quantity or bulk,

[1] *de Trinitate*, vi. 8.

which is found only in bodily things, and virtual quantity, which is estimated according to perfection of form or nature.

882   *Summa Theologica*, 1a. xlii. 1, *ad* 1

153. The fourth argument is taken from the degrees of reality we discover in things. Some are truer and better and nobler than others, so also with other perfections.[1] But more or less are attributed to different things in proportion as they variously approach something which is the maximum. Hence, there is something truest, and best, and noblest, and in consequence the superlative being, for the greatest truths are the greatest beings. Now the maximum in any order is the cause of all the other realities of that order. Therefore there is a real cause of being and goodness and all perfections whatsoever in everything; and this we term God.

497   *Summa Theologica*, 1a. ii. 3

154. The argument can be gathered from words let fall by Aristotle in the *Metaphysics*.[2] He says that the truest things are also the most real; and again, that there is a superlative truth.[3] One piece of architecture is more sham than another, one more genuine; throughout a comparison is implied with what is true without qualification and most of all. We can go farther and conclude that there is something most real, and this we call God.

1 *Contra Gentes*, 13

155. That there is a universal cause from which all other things go forth into reality can be established on three bases.

[1] The argument applies only to analogical perfections, forms admitting more or less within themselves, not to fixed or univocal meanings differentiated from without. All strictly metaphysical concepts are analogical.   [2] 993^b30.   [3] Cf. 1009^a1.

First, a perfection common to many things must be caused in them by a unique cause. A common perfection cannot belong to two things of themselves because of themselves they are distinct from one another; diversity of cause would produce diversity of effect. Now since existence is common to all things, which yet considered of themselves are distinct from one another, it must be attributed to them, not of themselves, but from one cause. This seems to be Plato's line of reasoning, when before all multitude he expects a unity, a unity not merely of number, but of reality.

Secondly, when one perfection held by many things is shared in differing intensities, then it comes to those imperfectly possessing it from that being which perfectly possesses it. A note positively predicated according to degrees of more or less is judged by close or distant approximation to a constant. For if each thing essentially possessed it, there would be no reason why its strength should be greater in one than in another. The inference is inevitable; that there is one being, most perfect and truly being. This may also be proved from the conclusion that there is a principle of motion wholly motionless and most perfect, from which all other less perfect things must receive their being.[1]

Thirdly, that which is by another must be resolved into that which is of itself. We must affirm a being that is its own very being, proved because there must be some one first being, pure act, devoid of composition, from which all other beings are. They are beings by sharing, and their essence is not identical with their existence. This is the argument of Avicenna.[2]

Disputations, III *de Potentia*, 5

[1] Cf. *Metaphysics*, 993[b].
[2] Working from *Metaphysics*, 1045[b], 1049[b].

156. What is observed to be in something by participation must necessarily be caused there by that to which it belongs essentially, as when iron is made red-hot by fire. God is his very existence, moreover such subsisting existence cannot but be unique. Consequently all things other than God are not their existence, but share in existence. Things diversified by different degrees of existence, so as to be more or less perfect, must be caused by one first and most perfect being.

175, 204, 207, 436   *Summa Theologica,* 1a. xliv. 1

157. Did eternal mind not exist then no truth would be eternal.

Summa Theologica, 1a. xvi. 7

158. If all created being were wiped out, the pure meaning of essence would still persist; if all human individuals were destroyed, rationality would still remain a predicate of human nature.

viii *Quodlibet,* 1, *ad* 1

159. Because theoretical truths are eternal in their content it does not follow that our minds are eternal, but that there is an eternal foundation somewhere, namely the first truth which is the universal cause containing every truth.

1046   ii *Contra Gentes,* 84

160. Above the human mind there must be set a higher mind, from which our mind receives its powers of understanding. To that which shares and which is mutable and imperfect there must always be presupposed that which is perfect essentially and which is unchanging and perfect. The human spirit is called intellectual by sharing in intellectual power. A sign thereof is that the human spirit is partially and not wholly intellectual; also that it comes to an understanding of truth by research and discussion; also that it enjoys imperfect understanding, for it does not understand everything, and even if it did there would have been a transition from potentiality. Therefore some higher mind must exist to kindle our soul into understanding.

293, 645   *Summa Theologica*, 1a. lxxix. 4

161. Plato held that the forms of things subsist in themselves apart from matter, and that by sharing in these ideas, as he called them, the mind knows things; bodily matter becomes a stone by sharing in the idea of stone, our mind knows stone by sharing in the same idea. But since it smacked of heterodoxy to teach that the forms of things existing apart from matter should be creative substances such as pure life and pure wisdom, Augustine, who was imbued with the doctrine of the Platonists, in place of these ideas substituted exemplars existing in the divine mind according to which all things are formed and by the human soul also known.

630, 642, 647   *Summa Theologica*, 1a. lxxxiv. 5

162. Whatever is good yet not identified with its goodness is said to be good by sharing. A previous good must then be presupposed, from which is received the real form of derivative goodness. To go back to infinity is not possible especially as regards final causes, for indefiniteness is repugnant to the nature of purpose and the good has the force of a purpose or end. We must therefore reach some first good thing, which is not a derivative good by sharing, nor a good by reference to something else, but which is good essentially of itself. And this is God.

145, 690, 1047   [1] *Contra Gentes*, 38

163. Human bliss cannot consist in any created good, for it implies perfect good entirely satisfying the desire; were there still something left to desire it would not be the ultimate end. The object of the will or human appetite is universal good, just as the object of the mind is universal truth. Hence, nothing can still the desire of the will save universal good. There is no repose in any creature, but in God alone. A creature has only a share of good. Therefore God alone can satisfy the will of man, *He who fills thy desire with all good things.*[1]

145, 744, 767   *Summa Theologica*, 1a–2ae. ii. 8

VII. QUINTA VIA, THE ARGUMENT FROM FINAL CAUSES

164. Another proof, taken from the governance of things, is introduced by Damascene[2] and mentioned by Averroes.[3] Contrary and discordant elements, it runs, cannot always, or nearly always, work harmoniously together unless they be directed by something providing each and all with their tendencies to a definite end. Now in the universe we see things of diverse natures conspiring together in one scheme, not rarely or haphazardly, but approximately always or for the most part. There must be something, therefore, whose providence directs the universe.[4]

703, 1093   1 *Contra Gentes*, 13

1 Ps. cii. 5 (Vulgate).   2 *De Fide Orthodoxa*, i. 3.
3 Commentary, *II Physics*.
4 Two distinct arguments, of which the second is independent, are engaged in the *quinta via*. The first is the argument from design, based on the concept of external finality, that is the arrangement of different things in a working pattern. The second is the argument from purpose, based on the concept of internal finality, the rationalization of any activity in the light of an end which, at the last analysis, is intellectually appointed.

165. We observe that things without consciousness, such as physical bodies, operate with a purpose, as appears from their co-operating invariably, or almost so, in the same way in order to obtain the best result. Clearly then they reach this end by intention and not by chance. Things lacking knowledge move towards an end only when directed by someone who knows and understands, as an arrow by an archer. There is consequently an intelligent being who directs all natural things to their ends; and this being we call God.

336   *Summa Theologica*, 1a. ii. 3

166. An end must be prefixed to everything that acts by natural necessity; wherefore, say philosophers, the work of nature is the work of intelligence.

                              Disputations, 1 *de Potentia*, 5

167. When diverse things are co-ordinated the scheme depends on their directed unification, as the order of battle of a whole army hangs on the plan of the commander-in-chief. The arrangement of diverse things cannot be dictated by their own private and divergent natures; of themselves they are diverse and exhibit no tendency to make a pattern. It follows that the order of many among themselves is either a matter of chance or it must be resolved into one first planner who has a purpose in mind. What comes about always, or in the great majority of cases, is not the result of accident. Therefore the whole of this world has but one planner or governor.

354, 457   1 *Contra Gentes*, 42

168. The principle of things is outside the world; so also is their end.

320, 321   *Summa Theologica*, 1a. ciii. 2

169. One expects the best cause to produce an effect which is best on the whole. However, this does not mean that each part is best when taken in isolation by itself, but only in proportion to the whole. In the case of a higher organism, for instance, its value would be impaired were every part to have the excellence of an eye.

353   *Summa Theologica*, 1a. xlvii. 2, *ad* 1

170. A bodily creature is good in its nature, not unboundedly so, but in a partial and contracted manner. Hence the conflict of one thing with another, though both in themselves are good. Now because they judge things, not in their objective natures, but according as their own private convenience is affected, some people reckon those things to be absolutely evil which are harmful to them, not recognizing that what is harmful in one respect is beneficial in another, as regards either itself or something else.

476   *Summa Theologica*, 1a. lxv. 1, *ad* 2

171. If we wish to register the purpose of any whole and of its parts we should mark first, that each part is for its own proper activity, thus eye for seeing; second, that the lower is for the higher, thus senses for mind, or lungs for heart; third, that all parts are for the perfection of the whole, thus matter for form; fourth, that the whole man is for an extrinsic end, namely his enjoyment of God.

So it is with the parts of the universe: each creature exists first for its own proper activity and well-being; second, the lower creatures are for the higher, as plants and beasts are for men; third, each is for the integrity of the whole; last, the whole universe with all its parts is ordered to God as to its end, by copying and showing forth divine goodness to the glory of God.

Transcending this subordination, rational creatures in a special way have God as their end, for knowing him and loving him, they can reach him by their own activity.

744, 1117 *Summa Theologica*, 1a. lxv. 2

172. Organs are judged to be homologous or otherwise by the functions that are their purpose, thus the roots of plants, though at the bottom, are like the heads of animals.

Commentary, *II de Anima, lect.* 8

173. The causality of an end consists in this, that other things are desired for its sake. The more perfect the end so much the more does the desire for it embrace many more things and the farther does it go.

213 I *Contra Gentes*, 75

174. The art of sailing governs the art of shipbuilding.

III *Contra Gentes*, 80

VIII. CONVERGENCE OF THE FIVE WAYS

175. A thing whose existing is other than its essence has its existence caused by another. God is the first efficient cause, and therefore his essence cannot be distinct from his existence.

Existence is the actuality of every form and nature. Goodness and humanity do not signify actual things unless they refer to existents. Existence, therefore, is related to essence as actuality to potentiality. Since there is nothing potential in God, for he is motionless, his essence is not distinct from existence: on the contrary, his essence is his existence.

That which has existence, but is not existence, is a being by sharing. Were the divine essence not the divine existence, God would be an existent by borrowing and not by owning. He would not be the first being.

204, 206, 208, 231, 591   *Summa Theologica*, 1a. iii. 4

176. The arrangement of efficient causes corresponds to the arrangement of final causes. Man is directed to his ultimate end by the motion of the first cause, and to his proximate ends by the motion of subordinate movers, as the soldier is directed to victory by the high command, and to his tactical dispositions by the regimental commander.

Summa Theologica, 1a–2ae. cix. 6

III

Nature of God[1]

177. The existence of a thing having been ascertained, the manner of its existence remains to be inquired into if we would know about its nature. Since we cannot know what God is, but rather what God is not, our method has to be mainly negative.

First, therefore, we shall take treat in what manner he is not;[2] secondly, how he may be known;[3] and thirdly, how named.[4]

What manner of being God is not may be known by eliminating characteristics that cannot apply to him, such as composition, change, and so forth. Therefore the first question to be raised concerns his simplicity, which rules out composition. And because simple things are imperfect and partial realities when they are bodies, the next question concerns his perfection.

Summa Theologica, 1a. iii, Prologue

---

[1] After touching what is the essential note of godhead to the natural theologian, the argument moves on to the perfections of the divine being before discussing the nature of divine activity. The key to the grammar is found in the treatise on the names of God which inquires into the validity of predication when God is the subject, and strikes a balance between agnosticism at one extreme and anthropomorphism at the other. St. Thomas uses the phrases of the negative theology of Maimonides and the mystical writers, but surpasses its findings through the sustained application of analogy. Terms denoting pure perfections apply to God with greater force and propriety than to other things.

[2] 178–252.

[3] 253–63.

[4] 264–88.

I. INITIAL KNOWLEDGE

178. The question *what is so-and-so?* compares with *does it exist?* as the question *what is its reason why?* with *how did it come about?*

107 Commentary, *VII Metaphysics, lect.* 17

179. We cannot be aware of a thing's existence without in some way, at least vaguely, perceiving what it is. Knowledge of existence implies some knowledge of nature.

206 Opusc. xvi, Exposition, *de Trinitate*, vi. 3

180. Neither Christian nor pagan grasps the meaning of what God is in himself. The meaning that does duty is inferred in the medium of causality, using the method of enhancing perfections and eliminating imperfections. Both men use the same nominal definition when one denies, and the other affirms, that an idol is God. Were there a man entirely ignorant about God he could not even name God, except in the fashion of one who bandies words whose meaning he does not know.

99, 109 *Summa Theologica,* ia. xiii. 10, *ad* 5

181. When effects fall short of their causes any words applied to them both do not exactly coincide in significance. Nevertheless, some likeness can be discerned, for the genius of an efficient cause is to produce something somewhat like itself, since it is productive inasmuch as it is actual. The effective form in such a transcending cause is somehow reproduced in the product, with a variation of manner and meaning. Hence the epithet, equivocal cause. The perfections of all things are communicated by God; between them and him there is simultaneous likeness and unlikeness.

1 *Contra Gentes,* 29

182. Similitude, but no adequation.

Disputations, III de Potentia, 16, ad 7

183. That a creature in some way is like God may be granted, but not at all that God is like any creature. There is a mutual likeness when things are in the same class, but not between cause and effect:[1] we say that a statue is like a man, but not conversely.

Summa Theologica, 1a. iv. 3, ad 4

184. God and creatures are not comparable even like things of different kinds, for he is at once before and beyond all classification.

270, 436   *Summa Theologica, 1a. iv. 3, ad 2*

185. The name for a perfection should be applied more forcibly to the cause than to the effect.

Commentary, I Posterior Analytics, lect. 6

II. SIMPLICITY AND UNITY

186. The essence of God is his existence. Moses was taught this sublime truth when he asked: *If the children of Israel say to me, what is his name; what shall I answer them?* The Lord replied: *I am who am; so shalt thou say to the children of Israel: he who is has sent me to you.*[2]

288   *I Contra Gentes, 22*

187. Existence itself is the most perfect reality, related to everything as actuality. Therefore existence is the actuality of all beings, even of forms, and must be related to all else as received, not as receiving.[3]

435   *Summa Theologica, 1a. iv. 1, ad 3*

[1] Pseudo-Dionysius, *de Divinis Nominibus*, x. 7.
[2] Exod. iii. 13–14.
[3] Existence and essence are really distinct as real actuality from real potentiality, not as distinct things.

188. Since there is no composition of quantitative parts in God, for he is not a body; nor a composition of matter and form; nor are his nature and complete substantiality distinct; nor his essence and existence; nor is there a composition of genus and difference; nor of subject and accidents—it is plain that God is altogether simple and nowise composite.

Summa Theologica, 1a. iii. 7

189. The plurality of names for divine perfections does not militate against divine simplicity. Perfections which are diversified in other things by different forms exist in God by identical virtue. An analogy may be drawn from the faculties of knowing. The single ability of mind knows all things which the sensibility knows by diverse abilities—and many other things besides. Every kind of perfection, which other things obtain only in varied diversity, is possessed by God in his own single and simple being—yea and many more.

439   1 *Contra Gentes,* 31

190. It is not profitless for the mind to formulate compounding or dividing judgements about God despite his entire simplicity. Though we come to know about him through intricate thoughts, we appreciate well enough that the object corresponding to them is simply one. For the mind does not attach to its objects the mode of its own understanding; it does not suppose that a stone is spiritual because it is understood spiritually. The verbal composition of a judgement is a sign of unity, for it proposes the unity of a thing.

39, 40, 616   1 *Contra Gentes,* 36

191. Some have taught that God is the world-soul—this is supposed to have been the theory of the followers of Amaury de Bènes—while others that he is the formal principle of all things; others, most foolishly, taught that he is primary matter.[1] All make the same mistake of thinking that in some way God can enter into composition with other things. He is the first efficient cause, and an efficient cause is not numerically identical with its effect. He is the essential efficient cause, immediately and directly active. This cannot be said of any part of a composite, where the whole thing is the active cause; to speak with accuracy, it is not the hand that acts, but the man through his hand. God is the first thing absolutely speaking, and no part of a whole can be that.

234 *Summa Theologica*, 1a. iii. 8

192. Divinity is said to be the being of all things, not as their pith, but as their maker and exemplar cause.

102 *Summa Theologica*, 1a. iii. 8, *ad* 1

193. *One* signifies, not only that which is indivisible or continuous, but also that which is perfect, as when we say one man or one house.

Summa Theologica, 3a. lxxiii. 2

194. The unity convertible with being does not add anything to being, but the unity which is the principle of number adds a reality in the category of quantity.

429 *Summa Theologica*, 1a. xi. 1, *ad* 1

195. Unity as the principle of number is contrasted with numerical multitude. But unity as convertible

---

[1] Amaury de Bènes (d. 1206–7) and his contemporary David de Dinant (or Dinan), who were condemned together during the period of the first official reactions to the revival of Aristotle. Thèry suggests that St. Thomas's unwonted fling was in order to show that the cause of true Aristoteleanism was not compromised by the censures: it is possible that the term *folly* is not so much a piece of invective as a conventional expression for what was untutored and silly in the archaic sense.

with being is contrasted with the kind of multiplicity that spells defect; thus what is single is contrasted with what is in pieces.

448   *Summa Theologica*, 1a. xi. 2

196. The number relevant to pure spirits is not that of discrete quantity caused by division of continuous quantity, but the number arising from distinction of forms: in this sense plurality is reckoned among the transcendentals.[1]

432   *Summa Theologica*, 1a. l. 3, *ad* 1

197. Taken as a principle of number, unity is not to be predicated of God; it applies only to things having existence in matter.

447   *Summa Theologica*, 1a. xi. 3, *ad* 2

198. Were there two or more gods they would differ. One would have something the other lacked. In this case the perfection of one would be wanting in the other. Neither would be absolutely perfect.

436   *Summa Theologica*, 1a. xi. 3

199. Though God is wholly simple we must still address him with a multitude of names. Our mind is not able to grasp his essence. We have to start from the things about us, which have diverse perfections though their root and origin in God is one. Because we cannot name objects except in the way we understand them, for words are the signs of concepts, we can name God only from the terms employed elsewhere. These are manifold, therefore we must make use of many terms. Were we to see God in himself we would not call on a multitude of words; our knowledge would be as

[1] Realities or forms, such as truth and goodness, not limited to specific classes.

simple as his nature is simple. We look forward to this in the day of our glory; *in that day there shall be one Lord and his name one.*[1]

40, 258   Opusc. XIII, *Compendium Theologiae*, 24

III. PERFECTION

200. We praise God, not for his benefit, but for our own.

Summa Theologica, 2a–2ae. xci. I, *ad* 3

201. Though our lips can only stammer, says Gregory, we yet must sing the high things of God.[2] What is not made cannot be called perfect in the original sense of the word.[3] Yet because we speak of perfection in connexion with things which are achieved from potentiality, the term can be extended to mean whatever is not wanting in actual being, whether produced or not.

Summa Theologica, 1a. iv. I, *ad* 1

202. All perfections whatsoever and wherever discovered exist primordially and superabundantly in God.

Opusc. XIII, *Compendium Theologiae*, 21

203. The divine essence is a universal medium, not in the style of a universal form, but of a universal cause.

104   Disputations, II *de Veritate*, 4, *ad* 7

204. When God is called universally perfect because no kind of perfection is wanting in him, the statement can be supported on two counts. First, everything brought to perfection pre-exists in the producing cause in a more excellent mode. Dionysius touches this when he declares that God is not this or that, but is all as the

---

[1] Zach. xiv. 9.   [2] *Moralia*, v. 36.
[3] *Perfectus*, from *perficio, facio*, to make.

cause of all.[1] Secondly, God is pure existence subsisting essentially and consequently contains within himself the whole perfection of existence: all perfections are embraced in the perfection of existence, and therefore no single perfection is lacking in God. Dionysius also refers to this in maintaining that God does not exist in any special manner, but holds beforehand within himself all being, absolutely, boundlessly, uniformly.[2]

291, 515   *Summa Theologica*, 1a. iv. 2

205. Mingled things are more pleasing than simple things, a chord more so than a single bass or treble note.

                                    Commentary, *III de Anima*, lect. 2

206. Though sheer existence is more perfect than life, and life itself more perfect than wisdom, yet if these terms be taken to represent different levels, a living thing is more perfect than a merely existing thing, because it is also existing, while an intelligent thing is more perfect than either, because it is both existing and alive. Existence, then, in this vaguest sense does not necessarily include life and consciousness; that which shares in existence need not share in every mode of existence. Nevertheless, the very existence of God embraces life and wisdom, because not one of the perfections of full existence can be wanting in him who is essential existence himself.

175, 503   *Summa Theologica*, 1a. iv. 2, *ad* 3

207. It is true that things that both exist and live are more perfect than those that merely exist, nevertheless God is really and completely perfect because he is his existence. And when I say completely perfect, I mean that nothing of any kind of excellence is lacking. Every excellence in things is existential; wisdom would be no

---

[1] *de Divinis Nominibus*, v. 8.   [2] Ibid. v. 4.

virtue unless thereby a man was actually wise, and similarly with other virtues.

The manner of a thing's being is that also of its excellence, for in proportion that a thing is limited to a special style, greater or less as the case may be, so also is it said to be more or less excellent. But if there is a thing possessing the whole virtue of existence, no nobility present anywhere else can there be absent. God is wholly his being and possesses existence to the full power of existence itself. Every excellence and perfection belongs to a thing inasmuch as it is, every defect inasmuch as somehow it is not. God is totally existence, and is therefore unflecked with any imperfection.

397, 435, 498   1 *Contra Gentes*, 28

IV. GOODNESS AND BEAUTY

208. Whatsoever is good is called good by the divine goodness, as by the first exemplar, effective, and final cause of every good.

111   *Summa Theologica*, 1a. vi. 4

209. Goodness and being are identical in reality, but the term *goodness* conveys what the term *being* does not, namely, the quality of being desirable.

Summa Theologica, 1a. v. 1

210. Every being as being is good.

458   *Summa Theologica*, 1a. v. 3

211. Since goodness is what strikes us as desirable, it affects us as a final cause. Initial causality is final causality, for a producer does not act except for some end, and by a producer is matter moved to form. Hence the end is called the cause of causes.

462   *Summa Theologica*, 1a. v. 2, *ad* 1

212. Goodness extends to non-existing things, not because it can be predicated of them but because it can cause them—if, indeed, by non-existents we mean those objects that are potential, not those utterly without being. For goodness compasses every goal, not only in which actual things find their completion, but also towards which tend even things merely potential. Being does not carry this sense; it implies the condition of a formal cause only, either intrinsic or exemplary, and its causality does not spread beyond existents.

Summa Theologica, 1a. v. 2, *ad* 2

213. All things desire God himself in desiring their own proper perfections, inasmuch as these are so many likenesses of him. Some know him for himself, and this is proper to rational creatures; others know some share of his goodness as stretching into the life of the senses; others have purely natural and unconscious appetites for him, because they are directed to their ends by a higher intelligence.

725   *Summa Theologica*, 1a. vi. 1, *ad* 2

214. Divine goodness neither depends on, nor can gain from, the goodness of the universe. The perfection of the universe is necessarily committed to the particular goods of its essential components, and its well-being is supplemented by factors of safety and adornment. The idea behind divine volition may be sometimes of what is fitting, sometimes of what is useful, sometimes of what is hypothetically necessary on the supposition that the present scheme of things should work. But absolute necessity is present only when God wills himself.

429   1 *Contra Gentes*, 86

215. Goodness is an analogical idea, divided into the honourable, the delightful, and the useful, and not predicated of them equally, but according to that order of priority. The division is rather of contrasted notions than of different things. Those goods are honourable and of true worth which are dear in themselves. Those things are delightful that give us pleasure, though sometimes they may be harmful or unworthy. Utilities have no attraction in themselves, but are desired, rather like bitter medicine, as leading to something else.

374   *Summa Theologica*, 1a. v. 6, *ad* 2, 3

216. Augustine declares that nobody rightly uses God, for he is to be enjoyed. The last end is not a utility.

Summa Theologica, 1a–2ae. xvi. 3, *sed contra*

217. What is worthy and what useful, is for the reason to decide; what is delightful is decided by the desire, which may not match the reason. Therefore every delight may not have moral goodness.

Summa Theologica, 1a–2ae. xxxiv. 2, *ad* 1

218. Delight is not best just because it is delight, but because it is repose with the best.

Summa Theologica, 1a–2ae. xxxiv. 3, *ad* 3

219. The desire for goodness, beauty, peace, does not end up with different things.

Disputations, xxii *de Veritate*, 1, *ad* 12

220. The good and the beautiful are the same in substance, for they are established on a single real form; but they are different in meaning, for the good answers to appetite and acts like a final cause, while the beautiful answers to knowledge and acts like a formal cause. Things are called beautiful which give delight on being seen.

Summa Theologica, 1a. v. 4, *ad* 1

221. There is nothing that does not share in goodness and beauty. Each thing is good and beautiful by its proper form.

Opusc. xiv, Exposition, *de Divinis Nominibus*, iv, *lect.* 5

222. Three conditions of beauty—first, integrity or completeness, for broken things are ugly; second, due proportion and harmony; third, brightness and colour.

1122   *Summa Theologica*, 1a. xxxix. 8

223. Clearness and proportion go to compose the beautiful or handsome. Dionysius says that God is beautiful for he is the cause of the consonance and clearness of all things. Bodily beauty consists in well-shaped members with freshness of complexion; spiritual beauty, which is the same as honourable good, in fair dealing according to the candour of reason.

Summa Theologica, 2a–2ae. cxlv. 2

224. Clearness and proportion are both rooted in mind, whose function it is to order and light up a symmetry. Hence beauty, pure and essential, dwells in the contemplative life, wherefore it is said of the contemplation of wisdom; *and I became a lover of her beauty.*[1] Beauty is shed on the moral virtues in so far as they shine with the order of reason, especially on temperateness, which clears the lusts that fog the light of intelligence.

Summa Theologica, 2a–2ae. clxxx. 2, *ad* 3

225. Delight of mind does not clog the use of reason; on the contrary we are more intent on what we more enjoy.

751, 1004   *Summa Theologica*, 1a–2ae. xxxiii. 3

[1] Wisd. viii. 2.

226. Then does sense act best when bent on its most congenial object.

988 Commentary, *X Ethics, lect.* 6

227. The senses most charged with knowledge are the most set on beauty. The beautiful is the same as the good, but with a difference of accent. Good is what all desire; therefore is it of the essence of beauty that at the knowledge and sight of it the desire is stilled. The senses closest to mind, namely sight and hearing, are most engaged by beauty. We speak about beautiful sights and sounds, but not about beautiful tastes and smells. And so beauty adds to the meaning of goodness a relationship to the power of knowledge. The good is that which simply pleases desire, the beautiful that which pleases on being perceived.

628 *Summa Theologica,* 1a–2ae. xxvii. 1, *ad* 3

228. Variety belongs to beauty; as the Apostle says, *in a great house there are not only vessels of gold and silver, but also of wood and earth.*[1]

428 *Summa Theologica,* 2a–2ae. clxxxiii. 2

229. Homes are not beautiful if they are empty. Things are beautiful by the indwelling of God.

Exposition, *in Psalmos,* xxv. 5

V. INFINITY

230. *Infinite* is used in two senses, first to mean the privative infinite attributed to things which should have limits naturally but which lack them; this applies only to quantities. Secondly, to mean the negative infinite which simply has no limit. In the first sense God is not infinite, because he is without quantity and further-

[1] 2 Tim. ii. 20.

more is exempt from the imperfection it denotes. In the second sense *infinite* applies to all his perfections.

418, 423   Disputations, 1 *de Potentia*, 2

231. Matter is perfected and made definite by form. Infiniteness attributable to matter is imperfect and amorphous. On the other hand, form as such is not perfected by matter but contracted rather; hence infiniteness attributable to form is perfection. Now of all realities existence is most form, and since the divine existence is not a reality received in a subject, for God is his own subsisting existence, it is clear that he is infinite and perfect.

175, 292   *Summa Theologica*, 1a. vii. 1

232. Boundlessness does not exclude plurality, except in so far as it rules out determinateness, which is the first principle of plurality. There are two kinds of determinateness, namely of limitation and of distinction. In the divine nature there is no kind of limitation, but there is distinctiveness, and in two ways: first, as being distinguished by essence from creatures, as the unlimited from the limited; second, according to the distinction of persons by the relation of origin, which distinction is because of the contrast in relations, not because of limitation.

447   VII *Quodlibet*, 6[1]

233. Within God there can be an opposition of relation, for that does not imply imperfection in either relative: but no other kind of opposition is possible, because then one of the extremes is always by way of being imperfect,

---

[1] Quodlibets, *quaestiones quodlibetales*, debates on special occasions about a selected topic, freely arising and willingly debated, additional to the series of connected disputations, the *quaestiones disputatae*, forming part of a course for an academic term, or year.

either as a non-being, as in the case of simple negation, or as mixed with non-being, as in the case of privation.

Disputations, VIII *de Potentia*, I, *ad* 13

234. Since the infinite must be everywhere and in all things, we have now to consider whether this applies also to God. God is in all things, not, indeed, as part of their essence, or as a quality, but in the manner that an efficient cause is present to that on which it acts. An efficient cause must be in touch with the product of its action immediately, and this by its own power. Now since God's very essence is his existence, created existence is his proper effect. This effect God causes, not only when things first begin to be, but so long as they continue to be. While a thing endures, therefore, God must be present to it according to its mode of being. Existence is most intimate to each and deepest in all reality since it is the heart of all perfection. Hence, God is in all things, and intimately.

285, 359 *Summa Theologica*, 1a. viii. 1

235. Were the divine being the formal being of everything, all things would be absolutely speaking one.

429 1 *Contra Gentes*, 26

236. God is everywhere and in every place, first because he is in all things giving them substance, power, and operation. Since place is real he is present there. Also things are in place because they fill it, and God fills every place, but not as a body, for so one occupant excludes another, whereas he displaces nothing.

229, 361, 376 *Summa Theologica*, 1a. viii. 2

237. Spiritual things are in place, not like bodies by the contact of dimensive quantity, but by the contact of power.

533 *Summa Theologica*, 1a. viii. 2, *ad* 1

238. In two senses creatures are said to be in God. First, in so far as they are contained and preserved by the divine power, even as we say that things within our power are in us. So by their own very reality are creatures in God. This is the meaning of the Apostle's words; *in him we live and move and have our being*.[1] Secondly, things are said to be in God as in the one who knows them, in which sense they are in God by their especial meanings, which in God are none other than the divine essence. Things in God are the divine nature. And because the divine essence is life, though without a process of coming to be and dying away, we can say in this context that things are living and deathless in God.

374, 375   *Summa Theologica*, 1a. xviii. 4, *ad* 1

VI. ETERNITY

239. God is pure act without alloy of potentiality.

175   Opusc. xiii, *Compendium Theologiae*, 11

240. He is infinite and comprehends within himself the plenitude of all perfection of all being; he cannot acquire anything new or attain to what has not already been achieved.

369   *Summa Theologica*, 1a. ix. 1

241. God alone is wholly immutable. Every creature is mutable, at least in the sense that it is drawn out of nothingness by divine will and could be allowed to fall back.

408   *Summa Theologica*, 1a. ix. 2

242. Nothing wanes or waxes in God, for he is unchangeable and his being is entire all at once.

386   Opusc. xiii, *Compendium Theologiae*, 8

[1] Acts xvii. 28.

243. We can mark three general levels of reality: first, above eternity, proper to the first cause; second, with eternity, proper to intelligences; third, under eternity but above time, proper to souls.

531, 568   Opusc. x, *de Causis, lect.* 6

244. As we have to penetrate composite things in order to reach simple things, so we must go through time to come to the knowledge of eternity. In successive changes where one part follows another we apprehend time by numbering the before and after in movement. There is no before and after to be reckoned in constant and changeless reality. The form of eternity lies in the apprehension of that uniformity. Furthermore those things are measured by time which have a temporal beginning and end; what is wholly invariable and without succession has neither beginning nor end. So therefore eternity is signified by these two clauses: first, that a thing in eternity can be closed neither prospectively nor retrospectively; secondly, that it is entire all at once without any successiveness.

126, 664   *Summa Theologica,* 1a. x. 1

245. Some seize on this as the difference between time and eternity, that time has beginning and end, but eternity not. This difference, however, is quite incidental and not essential; for even granting that time always was and always will be, there still remains this difference between them, that eternity is simultaneously whole, whereas time is not. Eternity is the measure of permanence; time the measure of change.

413   *Summa Theologica,* 1a. x. 4

246. We determine the reality of time when we divide motion into two terms with a midway between them.

Commentary, *IV Physics, lect.* 17

247. In time there are two notes to be thought of: time itself, which is successive; and the *now* of time, which is imperfect.

Summa Theologica, 1a. x. 1, *ad* 5

248. The apprehension of time is caused by the perception of the changing instant, the apprehension of eternity by that of the enduring instant.

766   *Summa Theologica*, 1a. x. 2, *ad* 1

249. The *now* of time is not time, the *now* of eternity is really the same as eternity.

Commentary, *I Sentences*, xix. ii. 2

250. In appreciating what happens in time, we should remark that a mind bound up in it is differently placed from a mind entirely outside its series. When many are travelling the same road, each of the company knows those ahead and those behind; he sees his immediate companion, he has seen those who have gone ahead, but those well behind he cannot see. But he who is no part of the throng but watches from high above is in a position to take in the whole convoy. He is able to see simultaneously all who are on the march, not as met before and after, but as all together in their order.

Because our knowledge is enclosed in the order of time, either directly or indirectly, the time-factor enters into our calculations, and our knowledge reckons things as past, present, or future. Past, in memory; present, in experience; future, by anticipation in present causes. Future events are either certainties, when they are wholly predetermined in their causes, or conjectures, when they can usually be forecast, or unknown, when their causes are not yet committed to action.

God, however, is entirely above the order of time. He is at the peak of eternity, surmounting everything all at once. Thence the stream of time can be seen in one simple glance.

305, 310   Commentary, *I Perihermenias, lect.* 14

251. Eternity is compared to time as an indivisible to a continuous stretch. There is diversity of parts in time according to a before and after of successive events, as in a line there are points in different places yet related to one another. Eternity, however, has no before and after, and is simultaneously entire.

Opusc. xxvi, *de Rationibus Fidei ad cantorem Antiochenum,* 10[1]

252. Delight as such is not in time, for it is of a good possessed, which is like the term and end of change.

369, 767   *Summa Theologica,* 1a–2ae. xxxi. 2

VII. HUMAN KNOWLEDGE OF GOD

253. God is not in a class; so it is clear that he cannot be defined, or given a formula by genus and difference.

390   1 *Contra Gentes,* 25

254. Though in himself supremely knowable, God surpasses the power of a limited intelligence by very excess of truth. The bat blinks in the blaze of the sun. Impressed by this thought, some have concluded that no created intellect can see the nature of God.

But it is an awkward conclusion. For since man's ultimate happiness consists in his highest activity, were he never able to see God, then either he could never reach his bliss or this would lie in something other than God, which is alien to Christian belief. Moreover, it is philosophically unsound, for there is an inborn desire

---

[1] Written in 1264, four years before Antioch ceased to be an outpost of the West, for discussions with Saracens, Greeks, and Armenians.

of knowing cause when effect is seen—this is the spring
of wonder. If, therefore, the mind of rational creatures
could never see the first cause of things this natural
desire would be pointless.

744, 912   *Summa Theologica*, 1a. xii. 1

255. But through no created likeness can the nature of
God be seen.

Summa Theologica, 1a. xii. 2

256. What is seen in imaginative visions is not God's
nature, but images which represent him after a fashion,
as do the metaphorical figures in holy writ.

Summa Theologica, 1a. xii. 3, *ad* 3

257. By native power no created mind can see the
essence of God. Knowledge implies the presence of the
known in the knower in the knower's own way. To
know subsisting being is natural to the divine mind
alone. It is above the natural ability of created mind.
Therefore a created mind cannot see the divine essence
except God by his grace shows and gives himself.

496   *Summa Theologica*, 1a. xii. 4

258. The divine essence is being itself. As other intelligible forms, which are not their own very being, are
united to the mind through a mental likeness whereby
they inform and make actual the intellect, so the divine
essence can be united to created intellect as that which
is both actually understood and of itself making the
intellect actual.

293   *Summa Theologica*, 1a. xii. 2, *ad* 3

259. God is not to be comprehended, for he is infinite
and cannot be contained in any finite being. So much
for comprehension in the strict and proper sense. But
when the word is used more widely in contrast to non-

attainment, God is reached by the blessed, according to the words of the Song of Songs; *I held him and will not let him go.*[1]

Summa Theologica, 1a. xii. 7, *ad* 1

260. God is called incomprehensible because he cannot be seen by us as perfectly as he is capable of being seen, not because anything about him will escape sight.

Summa Theologica, 1a. xii. 7, *ad* 2

261. The difference between that blessed vision and the present argument is like that between seeing and not seeing, not like that between seeing better and not seeing so well.

Disputations, xviii *de Veritate*, 1

262. Our natural knowledge begins with sensation, and therefore can be led as far as sensible things can take us. Through these effects, which do not equal the virtue of their cause, we cannot know the full power of God or, consequently, see his essence. Nevertheless they are his effects and dependent on their cause. We can be led by them so far as to know of his existence and some necessary attributes. He is the first universal cause surpassing all his effects, and we can know his relationship to creatures and their difference from him.

903   *Summa Theologica*, 1a. xii. 12

263. When you reach a proper appreciation of a thing through negative demonstration you know where it differs from other things, but not what it is in itself. We have such knowledge about God through demonstration. It is not enough for our contentment.

105   iii *Contra Gentes*, 39

[1] Cant. iii. 4.

VIII. THE NAMES OF GOD

264. A thing can be named to the measure that it can be known. In this life we cannot see God's nature, but we can know about him from the bearing he has on creatures as their principle. The method we employ will require intensification of perfections and elimination of imperfections.[1]

631 *Summa Theologica*, 1a. xiii. 1

265. We come to the knowledge of God from creatures and so we name him; the sense of the terms employed is appropriate to material creatures at the level of our natural knowledge. Now because perfect and subsisting things in our present environment are composite, their form being but a partial reality whereby they are things of a certain kind, terms used to signify a thing in the round are concrete, whereas terms that signify pure forms are abstract.[2]

Summa Theologica, 1a. xiii. 1, *ad* 2

266. We can discuss simple things only as if they were like the composite things about us from which we draw our knowledge. In speaking of God, then, we must use concrete names to signify his complete existence, for the only things that are complete existents in our environment are composite things; and we must use abstract names to signify his simplicity.

69 *Summa Theologica*, 1a. iii. 3, *ad* 1

267. What is most strikingly certain is that the first cause surpasses human wit and speech. He knows God

---

[1] The *via excellentiae* of affirming perfections at their highest strength; the *via remotionis* of denying any creaturely mode. Thus God is supreme mind, but his mind is not a faculty distinct from his substance.

[2] Thus, a *good thing* and *goodness*.

best who owns that whatever he thinks and says falls short of what God really is.

Opusc. x, Exposition, de Causis, lect. 6

268. It is not merely that God is not a stone or a sun or any such thing we perceive by our senses, but that he is not such life or essence as can be perceived by the mind.

Opusc. xiv, Exposition, de Divinis Nominibus, Prologue

269. We postulate substance and existence in God; substance to mean what is self-supporting, but not a substrate to supervening reality; existence to mean what is simple and perfect, not inhering.

Disputations, 1 de Potentia, 1

270. Obviously negative and relative terms do not signify the substance of God at all; they respectively rule out something or indicate the relationship something bears to him.

The controversy hinges on affirmative and absolute terms, such as good and wise. Notwithstanding the positive force of these terms, some hold that when they are used about God they serve to remove rather than to attribute something to him. They say that when we talk about the living God we mean that he is not like a dead thing, and so, likewise, with other terms. Maimonides speaks in this sense.[1] Others hold that these terms are used to signify his bearing to creatures: when we say that God is good, the sense is that he is the cause of goodness in things, and so likewise with other terms.[2]

Both these positions, however, present difficulties, which may be grouped under three headings. First,

[1] *The Guide for the Perplexed*, i. 58. Moses Maimonides, the Rabbi Moses, born at Cordova, 1135, died in Egypt, 1204, of whom St. Thomas always speaks with respect.

[2] Alain of Lille. Died as a Cistercian, 1202.

neither can explain why one name should be used in preference to another; God is the cause of bodies as he is the cause of goods, and therefore with equal force might be called a body. In fact, calling him a body might even have the advantage of clearing him from being a purely potential reality, such as primary matter. Secondly, it would follow that all the names predicated of him would be used in a secondary sense, as health is applied to a drug in a derivative sense, for it is merely an agent of health in an animate organism, which latter is primarily the healthy thing. Thirdly, the suggested interpretation runs counter to the intention of those who speak of God, for when they speak of the living God they mean more than that he is the cause of life, or that he differs from dead things.

Therefore we must conclude otherwise. Such absolute and positive terms signify the divine substance and are predicated essentially of God, though they represent him inadequately. Let me explain what I mean. Terms signify God to the extent that the mind knows him. In knowing about him from creatures, the mind knows him to the extent that they represent him. God in himself possesses beforehand all the perfections of creatures; he is unrestrictedly and universally perfect. Every creature represents him and is like him to the measure of its perfection; though God is their surpassing principle and not in the same class, nevertheless, some likeness is present. Creaturely terms can signify, though imperfectly, the divine substance, even as creatures imperfectly represent him.

When it is said God is good, the sense is not that God is the cause of goodness, nor yet that God is not evil, but, that what is meant by goodness in creatures preexists in God, and indeed more intensely. It does not follow that goodness is attributed to God because he causes goodness, but rather conversely, that because he is good he diffuses goodness.

155, 1074 *Summa Theologica*, ia. xiii. 2

271. The understanding of negatives is always based on affirmatives, as is shown by the rule of proving one by the other. Unless the human mind could make affirmations about God it would be unable to deny anything about him. Something must first be verified in a positive sense.

Disputations, vii *de Potentia*, 5

272. Two shades of meaning should be distinguished in any name we attribute to God, the very perfection signified, goodness or life as the case may be, and the mode of signification. As regards the former, perfections belong to God properly, and more properly than they do to creatures, for they are his in the primary sense. But as regards the latter, no human term is attributable to God, for it has a mode of signification befitting creatures.

Summa Theologica, ia. xiii. 3

273. Terms that designate unadulterated perfection, such as goodness, wisdom, being, may be predicated of God and of other things as well, because every perfection of creatures resides in God, though in another and more eminent way. Terms that designate perfections bound up with a creaturely mode of existence cannot be applied to God save by a figure of speech or metaphor, as when a man is called a blockhead on account of the hardness of his understanding. All terms expressing created types are of this sort, such as man or stone; also terms expressing specific properties. Such terms as first being, supreme good, which express perfections at their highest, are used of God alone.

When I say that terms may express perfection without defect, this must be taken with regard to their core of meaning, because at present we surround our meanings with imperfection. We can express things only in the manner we can conceive them in the mind. Such terms, as Dionysius notes, can be affirmed as well as denied of God; affirmed because of the meaning of the word, denied because of the mode of meaning.

The manner of superexcellence according to which pure perfections are found in God cannot be signified by the names we impose unless they are qualified by a negation, as when we speak of the infinite good, or by a relationship, as when we speak of the first cause or the supreme good.

509   1 *Contra Gentes*, 30

274. Some terms signify perfections deriving from God into creatures in such a way that the imperfect creaturely mode according to which the divine perfection is shared is involved in the very meaning; stone, for instance, is entirely committed to material being, and cannot be attributed to God save metaphorically. But there are other terms, such as being, good, alive, which signify perfections having no particular mode of sharing involved in their meaning, and these can be applied to God in their proper sense.

Summa Theologica, 1a. xiii. 3, *ad* 1

275. What are the signs of passion in us are credited metaphorically to God by the names for those passions.

Summa Theologica, 1a. xix. 11

276. Some emotions, though not existing as such in God, contain in their specific meaning nothing repugnant to divine perfection, and among them are delight and joy.

821   1 *Contra Gentes*, 90

277. Terms that are applied metaphorically to God are primarily used of creatures, not of God; whereas terms that signify pure perfections as regards the very value signified are primarily used of God and not of creatures, for these perfections derive from him, though on the point of linguistics they may have been applied to creatures in the first place.

Summa Theologica, 1a. xiii. 6

278. In language the subject of the etymology is sometimes other than the object of the real definition.

Summa Theologica, 1a. xiii. 2, *ad* 2

279. A term may be predicated of various subjects in three ways, univocally, equivocally, and analogically. Univocally, if the same term and meaning is used in exactly the same sense, as when *animal* is predicated of a man and a donkey, for to both the definition of animal applies, namely sensitive animate substance. Equivocally, if the term is the same but the meaning and definition different, as when *dog* is used of an animal and a star. Analogically, if various objects, though diverse by meaning and definition, bear on some one common meaning, as when *health* is ascribed to organic body and urine and drink, but not with the same force, for in the first case the subject is given, in the second a symptom, in the third a cause.

Opusc. II, *de Principiis Naturae ad fratrem Silvestrum*

280. It is impossible for a term to be predicated univocally of God and creatures. For every effect which does not exhaust the power of the cause receives the likeness of that cause incompletely. When a term of perfection is applied to a creature it signifies that perfection as distinct from another, thus human wisdom signifies a certain quality distinct from human substance, being,

and power. But when we apply it to God we imply no
such limitations. Man it fixes and stylizes, but not God,
who is left unenclosed and escaping the bounds of the
term's significance. Consequently it is clear that *wise* is
not given exactly the same sense when applied to God
and to men, and the same holds true with other perfections. Therefore terms are not univocal between
them.

Nevertheless, they are not purely equivocal, as some
have thought. This would mean that nothing could be
known or proved about God from creatures, for we
should always fall into the fallacy of equivocation in the
attempt.

It should be concluded that these terms are used
according to analogy. Creatures are shaped to God as
to their principle; their perfections surpassingly pre-
exist in him. This method in common use lies midway
between pure equivocation and simple univocation.
The meaning is not fixed and identical, as with univocal
terms, nor wholly different, as with equivocal terms, but
is used flexibly to signify different proportions to one
constant, as *health* is used of urine to mean the sign,
and of medicine to mean the cause, of animal health.

Summa Theologica, 1a. xiii. 5

281. All divine perfections in reality are identical. A
comparison with the faculties of knowledge will make
this clearer; a higher power by one and the same idea
understands what a lower power must needs take in
many pieces.

295   Opusc. iii, *Compendium Theologiae*, 22

282. Yet the diverse names we give to God are not
synonyms, for they convey diverse meanings, though
everything is one in his reality.

315   Opusc. xiii, *Compendium Theologiae*, 25

283. Though they signify one identical thing, nevertheless the names attributed to God signify him according to many and various aspects, and are therefore not synonymous.

Summa Theologica, 1a. xiii. 4

284. Perfections manifold and divided in other things are simple and united in God.

Summa Theologica, 1a. xiii. 4, *ad* 3

285. Since God is outside the whole scheme of creatures, though all of them are ordered to him, and not conversely, it is clear that while creatures are really related to God, in God there is no real relation to creatures, but only a logical one. However, there is nothing to prevent the attribution to God of terms implying relationship in time. They denote a change in his creatures, not in him: thus a column becomes on the right-hand side of an animal without undergoing change in itself, through the animal's shift of position.

234 *Summa Theologica,* 1a. xiii. 7

286. The sole word that perfectly utters God is the Eternal Word.

314 Commentary, *I Sentences,* 11. i. 3

287. Having pondered on how God is apart from all and yet the cause of all, theologians sometimes have said that he is ineffable and at other times have attributed to him all manner of names. Such was demanded of the angel who had the appearance of God: Tell me, by what name art thou called? But he answered, to forestall misunderstanding that might come from naming God, Why dost thou ask my name?[1] Truly this name is exalted[2] and above every name that is

---

[1] Gen. xxxii. 29.   [2] Phil. ii. 9.

named, not only in this world but also in the world that
is to come.[1]

Yet God is praised in holy writ not only as ineffable
but also as having many names. God calls himself, I
am who am;[2] the way, the truth, and the life;[3] the
light of the world;[4] the God of Abraham.[5] Prophets
and apostles praise him as good,[6] beautiful,[7] the beloved
of the beloved,[8] the God of gods.[9] As great and
terrible,[10] remaining for ever,[11] thou who alone art,[12]
before the ages began.[13] As the giver of life and breath,[14]
as wisdom,[15] understanding, reason, righteous and
mighty to save.[16] As inspiring,[17] and yet in whom are
hid the treasures of all knowledge.[18] As our witness,[19]
declaring his strength,[20] the king of kings and lord of
lords,[21] the ancient of days,[22] without change or shadow
of alteration.[23] As God with us,[24] sanctification and
redemption,[25] as greatness walking above the poles of
heaven.[26] As after the earthquake and the fire in a still
small voice.[27] He is in our hearts, and souls[28] and bodies;[29]
he fills heaven and earth,[30] he is in the world,[31] and above
all his works.[32] His kingdom is over all;[33] heaven is his
throne and earth his footstool.[34] He is compared to the
sun,[35] the bright and morning star;[36] to fire,[37] water,[38]

---

[1] Eph. i. 21. [2] Exod. iii. 4. [3] John xiv. 6.
[4] John viii. 12. [5] Exod. iii. 6. [6] Luke xviii. 19.
[7] Cant. i. 4. [8] Cant. v. 1. [9] Ps. xlix. 1.
[10] Dan. ix. 4. [11] Baruch iii. 3. [12] Job xiv. 4.
[13] Ecclus. xxiv. 10. [14] Acts xvii. 25. [15] 1 Cor. i. 21.
[16] Isa. lxiii. 1. [17] 2 Tim. iii. 16. [18] Col. ii. 3.
[19] 1 Cor. iv. 9. [20] Ps. lxxviii. 14. [21] Apoc. xix. 16.
[22] Dan. vii. 9. [23] James i. 17. [24] Matt. i. 23.
[25] 1 Cor. i. 30. [26] Job xxii. 14. [27] 3 Kings xix. 12.
[28] Eph. iii. 17. Wisd. v 27.
[29] 1 Cor. vi. 19. [30] Jer. xxiii. 24. [31] John i. 10.
[32] Ecclus. xliii. 30. [33] Ps. cii. 19. [34] Isa. lxvi. 1.
[35] Mal. iv. 2. [36] Apoc. xxii. 16, [37] Deut. iv. 12.
[38] John iii. 5.

wind,[1] dew,[2] cloud;[3] to the corner-stone[4] and the rock.[5]

Opusc. xiv, Exposition, *de Divinis Nominibus*, i, *lect.* 3

288. This name, *He Who Is,* is the most proper name for God, and for three reasons. First, for denotation; it does not signify a kind of form, but being itself. Second, for universality; it determines no mode of being, but names the boundless sea of substance. Third, for connotation; it intimates being entirely present, free of past and future.

175, 435   *Summa Theologica,* 1a. xiii. 11

[1] Joel ii. 28.   [2] Hos. xiv. 6.   [3] Hos. vi. 3.
[4] Ps. cxvii. 22.   [5] 1 Cor. x. 4.
(The references are to the Vulgate.)

IV

Activity of God[1]

289. Leaving behind truths about the divine substance, let us now turn to truths about divine operation. Since operations in general are divided into those that remain within and those that issue into external effects, we shall treat first of the activities of mind and will, for knowing is in the knower and loving in the lover, and then afterwards of divine power taken as the principle of productive activity.

497 *Summa Theologica*, 1a. xiv, Prologue

290. The absolute and the relative differ logically in God, but not really.

Disputations, VII *de Potentia*, 1, *ad* 6

I. DIVINE MIND

291. Hold steadily to the truth that God has most assured knowledge of all things knowable at any time and by any mind: it cannot be otherwise.

[1] The divine stillness is the immobility of perfection, not imperfection; of full activity, not inertia. With safeguards against introducing our own divisions into the godhead, the divine powers and operations are specifically studied. They are grouped round the two abilities of mind and will. True to his intellectualism St. Thomas takes knowledge first; in marking its special quality of possessing without destroying and its immunity from the fatal generations of physical processes, he firmly rejects the notion of an unconscious deity. On the contrary, divine knowledge runs from the comprehending identity of God with himself to the creative perception of the least and most fugitive reality.

Mind sets the measure for will, the joy of God in himself and the artist's love whereby he freely and generously establishes good

His being is identical with his understanding. As his substance is pure existence so also is it pure understanding. Here nothing is lacking that can relate to knowledge, for every hint of knowledge is held in the sheer form of knowledge. Since his being is one, simple, firm, and enduring, it follows that by one single insight God enjoys eternal and unwavering knowledge of everything.

Indeed in the first cause things exist more nobly even than they do in themselves, for what exists in another exists according to the mode of that one's substance, and the substance of God is his understanding. Everything that is in any way real, therefore, exists intelligibly in God at the height of his substance, and is there known completely.

Were the godhead unconscious it would be like a man who slumbers and worthy of no great reverence.

587, 639, 662   Opusc. VII, *de Substantiis Separatis ad fratrem Reginaldum socium carissimum*, 12[1]

292. In God knowledge is consummate—this grows on us when we reflect that unconscious things have no other form but their own, whereas conscious things have a natural capacity to possess the forms of other things as well. That is the root difference between them. Unconscious nature is more restricted and limited, while conscious nature has a greater breadth and reach. Aristotle had this in mind when he spoke of the soul as being somehow all things.[2]

Now the restriction of form comes from matter, and therefore the less material a form the ampler it is. The

things outside himself. His omnipotence is able to play with all the possibilities of being; his providence to direct them in every detail; his life to communicate its happiness.

[1] Reginald of Piperno, his secretary.

[2] *de Anima*, 431^{b}21.

non-materiality of a thing is the reason why it can know, and the mode of its non-materiality sets the measure of its knowledge. Plants are unable to know because they are earthbound, but sense is cognitive for it receives non-material impressions, while the mind is freer still and less involved in matter. Since God is at the summit of non-materiality he is at the summit of knowledge.

231, 305   *Summa Theologica*, 1a. xiv. 1

293. Since there is no potentiality in God, for he is pure act, knower and known must there be identical in every way, so much so that his mind neither lacks a concept, as our mind does before it knows, nor is this concept other than his substance, as it is with us. The intelligible form is the divine mind itself, understanding itself by and through itself.

497   *Summa Theologica*, 1a. xiv. 2

294. The knowing mind and the object of knowledge and the concept and the activity, all these are here wholly identical.

Summa Theologica, 1a. xiv. 4

295. He knows all things by knowing his own essence, and this he does without forming a judgement. For he knows himself just as he is without any composition.[1] It does not follow that he is ignorant of logical statements, for his essence, though one and simple, is yet the exemplar of all multiple and compound things.

34   1 *Contra Gentes*, 58

296. As he knows material things spiritually and compound things simply, so he knows propositions by simple intelligence, not by passing affirmative or negative judgements.

Summa Theologica, 1a. xiv. 14

[1] Of subject and predicate.

297. He does not consider one thing after another successively, but everything simultaneously. His knowledge is not reasoned or discursive, though he knows all reasonings and processes.

250   1 *Contra Gentes*, 57

298. Let us make quite clear that there is no discursiveness in divine knowledge. In our knowledge there is a double process; one of succession only, when from actually understanding one object we turn our attention to another; the other of causality, as when we arrive at conclusions through principles. The first process cannot apply to God, for the multiple objects we understand successively when they are taken in themselves, can be understood all at once when they are seen in one principle. God sees everything in one, namely, in himself alone. Nor does the second process apply; first, because it entails succession, for in working from principles to conclusions we do not simultaneously consider them both; secondly, because it is a process from the known to the unknown.

324, 582, 666   *Summa Theologica*, 1a. xiv. 7

299. He knows himself perfectly. To know a thing its power must be gauged perfectly, which involves the knowledge of all things to which its power can extend.

Summa Theologica, 1a. xiv. 5

300. Lest anyone should fancy that God stands utterly aloof and apart from everything, that on our part he is beyond our ken, while he for his part does not cherish what is below him, Dionysius adds that divine knowledge is circumapprehensive of all things because it knows all properties and circumstances, and comprehensive because it perfectly knows all natures, and pre-apprehensive because it does not acquire knowledge from things but as their cause forestalls them.

Opusc. xiv, Exposition, de Divinis Nominibus, i, lect. 3

301. Some would withhold the knowledge of singular facts[1] from the perfection of the divine mind and they would maintain their position along seven lines of reasoning.

First, from the very condition of singularity. It is alleged that no spiritual power can know determinate matter which is the principle of singularity, for knowledge results from an assimilation of knower and known; whence in our case only those powers using material organs can apprehend singulars. The pure intellect cannot know them because it is spiritual, much less therefore can the divine intellect, which more than any other is far away from matter.

Second, singulars are not eternal. Either they are always known by God or they are known at one time and not known at another. The former alternative is ruled out because there is no true science of what is not, science being about true things, and non-existents are not true things. The latter alternative is ruled out because divine knowledge is altogether invariable.

Third, some singulars happen contingently and are not produced of necessity. They can be objects of certitude only after they have actually happened. Certitude is infallible, whereas the anticipation of a contingent event is fallible; if the opposite could not come about the event would be already necessary. We can enjoy no certitude about a future contingency, though we may hazard a shrewd guess. But all divine knowledge must be supposed to be most certain and infallible.

[1] Real individuals, such as *Justinian*; not merely particularized generalities, such as *an emperor*.

Fourth, some of these singular effects are caused by will. Now before it has taken place an event can be known solely in its cause. But the motion of will can be known with certitude by him alone in whose power the decision lies. Therefore God cannot have certain foreknowledge of singular events that depend on what we are freely going to do.

Fifth, an argument from the very infinity of singulars. The infinite, that is the indefinite, is unknowable as such, for everything known is measured by mind; on this account art scorns shapelessness. Singulars, however, are infinite, at least potentially. Therefore it seems impossible that God should know them.

Sixth, from the paltriness of singulars. Since the nobility of a science is pitched according to the dignity of its object, so the triviality of an object redounds on the corresponding knowledge. The divine mind, however, is of all the most elevated and the least tolerant of pettiness.

Seventh, from the wickedness present in some singular events. Since the known is somehow in the knower and evil cannot exist in God, it seems to follow that God simply does not know the evil and deprivation appropriate to imperfect minds.

Let us sift these arguments so that we may throw away what is contrary to the truth and show forth the perfection of divine knowledge. We shall show, first, that the divine mind knows singulars;[1] second, and things not yet actual;[2] third, and future contingencies with infallible knowledge;[3] fourth, and the motions of the will;[4] fifth, and infinites;[5] sixth, and the humblest and vilest things;[6] seventh, and all evils, deprivations, and defects.

1 *Contra Gentes*, 63–4

[1] 302.   [2] 303–7.   [3] 308–10.
[4] 311.   [5] 303.   [6] 312.   [7] 313.

302. To know things properly means knowing them, not merely in the mass, but also in their distinctiveness from one another. So does God know things, *piercing even to the dividing asunder of soul and spirit, and of the joints and marrow, a discerner of the thoughts and intents of the heart, neither is there any creature that is not manifest in his sight.*[1]

Some have slipped into the mistake of thinking that God knows things in general because everything shares in the common nature of being, and that by knowing himself as the fount of being, he knows the nature of being and all things in so far as they belong to being.[2] But this will not do, for to know something in general and not in its peculiarities is to know it imperfectly. Our mind, bringing out what is latent to begin with and going on to develop its full activity, starts with universal and confused knowledge before reaching to proper understanding.

We should say, then, that God knows things other than himself, not only inasmuch as they share in the general nature of reality, but also according to their special characteristics. Some have attempted to illustrate how God can understand many things in one knowledge by the example of a conscious centre that would know all radii, or a conscious light that would know all colours. But such examples, though well enough as illustrations of universal causality, fail here because multiple and diverse things derive from such a unitary principle in what they share in common, not in what makes them peculiar; and so by it they would be known in general, not in detail.

In God it is otherwise. Whatsoever is of value in any creature pre-exists in God; all perfections are all to-

---

[1] Hebr. iv. 12.
[2] An opinion attributed to Averroes.

gether and contained in him superbly, not only for what they have in common, namely being, but also for their special notes of difference. Every kind of form is a perfection. So all are anticipated in God, not merely where they agree with one another, but also where they are exclusively themselves. Consequently God, who contains all perfections, should not be compared to created natures as common to proper, nor as unity to number, nor as centre to radii, but as perfect actuality to imperfect actualities.

It is clear that imperfect realizations can be known by a perfect actuality with distinctness, not merely in a sweeping generalization. The essence of God contains whatever is of value in other things, and much more besides, and so God can know things other than himself with proper knowledge. The proper nature of each consists in this, that in some degree it participates in the divine perfection. God would not know himself perfectly did he not also know how his perfections could be shared; neither would he perfectly know the very nature of being unless he knew all the variations on being.

21, 62, 436 *Summa Theologica*, 1a. xiv. 6

303. God knows all things that are real in any way whatsoever. Things that are not real absolutely may be real relatively. Things are real absolutely when they are actual and exist. Things that are not actual may be in the power of God or in the power of the creature, whether in active power or passive potentiality, whether in the ability of thought or imagination to invest an object with any sort of meaning or interest. Whatever they are and however they can come about or be thought of or alluded to, all are known by God, though actually they do not exist.

Yet some difference should be noted among the things that are not actual. Though some of them are not actual now, nevertheless they have been or will be actual, and all these are said to be known by the knowledge of vision. For since God's act of understanding, which is his being, is measured by eternity which is without succession and comprehends all time, the instantaneous glance of God falls on all things in any period of time as on things present to him. But there are other things in the power of God or the creature which are not, nor have been, nor ever will be; these he is said to know by the knowledge of simple intelligence, not of vision, for vision implies a real object apart from the viewer.

254, 346   *Summa Theologica*, 1a. xiv. 9

304. By his art an artist may know even those things he has not yet wrought. The forms of art flow from his knowledge into external material there to constitute works of art. There is nothing to prevent his entertaining thoughts about forms that have not yet outwardly appeared.

1 *Contra Gentes*, 66

305. The divine essence contains all real nobilities by transcending rather than by combining them all. Every form, peculiar and generic alike, is a perfection, for it accentuates reality, and betrays imperfection only when it falls short of authentic reality. The divine mind, therefore, in its own essence can comprehend what is innermostly peculiar to all things, understanding where they succeed and where they fail in rendering divine perfection. So the divine essence, itself sheerly perfect, can be taken as the proper reason of singular things. Now because the special character of one thing is distinct from the special character of another, we can attribute to the divine mind a distinction and plurality

as regards the objects understood, for within the divine mind is the proper reason of each and all. This is because God understands the proper relation of similarity which they bear to him. In consequence the reasons of things in the divine mind are many and distinct just because God knows how things are assimilable to him in many and diverse ways. Augustine speaks about God making a man by one reason and a horse by another; he says also that the reasons of things are many in the divine mind. This in some measure safeguards the opinion of Plato, who postulated ideas according to which are formed all things existing in matter.

582   1 *Contra Gentes*, 54

306. God knows singulars, not merely in their universal causes, but also according to the proper and unique nature of each one of them.

658   Disputations, 11 *de Veritate*, 5

307. Some maintain that God knows singular things through universal causes, and they cite the example of the astronomer who can foretell future eclipses from his complete information about the general orbits of the heavenly bodies. But this will not serve, for the forms and powers of singular things deriving from universal causes, howsoever they be associated, are not individuated except by individual matter. He who knows Socrates because he is white, or the son of Sophroniscus, or for some such characteristic, does not know Socrates intimately as this individual man. On this theory God would not know singular things in their singularity.

Then others aver that he knows singular things by applying universal causes to particular effects. Neither will this serve, for no one can apply something to another unless he first knows the other. Far from giving

the reason why particulars can be known, the application they invoke presupposes the knowledge of singulars.

Therefore another explanation must be proposed.
Since God is the cause of things by his knowledge, his
knowledge reaches as far as his causality. The active
power of God extends not only to forms, the sources of
general meaning, but also even to matter. Therefore
divine knowledge must extend even to singulars individuated by matter. His essence is the sufficing principle
of knowing all things made by him, in general and in
detail. The same would hold true of a human artist's
knowledge were it productive of the whole being of
his effect and not merely of the form.

387, 447, 655   *Summa Theologica*, 1a. xiv. 11

308. A contingent event can be considered either in
itself or in its cause. In itself it is already actual and as
such is present, not future; it is already settled, not held
in suspense: accordingly it can fall under infallibly certain knowledge, as when I see that Socrates is sitting
down. In the light of its cause it is still a future event,
for the cause is not yet committed to one alternative
and being a contingent cause can take opposite courses;
accordingly the event does not fall within the range of
human certitude. Hence, when we know a contingent
effect in its cause we cannot go beyond conjecture.

Now God knows all contingent events, not merely
as they are in their causes, but also as each one of them
is actually in itself. Though they become actual successively, God knows them, but not as we do, that is
successively as they happen, but simultaneously. His
knowledge is rated by eternity, and eternity, being
simultaneously entire, comprises all time. All things in
time are present to God in eternity, not only, as some say,[1]

[1] e.g. Avicenna.

because he grasps the reasons of all things, but also because his glance takes in everything as present. Yet events remain future contingencies if their proximate causes are taken as the system of reference.

323, 359   *Summa Theologica*, 1a. xiv. 13

309. A contingent event escapes certitude because it is future, not because it is present.

1 *Contra Gentes*, 67

310. At the height of eternity God regards all things from above the movement of time. Events that come to be in time are already present to him. When I see Socrates sitting down, my knowledge is certain and infallible, but it imposes no necessity on Socrates to sit. And so God, in looking at things which to us are past, present, or future, infallibly and certainly knows them as present realities, yet without imposing on them the necessity of existing.

Opusc. xxvi, *de Rationibus Fidei ad cantorem Antiochenum*, 10

311. The will's mastery over its own activity, its inner poise to decide or not, excludes predetermination by another particular cause and violence from an external agent, but not the influence of a higher cause which is the principle alike of its being and of its activity. The causality of the first cause flows into movements of will, and so God in knowing himself knows these as well.

362, 692   1 *Contra Gentes*, 68

312. The knowledge of base things does not detract from the fineness of divine knowledge, but rather attests it.

For since the divine mind is of infinite strength fittingly does it penetrate into the remotest corners.

Everything considered in itself is noble enough. Lower only makes sense in comparison with a higher, and from this point of view the noblest creature falls no less short of God than the lowest creature falls short of the highest.

The meanness of objects does not necessarily cheapen the knower, but only accidentally when his mind is distracted from nobler thoughts or contaminated by inordinate affections, neither of which situations can occur for God.

Power is not called slight because it can deal with slight things, but because it is limited by them. Ability to do mighty things spells ability to do puny things as well.

All this agrees with what is said of divine wisdom reaching *everywhere by reason of her purity, for she is a vapour of the power of God and a certain pure emanation of the glory of the almighty God: and therefore no defiled thing cometh into her.*[1]

1 *Contra Gentes*, 70

313. It does not follow that the divine knowledge is discursive for knowing evil through good. The good is, as it were, the reason for the knowledge of evil, since evil is naught else but the deprivation of good. Evil is known in good as an implication in a definition, not as a conclusion in premisses.

459　　　　　　　　　　　　1 *Contra Gentes*, 71

314. The Logos implies a relationship to creatures, for God in knowing himself knows them all. The word conceived in the mind represents everything actually understood. Whereas in our minds there are diverse words for the diverse things we utter, God knows himself and all other things besides in one act by a unique word, and that word is expressive of God and of crea-

1 Wisd. vii. 24–5.

tures. Of himself his knowledge is contemplative; of other things both contemplative and productive. The Word in the Father is expressive; with respect to creatures it is expressive and operative. *For he spake and it was done*;[1] the poetic reasons of all things made are in the Word.

4, 94, 286   *Summa Theologica*, 1a. xxxiv. 3

315. If we speak of an idea in the strict sense as a form producible in being, then one idea comprehends the singular together with the species and genus there individualized, for in a single reality Socrates, man, and animal are not distinct. But if we speak of an idea in the wide sense as a likeness or meaning, then there are correspondingly different ideas, since we can separately consider Socrates as Socrates, as man, and as animal.

283   Disputations, III *de Veritate*, 8, *ad* 2

316. God's knowledge is the cause of things, related to creatures as any artist's is to his works of art. One intelligible form relates to opposites and the same science deals with contraries, and therefore knowledge does not produce a decision unless influenced by appetite. Hence the cause of things is the divine knowledge, but as having will conjoined. This is customarily called the knowledge of approbation.

698   *Summa Theologica*, 1a. xiv. 8

317. Knowledge does not involve causality until the will joins in.

913   *Summa Theologica*, 1a. xiv. 8, *ad* 1

II. DIVINE WILL

318. From its inner nature does one thing turn toward another; furthermore, according to the differences of

[1] Ps. xxxii. 9 (Vulgate).

natural conditions are the differences of natural bents. Material things are, as it were, bound and stiffened with matter and so they are not self-directing; their tendencies follow a physical determinism and are shaped by the outside principle of their nature. But non-material substances are freer from matter; in various degrees they act and desire spontaneously and from within. Were the artist's idea of a house a natural form,[1] he would not be free to design or not to design a house, or to make it in this style or that. In sensitive substances forms are received to some extent without matter, yet they are not completely spiritual and without material conditions, for the play of physical organs is engaged. Their tendencies are not wholly free, though an imitation and likeness of freedom is there.[2] But in intellectual natures, where forms are received without matter, the full play of freedom is ensured and with it the ability to will. To material things, then, natural appetite is attributed; to animals a sensitive appetite; to intellectual substances a rational appetite or will, and the more spiritual they are the greater the power of will. Since God is at the summit of spirituality, he possesses supremely and most properly the character of will.

670, 692   Disputations, xxiii *de Veritate*, 1

319. Will belongs to every intelligent being as feeling belongs to every sensitive being. Because there is mind in God there is also will. His knowing is his being, and so is his willing.

Summa Theologica, 1a. xix. 1

[1] Physical, as contrasted with intentional, ideal, volitional. Cf. 586, 595, 596, 670, 697.
[2] They are voluntary in the broad sense of the term, but not deliberate. Cf. 671, 682.

320. He wills himself and things other than himself; himself as the end, other things as ordered to that end. It befits the divine goodness that other things should be partakers therein.

Summa Theologica, 1a. xix. 2

321. His own goodness is sufficient; but that he can will naught else is not a consequence.

Summa Theologica, 1a. xix. 2, *ad* 3

322. Of necessity he wills his own perfect and independent goodness. He can gain no perfection from other things. Hence, he does not will them by absolute necessity but by hypothetical necessity, namely on the supposition that what he does will he cannot unwill.

242   *Summa Theologica,* 1a. xix. 3

323. The will of God is the cause of things. That God acts through his will, and not, as some have supposed, from natural necessity, appears on three grounds.

First, from the system of active causes. Mind and nature both act for a purpose. Ends are prefixed to natural forces by intelligence, as when an archer accurately flights an arrow to its target. An intellectual and voluntary agent must be prior to natural forces. Therefore, since God is first in the order of efficient causes he acts by mind and will.

Second, from the very nature of efficient causes. A natural cause is determined to the production of one effect, for nature, unless interfered with, acts in a constant manner. But the divine being is not a special kind of thing, but contains within itself the whole plentitude of being. Unless it causes an indeterminate and infinite being, which is out of the question, it cannot act by necessity of nature. Determinate effects proceed from its infinite perfection by a decision of mind and will.

Third, from the relationship of effect to cause. Effects pre-exist in the cause and according to its mode of being. Since the divine being is the divine understanding, effects pre-exist there in an intelligible manner. They proceed from him intelligibly and consequently through will.

167, 388   *Summa Theologica*, 1a. xix. 4

324. As in one act God understands everything in his essence, so by one act he wills everything in his goodness. As his understanding of a cause is not the cause of his understanding the effect, though he understands the effect in the cause, so his willing an end is not the cause of his willing the means, though he wills means to be directed to end. In other words, he wills this to be for that, but his willing this is not because of his willing that.

298, 694   *Summa Theologica*, 1a. xix. 5

325. An event may escape from the scheme of a particular cause, but never from that of a universal cause which includes all particular causes. If any particular cause fails in its effect this is because of the hindrance of some other particular cause, itself contained in the universal scheme. Therefore no effect can possibly be a freak to the universal cause. Since God's will is the universal cause of things, it is quite impossible that it should fail in its projects.

Summa Theologica, 1a. xix. 6

326. When a cause is vigorous the effect is covered not merely as to its substance, but also as to its manner of becoming or being done. Since the divine will is supremely effective, it follows not only that those things are done which God wills to be done, but also that they are done in the way that he wills. He wills some to come about necessarily and others contingently, so that there may be a pattern of things for the complement of the universe. And therefore he prepares necessary causes for some effects, unfailing causes whence effects derive of necessity, and contingent and defective causes for other effects, causes from which events derive contingently.

Summa Theologica, 1a. xix. 8

327. The love for a thing may be measured either on the side of the act of will or on the side of the object loved. The act of will may be more or less intense, and from this point of view God does not love one thing more than another, for he loves all by one simple and always constant act of will. But as regards the object, as we may be said to love that person the more to whom we wish the greater good, though the intensity of the act may not be greater, so we can say that God loves some more than others. Since his love is the cause of goodness in things, one thing would not be better than another did he not love it more.

432, 961   *Summa Theologica*, 1a. xx. 3

328. The evil of sin in no real sense is willed by God. It offends against the advance to divine goodness. He wills physical and penal evil by willing the good that is conjoined to them: the love of justice may imply punishment, and the love of the order of nature implies allowing some things to decay.

488   *Summa Theologica*, 1a. xix. 9

329. Hatred of anything cannot be ascribed to God. He wills things for their likeness to his goodness; this assimilation is the good of each and every thing. All active causes love their products after their fashion; parents their children, poets their poems, craftsmen their handiwork. Much less than any of them can God hate a single thing, for he is the cause of everything. *Thou lovest all things and hatest nothing of the things thou hast made.*[1]

Yet he may be said to hate by using a figure of speech, and this for two reasons; first, by willing good to things he wills evil—the contrary of good—not to be; secondly, by willing a greater good ruling out a lesser good. So may he be said to hate, though in truth it is the greater love.

407, 477   1 *Contra Gentes*, 96

330. There are two kinds of justice, commutative and distributive justice. The former enters into the exchange of goods, and does not apply to God, since as the Apostle says, *Who hath first given to him and recompense shall be made to him?*[2] The other enters when things are shared out, as when a ruler or steward gives to each according to his deserts. In a well-ordered state or household this kind of justice is displayed by the lord and master. So the order of the universe, embracing natural and voluntary things alike, manifests the justice of God.

454   *Summa Theologica*, 1a. xxi. 1

331. Mercy is supremely God's—effectively rather than affectively.

Summa Theologica, 1a. xxi. 3

332. The work of divine justice always presupposes the work of mercy and is founded thereon. Creatures have no rights except because of something pre-existing or pre-considered in them, and since we cannot go back and back, we must come to something founded on the sole generosity of the divine will, which is the ultimate end. The possession of hands is owing to human nature

---

[1] Wisd. xi. 25.   [2] Rom. xi. 35.

because of the rational soul, the possession of a rational soul is demanded if we are to be men, but why should we have human nature except because of divine generosity? And so mercy is the root in each and every divine work, and its virtue persists in everything that grows out of that, and even more vehemently flourishes there. The first cause enters into effects more strongly than do secondary causes. Even with regard to things that are a creature's due, God more abundantly dispenses them than the proportion of the claim demands. The order of justice would be served by much less than in fact is granted by divine generosity, which far exceeds what is owing.

390, 392, 1074 *Summa Theologica,* 1a. xxi. 4

333. Presumption is less a sin than despair, for it is more characteristic of God to pity and spare than to punish. Mercy springs from himself, punishment is occasioned by our fault.

940 *Summa Theologica,* 2a–2ae. xxi. 2

III. PROVIDENCE

334. Everything is provided for in the scheme of the universal cause; nothing can evade it.

1043 *Summa Theologica,* 1a. xxii. 2, *ad* 1

335. Divine causality reaches to all beings, not only in their specific but also in their individual principles, not only in immortal but also in mortal beings. In whatsoever sense they can be said to exist, all things are divinely directed to their ends.

Summa Theologica, 1a. xxii. 2

336. When a master sends two servants to the same place, their meeting may seem to them a chance encounter. So a happening may seem haphazard or casual

with respect to lower causes when it appears unintentional, but there is nothing fortuitous about such events with respect to a higher cause.

Opusc. xii, *Compendium Theologiae*, 137

337. Providence, properly speaking, is the plan of ordering things to an end and is the principal part of the virtue of prudence.

Summa Theologica, 1a. xxii. 1

338. There are two elements in providence, the plan and its execution, which is called government. As regards the former, God's plan is immediate to everything, for in his mind is the reason for everything, even for the very least. As regards the latter, there are intermediaries, for the divine rule governs lower by higher, not from any defect of power, but from abundance of goodness endowing creatures with the dignity of causing.

Summa Theologica, 1a. xxii. 3

339. A twofold process can be watched at work, one according as things emerge from their principle, the other according as they are directed to an end. Disposition concerns the former, for things are said to be disposed according as they are arranged in different grades by God, thus an artist variously arranges the parts of his work, and thus composition is a part of art. Providence concerns the direction of things, and so it differs from divine art and disposing. Divine art is exercised in the production of things, disposition in their order, providence in their direction to an end.

Disputations, v *de Veritate*, 1, *ad* 9, *i*

340. Some of the ancient philosophers postulated merely a material cause, and since they did not accept efficient causality they could not admit final causality.

Afterwards others accepted the former, but said nothing of the latter. Both sets imagined that the world-process happens from the determinism of preceding causes, either material or efficient. This can be disproved by philosophical science.

Disputations, v *de Veritate*, 2

341. It may be said that in human affairs the same fate attends good and bad alike; *All things happen equally to the just and the wicked;*[1] and therefore that human affairs are not ruled by providence. It may indeed strike us that there is no rhyme or reason in the result because we are ignorant of the particulars of divine dispensation, yet we need have no doubt there is a good reason. A man goes into a smithy and judges that the tools are needlessly numerous, but that is because he has no knowledge of the craft, for they are all serviceable and are designed for a proper purpose.

Disputations, v *de Veritate*, 5, *ad* 6

342. Does divine predestination impose necessity on human acts? In this matter we must proceed cautiously so that truth may be strengthened and error avoided. For it is equally false to say that human acts and events do not fall under divine foreknowledge and that foreknowledge and divine predetermination load human acts with necessity, for that would abolish freedom, the opportunity of giving counsel, the usefulness of laws, the care for acting aright, and the fairness of rewards and punishments.

691   Opusc. xxvi, *de Rationibus Fidei ad cantorem Antiochenum*, 10

343. Fate is the ordering of secondary causes to effects foreseen by God, and so whatever is subject to secondary

[1] Eccles. ix. 2.

causes is subject also to.fate. But whatever is done immediately by God is not subject to secondary causes, nor therefore to fate, for instance the creation of things, the glorification of spiritual substances, and the like. Hence Boethius says that things nearest to godhead are steadfast and escape the changeable order of fate, and that the farther a thing is from the first mind the more deeply it is involved in the meshes of fate.[1]

1029 *Summa Theologica*, 1a. cxvi. 4

IV. DIVINE POWER AND ACTION

344. God is powerful, and strength of action is justly ascribed to him.

Divine power is his substance, divine power his action.

11 *Contra Gentes*, 7, 9

345. Power signifies a principle that puts into execution what knowledge directs and will commands.

Summa Theologica, 1a. xxv. 1, *ad* 4

346. God is the greatest actuality and the principal being, hence his action must close first of all on something real, though non-being may be a consequence. Therefore omnipotence cannot make affirmation and negation to be simultaneously true, or anything else involving such a contradiction.

Disputations, 1 *de Potentia*, 3

347. Whatever can have the nature of being is counted among the possibles, and God is called almighty with respect to these. Whatever implies contradiction does not fall within the scope of omnipotence, for it cannot

[1] *de Consolatione Philosophiae*, iv. 6.

begin to look possible. It is more appropriate to say that such things cannot be done, rather than that God cannot do them.

32, 303   *Summa Theologica,* 1a. xxv. 3

348. To sin is to fall short of a perfect action; and to be able to sin is to be able to fail, which is no trait of omnipotence.

480, 887   *Summa Theologica,* 1a. xxv. 3, *ad* 2

349. To undo the past is no function of omnipotence.

Summa Theologica, 1a. xxv. 4

350. Divine wisdom is not so restricted to any one particular scheme of things that another could not be produced.

32   *Summa Theologica,* 1a. xxv. 5

351. Concerning the institution of things we should discuss what their natures demand, rather than what God could have done.

Opusc. xxi, *Declaratio XXXVI Quaestionum ad lectorem Venetum,* 24[1]

352. When it is said that God could make things better, the proposition is true if *better* is taken substantively, for he could always improve on any one thing. But if the term is taken adverbially, referring to the mode of divine action, then God could not make things with greater wisdom and goodness.

925   *Summa Theologica,* 1a. xxv. 6, *ad* 1

353. Given the things that do in fact actually exist, the universe cannot be improved on. Were any one thing bettered in kind, the proportions of the whole

[1] Bassiano of Lodi.

scheme would be ruined, just as when a harp-string is overstretched the melody is spoilt.

Summa Theologica, 1a. xxv. 6, *ad* 3

354. It is ridiculous to say that the power of the sun is for the sake of the worms that breed in its heat; divine power even less is for the sake of its effects.

171   Disputations, 1 *de Potentia*, 1, *ad* 13

355. God does not seek his glory for his own sake, but for ours.

Summa Theologica, 2a–2ae. cxxxii. 1, *ad* 1

356. The operation of a thing is twofold, as Aristotle[1] teaches: one is immanent and is a perfection to the doer; the other issues into external reality and is a perfection to the thing made. Both belong to God: the first in that he understands, wills, loves, and rejoices; the other in that he produces things in being and sustains and fosters them. The first is termed an operation or activity, the latter rather a making.

II *Contra Gentes*, 1

357. All irrational nature is related to God as instrument to principal.

Summa Theologica, 1a–2ae. i. 2

358. As the impetus in the arrow's flight shows the archer's aim, so the spontaneous necessity of natural things declares the governance of divine providence.

Summa Theologica, 1a. ciii. 1, *ad* 3

359. It must be granted without qualification that God operates in all natural and voluntary activity. Through not appreciating the situation accurately, some have made the mistake of attributing all action exclusively to

---

[1] Metaphysics, 1050ᵃ18. Cf. Commentary, ix, *lect.* 8.

God and denying that natural things perform by their proper powers, as though fire did not heat, but that God creates heat.[1]

1091   Disputations, III *de Potentia*, 7

360. Similarly in other cases. Some have interpreted the workings of efficient causality as though no created power has any real effect on things, but that God alone is the direct cause.

This, however, is impossible, for it would abolish the order of cause and effect among created things, and this would reflect ill on the power of the creator; for to impart power of action to an effect comes from very strength of causality. Furthermore, the operative powers we notice in things would be futile were they destitute of real action.

Therefore we must so understand God's action in efficient causes as to leave intact their own proper actions. In order to make this clearer, bear in mind that, of the four classes of cause, the material cause is not a principle of action, but rather the recipient. But the others, namely the final, efficient, and formal causes, are principles of action and according to a well-defined precedence. As regards all three of them, God operates in every action.

First, as an end. Since every action is for the sake of some good, whether true or apparent, and since nothing is or appears good unless it shares in some likeness of the supreme good, which is God, it follows that he is the final cause of every action.

Second, as efficient cause. When there are many subordinate causes, the secondary always act in virtue of the power of the first. And so God is the first efficient cause of the actions of every cause.

---

[1] The doctrine of occasionalism, i.e. that creatures are not true causes, but occasions of divine causality.

Thirdly, as regards formal cause. Remember that God not only moves things to their actions by applying forms and powers to their activities, like a woodman setting his axe to cutting down a tree though he has not produced the form of axe, but that God gives created things their forms as well and preserves them in being, as the sun is said to be the cause of the display of colour. Now because form is intrinsic to a thing, and all the more so when it is comprehensive and primary, and because God himself is the proper cause of the very being of everything, it follows that he intimately works in everything. *Thou hast clothed me with skin and flesh; thou hast put me together with bones and sinews.*[1]

111, 117, 119, 236, 326, 442, 1047　　　*Summa Theologica*, 1a. cv. 5

361. God has so communicated his goodness to creatures that one thing can shed on another what it has received. To detract from the proper actions of things is to disparage divine goodness.

If creatures exerted no actions productive of real effects, we could never deduce their natures from their effects, and all natural science would go by the board.

442　　　　　　　　　　　　III *Contra Gentes*, 69

362. The same effect is not ascribed to God and to the natural cause engaged as though each were responsible for a part, for the whole effect proceeds from each, though in different ways.

III *Contra Gentes*, 70

363. Divine art is not exhausted in the production of creatures, and therefore can operate otherwise than according to the customary course of nature. But it does not follow that by acting against the general run

[1] Job. x. 11.

of things divine art contravenes its own principle, for an artist is well able to devise a work of art in a style different from his first production.

325   Disputations, vi *de Potentia*, 1, *ad* 12

364. When the three following rules are taken into account, namely that God is the cause of the being of natural things, that he has particular interest and care for each, and that he does not act by the compulsion of his nature, we can see how some particular effects need not agree with the usual course of nature. The effect may surpass the entire power of nature as regards the intrinsic being of the event, for example the quality of glory,[1] or as regards its happening in such and such a subject, for example sight in a blind man, or because it has demanded the suspension of the action of otherwise inevitable forces, for example the combustion of fire or the current of streams.

43   Disputations, vi *de Potentia*, 1

365. Such an event is not against nature simply speaking, because it is consonant with nature by and large, which covers the order of all creatures to God.

Disputations, vi *de Potentia*, 1, *ad* 1

366. There are three characteristics of a miracle; first, that it is above the power of natural forces; second, that it is beyond the natural disposition of the subject; third, that it is beside the normal course of events. These three notes are somehow present in every miracle, namely of difficulty for the first, beyond expectation for the second, rareness for the third. Effects which immediately come from God alone but which follow the grain of things, for example the infusion of the rational soul or of grace, are not miraculous.

1069   Commentary, *IV Sentences*, xvii. i. 5, *iii*

[1] In the beatific vision.

367. A miracle is an accredited witness pointing to divine power and truth.

Disputations, vi *de Potentia*, 5

368. Demons can work certain strange effects, but not miracles in the technical sense.

Disputations, vi *de Potentia*, 3

369. The perfect act of an intellectual nature is that activity whereby it grasps everything.

731, 737   *Summa Theologica*, 1a. xxvi. 2

370. The sum total of good things is in God, by mode of total simplicity, not of composition.

186   *Summa Theologica*, 1a. xxvi. 1, *ad* 1

371. Whatever the promise of any joy, whether it turns out to be well founded or illusory, pre-exists wholly and superlatively in the divine joy. As to contemplative happiness, God has the continuous and most certain contemplation of himself and everything else; as to active happiness, the government of the entire universe. As to earthly happiness, which lies in pleasures, riches, power, dignity, and fame, he possesses joy in himself and in all other things for his delight; instead of riches he has the complete self-sufficiency desired in riches; for power he has omnipotence, for dignity the sovereignty over all, and for fame the wonder of creation.

252, 767   *Summa Theologica*, 1a. xxvi. 4

V

Creation[1]

372. There are three phases in the going out of creatures from God. We ask first, what is their cause; second, how they come about; third, what is the principle of their staying.

Summa Theologica, 1a. xliv, Prologue

373. God's spirit is said to move over the waters as an artist's will moves over the material to be shaped by his art.

858, 860   *Summa Theologica,* 1a. lxvi. 1, *ad 2, ii*

I. CREATURES

374. By dwelling on creatures the mind is kindled into loving divine goodness. For all the perfections scattered throughout the universe flow together in him who is the spring of all goodness. If therefore the goodness, beauty, and freshness of creatures so draw our hearts, how much more then God who is their source? Creatures are but rivulets, he is the main stream. *Thou hast given me, O Lord, a delight in thy doings: and in the works of thy*

---

[1] The doctrine marks a decisive advance. It frees itself from physical incident or 'historic' fact; the philosophical theory is committed neither to the statement that once upon a time the world began nor to taking sides in the dispute about infinite numbers. Nevertheless, it goes beyond anything that Aristotle had said; causality is taken to the heart of being and not left with the transmutations of kinds or qualities of being, more or less profound. The need of a purely total cause is inferred, whose action produces, sustains, and activates all derivative realities, extending to all things and penetrating to every mode and part.

hands I shall rejoice.[1] And again: *They shall be drunk with the plenty of thy house,* that is the universe; *and thou shalt make them drink of the torrent of thy pleasure. For with thee is the fount of life.*[2]

300, 386   II *Contra Gentes,* 2

375. When affection is said to delight in something for its own sake, the phrase *for its own sake* can be understood either to mean the final cause, and in this sense nothing save the last end can be delighted in for its own sake, or to mean the formal cause, and in this sense one can take delight in whatever is delightful by its own form. A sick man delights in health for its own sake as in an end, and in pleasant medicine as having a good taste, though it is not the end he is after, but not in bitter medicine for its own sake, for it is a draught he takes solely on account of the end. Similarly one may say that man delights in God for himself as being the last end, and also in virtuous activities, not because they are ultimate, but because of the real worth held in pleasant things.[3]

215, 721   *Summa Theologica,* 1a–2ae. lxx. 1, *ad* 2

376. The being of creatures is not through anything else if the word *through* denotes the intrinsic formal cause; if it denotes the exemplar and efficient cause, then their being is through the divine being, not through themselves.

238   Commentary, *I Sentences,* viii. i. 2, *ad* 2

377. Science ensures right judgement about creatures. Their drawback is that they are occasions of our turning

---

[1] Ps. xci. 4.   [2] Ps. xxxv. 8–9.

[3] There is an analogy between efficient and final causes. As efficient causes may be secondary yet principal and not merely instrumental, so final causes may be penultimate ends and not merely means to an end.

away from God. Consequently the gift of science corresponds to the third beatitude: *Blessed are they that weep, for they shall be comforted.*[1]

Summa Theologica, 2a–2ae. ix. 4

378. Mortal creatures are not themselves direct causes of our sin, but occasions only, and accidental causes.

Disputations, v *de Veritate*, 3, *ad* 1

379. To curse irrational things as creatures of God is blasphemous, to curse them for themselves is valueless and vain.

Summa Theologica, 2a–2ae. lxxvi. 2

380. To hold creatures cheap is to slight divine power.

iii *Contra Gentes*, 69

381. By faith in God a man may be guided to his final goal; and nevertheless he may imagine that he is subject to certain forces when in point of fact he is above them, all because he is ignorant of nature and of his place in the cosmos. We are warned by Jeremiah: *Be not afraid of the signs of heaven which the heathen fear.*[2]

75   ii *Contra Gentes*, 3

382. The first cause, who is purely active without passivity, does not work to acquire an end, but intends solely to communicate his perfection.

Summa Theologica, 1a. xliv. 4

383. Art, the idea of a thing to be made in the mind of the maker, is possessed most authentically by God. *Wisdom, which is the worker of all things, taught me.*[3] To give, not for any return but from the very excellence

---

[1] Matt. v. 5.   [2] Jer. x. 2.   [3] Wisd. vii. 21.

and consonance of giving, is an act of liberality. God
is supremely liberal.

1 Contra Gentes, 93

384. It is congenial to good that something should
come from it, not that it should come from something else.

Summa Theologica, 1a–2ae. i. 4, *ad* 1

385. When they desire any good whatsoever, whether
by intellective, sensitive, or unconscious appetite, all
things desire God as their end, for nothing attracts but
for some likeness to God.

164   *Summa Theologica*, 1a. xliv. 4, *ad* 3

386. Multiplicity can proceed from unity in three
ways. First, by division, as when a whole is broken up
into many parts; such multiplication takes away the
integrity and completeness of the whole. Secondly, by
common predication, as when many species issue from
one genus, and many individuals from one species; what
are here multiplied are not subsisting things, but general
natures. Thirdly, by effusion, as when many rivers rise
from one source, and water from a spring spills into
many streams. In this last comparison there is some likeness to the going out and distribution of distinct goods
from the divine goodness, though here no lessening of
the original is involved in the separation and multiplication, for the divine goodness remains undivided in its
essence, unspent, and simple.

Opusc. xiv, Exposition, *de Divinis Nominibus*, ii, *lect.* 6

387. When they came to scrutinize the natures of
things, the ancients recapitulated the sequence in individual processes of human knowledge, which begins from
the senses and reaches to the understanding. The first

philosophers were occupied with sense objects and step by step climbed to intelligible truths. Now because accidental forms are sensible, unlike substantial forms, they imagined that all forms were accidents, and that substance was matter. Because substance suffices to account for the accidents emanating from its principles they invoked no other cause save matter. This was supposed to explain the events we witness among sense phenomena. Furthermore, they were convinced that matter itself had no cause and they roundly denied the existence of any other causes.

Later philosophers, however, began to address themselves after a fashion to substantial forms, yet without reaching to a universal judgement, since their chief preoccupation was with special forms. They postulated certain active factors serving to transmute matter, but these were not regarded as imparting being as such. According to this reading some material reality was presupposed to the action of the efficient cause, but the whole of being was not considered to derive from it.

Later philosophers still, such as Plato and Aristotle with their followers, reached the stage of considering being in general, and they were remarkable, as Augustine notes,[1] for professing a universal cause of reality from which everything issues forth into being.

59, 655, 1091   Disputations, III *de Potentia*, 5

II. CREATIVE ACTION

388. We must examine the emanation, not merely of particular things from particular causes, but also of the whole of being from the universal cause, designated by the name *creation*.

Summa Theologica, Ia. xlv. I

[1] *de Civitate Dei*, viii. 4, where Plato is praised, Aristotle not mentioned.

389. In studying the emanation of things in their entirety from the universal principle of being, matter, though not produced as a thing, must not be left out of account.[1]

398   *Summa Theologica*, 1a. xliv. 2, *ad* 1

390. That God can and does make something from nothing should be steadfastly held. Every efficient cause acts inasmuch as it is actual, and consequently the mode of its action corresponds to the actuality of its being. Now a determinate being is determinately actual, and on two counts: first in itself, for the entire substance is not actual, since it is a compound of matter and form, actual through its form; secondly in its actuality, which is limited to one class or kind, and does not include the perfection of every other actuality. It is active as a being of a determinate kind, not as being merely a being. As an efficient cause is, so does it act; and therefore a natural cause does not produce being absolutely, but being in a subject and being as realized according to this or that kind. Consequently a natural cause acts by transmutation, requires material on which to work, and is unable to produce something from nothing.

But God is otherwise; he is totally actual, both in himself, for he is pure act unmixed with potentiality, and with reference to actual beings, for he is their origin. The whole of subsisting being is produced by his action, to this action nothing is presupposed. He is the principle of being entire according to his entire simplicity; for which reason he can produce something out of nothing.

427, 436, 1013   *Disputations*, III *de Potentia*, 1

---

[1] Matter is a substantial reality, the potential principle in a complete material substance, or thing.

391. In saying that a thing is produced from nothing, the preposition *from* does not denote material stuff, but precedence, as when we say, noon comes from forenoon, that is it follows after. Note that the preposition can either include or be included in the negation expressed by the term *nothing*: in the former case a priority of previous non-being to what exists now is stated; whereas in the latter case the sequence is disclaimed, and the sense of *produced from nothing* is *not produced out of anything*, as when we say, he speaks of nothing, meaning that he does not speak of anything.

427   *Summa Theologica*, 1a. xlv. 1, *ad* 3

392. Creation implies a thing's existence in fact, not that it has been achieved as the result of a preceding process. No approach to being is involved, nor any transmutation. What is stated is just initial reality coupled with a reference to the creator. In this sense creation is original freshness related to God.

134   Disputations, III *de Potentia*, 3

393. In mutation there is a constant subject before and after. Therefore creation is not mutation, except by stretching the term.

125   *Summa Theologica*, 1a. xlv. 2, *ad* 2

394. Nothing is presupposed to the universal production of things; nothing to which anything could be owing. Only afterwards can claims be lodged. God depends on no other, nor looks to receive anything. He who acts because obliged by justice does not act simply from himself but because he is bound by something other than himself. The first cause owes no debt of justice. *Who hath first given to him and it shall be*

*recompensed unto him again? For of him, and through
him, and in him, are all things.*[1]

332   II *Contra Gentes*, 28

395. Nevertheless, in terms of a particular creature, a
just due may appear by referring back from what
comes after.

II *Contra Gentes*, 29

396. Being is what the mind first conceives as most
evident, and into which it resolves all conceptions. No
reality can be added to being as though it were something extraneous to being, as a difference can be added
to a genus or an accident to a substance. The only kind
of addition that can be entertained is the making
explicit of a special mode unexpressed in the general
term *being.*

This making explicit may take two forms. The mode
stated may be a special grade of being, for there are
degrees of being according to the different classes in
which things can be ranged. Or it may state a general
mode consequent on all being, whether in itself, thus
essence and *one*, or by relationship, thus *something, good,
true.*

429   Disputations, I *de Veritate*, I

397. Existence is all-pervading. When a particular man
comes to be, what first appears is existence, then life,
then humanity, for he is an animal before he is a man.[2]
And so back again, he first loses the use of reason and
life and breath remain, then he loses these, but existents
are left.

206, 207   Opusc. x, Exposition, *de Causis, lect.* I

[1] Rom. xi. 35.
[2] The priority is in the arrangement of realities; a succession
measurable by time is not alleged.

398. Properly speaking, *to be created* applies to things which properly speaking can be said *to be,* namely complete substances. As accidents and substantial forms are not complete things, for they are co-existents rather than existents, it is more exact to refer to them as concreated rather than created.

Summa Theologica, 1a. xlv. 4

399. Bare matter does not exist alone in reality by itself, since it is purely potential, not actual being.

510   *Summa Theologica,* 1a. vii. 2, *ad* 3

400. In its active sense creation signifies divine action invested with a certain logical relationship, and as such is uncreated itself. In its passive sense it signifies a real relation, which is a created entity; though to speak more precisely, a creature is a substance, and this real relationship is not a thing, but a reality inhering in a thing, and therefore concreated rather than created.

Disputations, III *de Potentia,* 3, *ad* 2

401. As regards the thesis that the action of God is interior and exterior, and that the exterior ceases with the object—if it be understood to mean that God acts by some exterior action that is not his substance, then the proposition is wholly false; but it can be defended when taken to mean that the action is exterior because of its object, not by reason of itself.

As regards the thesis that to create posits an object in time, and that therefore the act is temporal and subject to the rules of time and may not be before it is—this again refers to the object, but it is not happily phrased as seeming to signify the action.

Opusc. XXIII, *Declaratio cviii dubiorum ad Magistrum Generalem,* 71, 72[1]

[1] Arising from a commentary on the *Sentences* by a fellow

402. Creation is the primordial action, presupposing no other and presupposed to all others. Hence it is an action peculiar to God, who is the first cause.

Moreover, he alone is the universal cause of being. The first and proper cause of existence neat is the first and universal cause; other efficient causes are not the cause of being absolute, but of being such or such a thing.

204   II *Contra Gentes*, 21

403. While allowing that creation is the proper action of the universal cause, some have, nevertheless, supposed that inferior causes can be creative as instruments of the first cause. Even Peter Lombard[1] held that God can communicate creative power, in such wise that a secondary cause acts as a minister, not by its own authority.

This, however, cannot be the case. For a secondary instrumental cause does not share in the action of a principal except by working dispositively through its own proper power to the effect intended. Otherwise it would be futile to adopt it. Now the proper effect of creative activity is presupposed to all others, and no instrument can predispose to its production. Creation works without raw material requiring to be prepared by an instrumental cause.

43   *Summa Theologica*, 1a. xlv. 5

III. SUSTAINING ACTION

404. Every creature is to God as the air to the sun that lights it.

117, 234   *Summa Theologica*, 1a. civ. 1

Dominican, Peter of Tarentaise, afterwards Pope Innocent V. The Master-General of the Order was John of Vercelli.

[1] The author of the *Sentences*, the chief theological text-book of the scholastic period.

405. Positively considered the twist in creatures to nothingness is but their dependence on the causal principle of their being.

Commentary, II *Sentences*, XIX. i. 1, *ad* 7

406. If things emanated from God from all eternity it would be impossible to assign an instant or period when they first began: either, therefore, they were never produced, or their being is always emanating from God as long as they exist.

Augustine[1] says that when a man is building a house the edifice remains after he has ceased his work and gone away, whereas the world would not stand for a single instant if God withdrew his support. Here is rejected the position of those who argue as though a thing did not need an active cause except while it was in process of being made.

427 III *Contra Gentes*, 65

407. We can speak of the power of God either absolutely or relatively to his wisdom and prevision. To speak absolutely, God could withdraw his sustaining action and things would cease; but allowing for his wisdom and what he has freely disposed he will not have it so. *For God made not death; neither hath he pleasure in the destruction of the living. For he created all things that they might be;*[2] not that they might fall into nothingness.

329 IV *Quodlibet*, 4

408. As creatures come forth from nothing so could they go back there, did God permit.

Disputations, V *de Potentia*, 4, *ad* 10

409. To be able to be denotes the active power of the creator, not a passive potentiality in a subject. To be

---

[1] *de Genesi ad litteram*, iv. 2.   [2] Wisd. i. 14.

liable to lapse into nothingness does not imply a potentiality in the creature to non-being, but a power in the
creator of not communicating being.

    435, 436   *Summa Theologica*, 1a. lxxv. 6, *ad* 2

410. Were a thing to be annihilated, God could still
restore it with the same numerical identity.

                                          iv *Quodlibet*, 5

IV. ETERNITY OF THE WORLD

411. Creation precisely states a principle of origin, but
not necessarily a principle of duration.

    134, 250   Disputations, iii *de Potentia*, 14, *ad* 8

412. For time itself is contained in the universe, and
therefore when we speak about creation we should not
inquire at what time it happened.

                            Disputations, iii *de Potentia*, 17

413. The statement that something was before time
can be understood in two senses. First, before a period
of time and before anything temporal; in this sense the
world was not before time, for the instant of its beginning was temporal, though then it was not in time as in
a section of time but as in a point of time. But the
question can be directed to an instant before any other
instant; in this sense the world was before time. It does
not follow that the world is therefore eternal, for that
temporal instant before time is not itself eternal.

    131, 144   Disputations, iii *de Potentia*, 17, *ad* 5

414. That the world must have existed always is not a
necessary truth, nor can it be demonstratively proved.

                          Summa Theologica, 1a. xlvi. 1

415. That the world has had a beginning is credible,
but not demonstrable; that is, a beginning cannot be

strictly deduced either from the concept of an object of which the meaning is not temporal or spatial, or by an analysis of the causality involved in its production.[1]

138 *Summa Theologica*, 1a. xlvi. 2

416. Arguments for perpetual change and time are not cogent, yet even they necessarily imply an everlasting spiritual substance.

Commentary, XII Metaphysics, lect. 5

417. God is before the world in duration, yet *before* does not mean a priority of time, but of eternity, or perhaps, if you like, an endlessness of imaginary time.

Summa Theologica, 1a. xlvi. 1, *ad* 8

418. To be infinite in substance is one case, to be infinite in magnitude quite another. Granting there might be a body infinite in magnitude, it would not thereby be infinite in nature, for it would still be limited to a definite kind by its form and to an individual thing by its matter. We assume then that no creature can be infinite in substance. The question now remains open whether it can be infinite in magnitude.

Remember that a body, which is a complete magnitude, can be considered under two aspects; as a mathematical body, in which case quantity only is engaged, or as a natural body, in which case matter and form are included. That a natural body cannot be infinite is manifest, for it must have a determinate substantial form, from which determinate accidents result, quantity among them. So every natural body has a determinate quantity, great or small as the case may be. The same line of argument touches a mathematical body; if it be

[1] Other arguments, e.g. from the energy-entropy cycle, whatever their validity, would not be classed as demonstrations, but as 'probable' arguments proper to physics.

imagined as actually existing then it must be imagined as existing under some form. The form of quantity as such is figure, consequently such a body must have some figure. It would, therefore, be finite, for a figure is bounded by limits.

232   *Summa Theologica*, 1a. vii. 3

419. A geometrician is under no necessity of assuming that a given line is actually infinite, but merely that from a given actually finite line he can always subtract a quantity as required, which line he terms an infinite line.

Summa Theologica, 1a. vii. 3, *ad* 1

420. To be infinite is not irreconcilable with magnitude in general, but with the notions of the various kinds of magnitude, two-dimensional, three-dimensional, and so forth.

Summa Theologica, 1a. vii. 3, *ad* 2

421. The quantitative infinite is associated with matter, since by division of a whole we approach to matter, for parts are like matter; while by addition we approach to the whole, which is like form. Infinity is found in the division, not the addition, of magnitudes.

Summa Theologica, 1a. vii. 3, *ad* 3

422. Change and time are not actually whole but successively, therefore they have potentiality mingled with actuality. Magnitude, on the other hand, is an actual whole. Indefiniteness or infinite dimensions are ruled out, therefore, in the case of actual sizes; they may be applied, however, to change and time.

230   *Summa Theologica*, 1a. vii. 3, *ad* 4

423. Can there be an infinite number? Concerning this question two opinions have been advanced. Some, like

Avicenna and Algazel, while dismissing a multitude actually and essentially infinite, admit the possibility of a multitude accidentally infinite. A multitude would be termed essentially infinite when the very existence of something depended on an infinity of things, which is impossible, for its coming into existence would also depend on an infinity, and would therefore never be completed. A multitude is termed accidentally infinite when the infinity is not required but happens. The difference may be illustrated by an example. Blacksmith's work displays a multitude of causes, art in the mind, skill in the arm, a hammer, and so forth. Were these infinitely multiplied, the smithing would never be finished. Yet the number of hammers employed, resulting from the breaking of one after another, is a chance happening; it makes no difference whether one, or two, or many are used, or even an infinity if the work is performed in infinite time.

The other opinion professes to find this impossible. For every multitude in fact must be some kind of multitude. The kinds of multitude are like the kinds of numbers, of which none is infinite, for every number is a multitude computed by units. An actually infinite multitude, even taken accidentally, is on this account impossible. But a potentially infinite multitude is possible, for the increase of a multitude follows the division of a magnitude; the more you divide the more numbers result. Because there is a potential infinity in dividing a continuum (approaching as it were to matter), for the same reason there is a potential infinity in adding to a multitude.

145, 447   *Summa Theologica*, 1a. vii. 4

424. If it be urged that one conclusion may follow from another and so on and on, note that arguments do

not go round and round in circles, but they tend to advance in a straight line, as Aristotle notices, along which infinite motion or process is impossible.

Commentary, *I de Anima, lect.* 8

425. A thing which exists always is not exempted from needing another in order to exist.

117   Disputations, III *de Potentia*, 13, *ad* 1

426. Even had the world existed always it would not be co-eternal with God, for, as Boethius remarks, its existence would not have been entire all at once, which is the note of eternity, described by him as the perfect possession altogether of endless life.[1] The succession of time comes from change.[2] Variableness necessarily excludes true eternity, but not indefinite duration.

214   Disputations, III *de Potentia*, 14, *ad* 1, *ii*

427. Let us suppose, in agreement with Catholic belief and against some people's mistaken views, that in fact the world has not existed from eternity, but once had a beginning, as holy writ testifies. The doubt emerges, nevertheless, whether it could always have existed.[3]

In order to open out the truth of the matter let us begin by observing where we agree with our opponents and where we differ. If crediting eternity to something other than God is equivalent to meaning that it was not made by him, that would be an ungracious error, not against faith merely, but also against the doctrine of

---

[1] *Consolatio Philosophiae,* v. 6.
[2] *Physics,* 218[b].
[3] This *opusculum de Aeternitate Mundi* is, together with the *de Ente et Essentia* and the *de Unitate Intellectus,* the most celebrated of St. Thomas's smaller works, and is here quoted extensively as a typical example of his mode of arguing by methodic exclusion.

philosophers, who teach and prove that anything existing in any way whatsoever cannot exist unless caused by the greatest and truest being. If all that is meant, however, is that a thing always was, though caused by God in its entirety, then we are on the point of the debate.

Were this called impossible the reason alleged would be, either that God could not make something that always was, or that it could not be done even when allowances have been made for omnipotence. Both sides agree on the first proposition that God can do everything. What has to be looked into is the second proposition.

That it cannot be done will be supported on one of two grounds; either because such a reality would exclude passive potentiality, or because it would involve a contradiction in terms.

As to the first, let it be remembered that no process of becoming precedes the established being of a pure spirit; there is no passive potentiality before its existence, and no production of it from presupposed material. Nevertheless, God can produce a pure spirit in existence, and has done so. In this context it may be admitted that a thing caused by God could not exist always if this implied an eternally pre-existing passive principle. However, this is not entailed in the statement that God could make a reality that always was.

As to the second, we speak of an impossibility on account of the inherent repugnance of the ideas involved, for instance that contradictories should be simultaneously true. Though some hold that God can do the impossible, while others deny it because of the nonentity of the impossible, in truth it is out of the question for God to produce what would be a self-destructive object. Yet to affirm that God could do it would not be contrary to faith, though I hold that it would be false. For instance, to assert that what has happened has not happened is a contradiction in terms, and similarly that omnipotence may cause things that have happened to be as if they had not happened at all; whoever says this, remarks Augustine,[1] does not notice that what he is saying is that some things are true inasmuch as they are false. All the same some authorities have devoutly professed that God can so wipe out the past, nor were they deemed heretical.

Therefore we should look closely to see whether these two notes, namely *caused by God* and *always existing*, are incompatible. Whatever the merits of the case the charge of heresy cannot enter here, though, were the ideas mutually exclusive, I hold that an everlasting creature would be a figment. But if the ideas do not clash it would be otherwise, and to deny its possibility would be a mistake. Furthermore, it would derogate from omnipotence, which exceeds our power and understanding, to say that we could conceive of something God could not produce. Nor is sin at all relevant, for that as such is emptiness. The whole question, therefore, boils down to this: Are the ideas *entirely creaturely* and *without a beginning in duration* mutually exclusive or not?

That they do not cancel out may be shown as follows. Their mutual exclusiveness could only be on account of one or both of the following postulates; first, that a cause must precede its effect in duration; secondly, that non-being must precede being in duration, as when we say that creation is from nothing.

Observe that there is no need for the efficient cause, in this case God, to precede his effects in duration, unless he so wills it. To start with, no cause instantaneously producing effects necessarily antedates them in

[1] *Contra Faustum.*

duration, and God is a cause able to produce effects suddenly and not through a process of change. The major premiss may be made clearer by induction from sudden effects such as radiations and so forth, and may be proved by deduction as follows: when a thing is supposed to exist, at that very moment the beginning of its action can also be supposed, as appears even with things that come to be through natural processes, for at the very instant that fire begins so does heating. Now in an instantaneous action the beginning and the end are simultaneous, indeed identical. At the very instant an efficient cause is conceived of as producing its instantaneous effect, the term of its action is also posited. The action and the finish are instantaneous. Well then, it is not contradictory to conceive of a cause producing an instantaneous effect and not preceding it in duration. This of course would be inconceivable in the case of a cause producing its effects through successive stages; here the beginning must precede the finish. Because people usually deal with causality working through a process, they do not readily recognize that an efficient cause is not necessarily antecedent to its effect in duration—laying down the law on special problems is rather apt to go along with lack of experience.

It cannot be objected against this line of reasoning that God acts through his will, for the will does not necessarily precede its effects in duration, except when its action is deliberative, and far be it from us to attribute deliberation to God.[1]

Furthermore, a cause producing the whole substance of an effect is no less potent than is a cause producing the form, indeed, it is much more potent, for it does not merely educe a form from potential material. Yet a transforming cause may so act that whenever it exists its effects

[1] God does not calculate, or make up his mind in stages, as we do.

exist also, as with the light of the sun. With much stronger reason can God so act that his effect is whenever he is.

Then again, a cause that could not produce a contemporary effect would be lacking its complement, for a complete cause and its effect are simultaneous. But nothing is lacking in God. Therefore his effects may always be, on the supposition that he always is, and he is not bound to precede them in duration.

Lastly, the will of the willer does not diminish his power, least of all with God. The opponents of the Aristotelean argument—to the effect that creatures have always existed because like always makes like—urge that this is tantamount to treating God as a non-voluntary cause. But the same objection applies to what they would admit, namely that he is a voluntary cause but cannot unmake the things he has caused so as to make them as though they had never been.

Hence, to say that an efficient cause need not antedate its effect manifestly offers no violence to the mind. It now remains to inquire whether on account of its being made out of nothing it is impossible to conceive of a creature that never was not.

In the *Monologion*[1] Anselm shows that this is not a contradiction: the third interpretation, he says, of the words *made out of nothing* is when we understand that it is made, but that there is not anything out of which it is made. A similar turn of speech is employed when somebody grieving without cause is said to grieve about nothing. According to this construction no awkwardness follows if we mean that all beings, apart from the supreme being, are made out of nothing, that is, not made out of anything. Nor is precedence implied, such as would mean that once there was nothing, and then afterwards there was something.

[1] Chapter 8.

Even were precedence indicated, and the statement
to bear the sense that the creature was made after
nothing, this term *after* would mean precedence only
in the most general sense. For precedence may be of
nature or of duration. The general and universal does
not imply the particular and proper.[1] That the creature
is after nothingness does not imply that once in duration
there was nothing and then afterwards something was,
but merely that nothing is prior by nature to reality. For
that which a thing has of itself is prior to what it receives
from another; now a creature's reality is received from
another; therefore left to itself and considered in itself
it is as nothing, and there is nothing in it before being.

Nor would it follow that non-being and being would
be simultaneous unless nothing precedes being. For we
do not say that if creatures always were there would be
a time when there was nothing, but that creaturely
beings are such that they would be non-beings were
they left to themselves.

Clearly, then, there is no contradiction in affirming
that a thing is created and also that it never was non-
existent. It is certainly strange that Augustine did not
notice any, for it would have been a decisive disproof
of the eternity of the world, which he attacked on many
scores but not on that. On the contrary, he rather hints
that no contradiction is present.

There are other objections which I skip for the
present, partly because they are dealt with elsewhere
and partly because their very weakness lends force to
the position they oppose.

144, 145, 406   Opusc. IV, *de Aeternitate Mundi contra*
                       murmurantes

[1] That is, the general category of precedence, in things' natures,
does not entail the sub-category of precedence in duration.

VI

Variety[1]

428. Having considered the production of things in being, we now turn to the variety they display, beginning with the distinction of things in general[2] and going on to their distinctions in detail, first as regards good and evil,[3] then as regards spirit and body.[4]

Summa Theologica, 1a. xlvii, xlviii, Prologues

I. MONISM AND PLURALISM

429. Parmenides was among those who maintained that the whole world was one being. He seems to have clung to the meaning of formal unity. He argues as follows: whatever is outside being is non-being; now whatever is non-being is nothing; therefore whatever is outside being is nothing. But being is one. Whatever,

[1] Reflections about the spiritual value of the lyric and the metaphysical status of personality recoil on the perennial problem of the One and the Many. In St. Thomas, as in Aristotle, two streams converge; from the Ionians the strong sense of reality in motion, from the *Italikoi* the appreciation of formal pattern. The dualism of potentiality and actuality is taken into the heart of being. Hence, the multitude of things perceived by experience is established in metaphysics, not by a mixture of being and non-being, but by a composition of partial realities. The real distinction between essence and existence in creatures provides for their separation from the One, while preserving intact their substance; they are true things, not merely appearances. This central thesis of his metaphysics supports his universal use of analogy. The criticism of monism is conducted beyond the levels of sensibility and ethics and is sustained in theology; there is no suggestion of pantheism in his mystical theory, nor of scorn for creatures in his ascetical discipline.

[2] 429–57.   [3] 458–94.   [4] 495–516.

therefore, is outside this single reality is nothing. Evidently he banked on the formal notion of being, which seems to be one, so much so that anything supervening to diversify being is inconceivable, for it would be extraneous to being and therefore nothingness, which cannot diversify being. His mistake lay in treating the nature and meaning of being after the fashion of a generic object. But being is not a genus, but is predicated in manifold ways of different things.

193, 230, 396   Commentary, *I Metaphysics, lect.* 9

430. The very differences that divide beings among themselves are real. God is not the author of the drift towards nothingness, but of being; he is the principle, not of fault, but of multitude.

404   Disputations, III *de Potentia*, 16, *ad* 3

431. The fineness of the idiosyncrasies of created things within the pattern they make is missed by labouring the point that secondary causes are responsible for the variety, and they cannot match the simplicity of the first cause.

228   II *Contra Gentes*, 42

432. The distinction of things has been ascribed to various causes, and by some to matter, either alone or in conjunction with an efficient cause. Democritus, for example, and the old natural scientists, allowed no cause but matter; in their opinion the distinctiveness of things comes from the chance motions of matter. Anaxagoras introduced mind, which defines things by separating them from the swirl.

But this will not pass, and on two counts. First, because matter was created by God and consequently the distinctions flowing from matter must be traced

back to a higher cause. Secondly, because matter is for
the sake of form, not form for the sake of matter. Now
the distinction of things comes from their proper forms,
matter of itself being amorphous.

Others attributed the distinction of things to secondary causes, as did Avicenna. He held that God produced the first intelligence by understanding himself,
and this, since it was not identical with its own being,
consequently let in composition of potentiality and
actuality. The first intelligence, by understanding the
first cause, produced the second intelligence, and in
understanding itself to be potential produced the
heavenly bodies and motion, and in understanding itself
to be actual produced soul.

But neither will this pass, and also on two counts.
First, because things which cannot be caused save
through creation are produced by God alone, and to
this class belong all things not subject to physical
generation and corruption. Secondly, because the explanation proposed would amount to saying that the
universe of things does not issue from the intention of
the first cause but from the interplay of many efficient
causes, in other words from chance. Therefore the
finished arrangement of the universe, which requires
a diversity of things, would consist in a random collection.

Hence, we must conclude that the distinction and
multitude of things is established by the intention of the
first cause, which is God. For he brought things into
existence in order to communicate his goodness to creatures and to be reflected in them. And because one
creature alone was not enough for that manifestation,
he produced many and diverse things, so that what was
wanting in one might be supplied by another.

302, 307   *Summa Theologica*, 1a. xlvii. 1

II. ESSENCE AND EXISTENCE

433. Actuality and potentiality are wider terms than form and matter.

557   Opusc. xvi, Exposition, *de Trinitate*, v. 4, *ad* 4

434. Though there is pure actuality without potentiality, there is never in nature a potentiality that is not related to some actuality; thus there is always some form to primary matter.

254   Disputations, *de Spiritualibus Creaturis*, 1

435. The difference of essence between compound and simple substances is that the former are composed of matter and form whereas the latter are pure forms.

Two other differences ensue. One is that the nature of a compound substance can be signified as a whole or as a part, on account of individuation by matter; but the two significations are not interchangeable at choice; for instance, you cannot say that a man is his nature. But the nature of a simple thing, which is its form, cannot be signified except as a whole, for, save the form, nothing is substantial, for there is no material subject receiving the form. Therefore in whatever way you take it, the nature of a simple substance can be predicated of the thing.

The second difference is this: the essences of compound things are received in determinate matter and multiplied by its divisions, so allowing for things that are the same in kind but diverse in number; whereas the essences of simple things are not so received, and consequently no such multiplication is possible; in their case many individuals of the same species cannot be found, but as Avicenna expressly says,[1] there are as many species as individuals.

[1] *Metaphysics*, v. 2.

Notwithstanding the absence of matter, however, these forms are not entirely simple substances, for they are not pure actualities but mingled with potentiality, as will presently appear.

Whatever is not contained in the very concept of the essence or quiddity arrives from outside and enters into composition with the essence; no essence can be conceived without its essential parts. But every essence can be conceived of without postulating its existence in fact; I can talk about the natures of man or phoenix without deciding whether or not they do exist in real nature. Therefore it is plain that existence is different from essence, save in the case of a thing whose essence is existence.[1]

Such a thing necessarily would be unique and first. For plurality can result only from the addition of some difference, as when a genus is multiplied into its species, or when a form is propagated in diverse matters and hence a species is multiplied into many individuals, or when one reality is pure and another participates in it. But if there be a thing which is pure existence, and therefore subsisting existence,[2] this existence cannot receive the addition of a difference, otherwise it would not be pure existence but existence together with some other form besides. Still less can it receive the addition of matter, for then it would not be subsisting but material. Therefore we conclude that a thing identical with its existence must be unique.

It follows that in everything else the existing is one reality and the essence or nature another and distinct reality. With pure intelligences, then, existence is dis-

---

[1] The argument is not for a distinction between the mental concept of a thing's meaning and its reality, but between the principles respectively by which a thing *can be* and *is*.

[2] Subsisting, i.e. in itself, not in a subject.

tinct from form; which explains why an intelligence has been pronounced to be a form and an existence.[1]

What belongs to a thing is either caused by the principles of its nature, as a sense of humour in man, or comes to it from an extrinsic principle, as the light in the air from the sun. It cannot be that the very existence of a thing derives from its form or essence, I mean as from an efficient cause, for then a thing would be the cause of itself and would produce its own existence, which is impossible. Therefore it must have existence from another. And because anything that is by another must be resolved into something that is of itself as into its first cause, so there must be a being which is the cause of existence in all things because it is itself pure existence.

187, 204, 206,   Opusc. VIII, *de Ente et Essentia ad Fratres*
207, 231, 288   *Socios*, 5

436. In substance there is a threefold manner of possessing essence, namely as in God, as in spiritual substances, as in material substances.

God's essence is his very existing. Therefore we come across some philosophers who declare that God does not have a quiddity or essence, because his essence is none other than his existence.[2] From this it follows that he is not in a genus, for whatever is in a genus has a nature in front of its existence; generic or specific natures as such are not distinguished in diverse things but are repeated by diverse existences in them. Yet in saying that God is pure existence we should not fall into the error of those who hold that God is the universal existence whereby everything formally is.[3] For the very condition of God's

[1] An intelligence, i.e. a pure spirit. The argument repeats Avicenna. Note that essence and existence are not distinct 'things'.
[2] Avicenna.
[3] The followers of Amaury de Bènes.

existence is that no addition can be made to it. It is existence distinct from every other by its very purity, whereas the concept of common existence neither includes nor excludes any addition, otherwise something could not be conceived of that added to common existence. So it is that no perfection or nobility is wanting in pure existence; rather God embraces the perfections found in all classes. The Philosopher[1] and the Commentator[2] call him the absolutely perfect, having all perfections in a more excellent manner than do other things: perfections that are diverse among them are one in him, and all agree together in his simple existence.[3]

In the second manner essence is possessed by created intellectual substances. Their essence is other than their existence, though their essence is without matter. For this reason their existence is not absolute, but received and limited and defined by the capacity of the receiving nature, though this last is unrestricted and unreceived by any matter. The *Liber de Causis*[4] notes that pure intelligences are finite from above, but infinite from below. They are finite as regards the existence they receive from above, but they are not defined from below, because their forms are not limited by the capacity of any matter receiving them. Therefore, among such substances, a multitude of individuals of the same species can be found.

[1] Aristotle, *Metaphysics* 1021[b]30.

[2] Avicenna, *in loco*.

[3] The argument turns on the distinction between sheer existence, in which every value is implicit, and common, or as we say *mere*, existence, which is but a premiss to more vivid conclusions.

[4] Cf. St. Thomas, Commentary, *V Metaphysics*, *lect.* 4. The *Liber de Causis* was an extract from Proclus, commented on by many scholastics, ascribed to Aristotle before the time of St. Thomas.

An exception, however, must be made in the case of the human soul, on account of its union with the body. Though the individuation of the soul depends on the body as the occasion for its starting off, for the soul does not obtain individualized existence except in the body of which it is the actuality, it does not follow that when the body is taken away the individuality of the soul also perishes, for since it has spiritual reality on which it gains the individual existence of being the form of this body, that existence still remains individual. Therefore Avicenna says that the individuation and multitude of souls depends on the body in the beginning but not in the end.[1]

Now because their essence is not existence, spiritual substances can be discussed according to the categories; genus, species, and difference can be applied to them, though their specific differences are unknown to us. Even in sensible things these differences are unknown and have to be signified by accidental differences springing from essential principles, as causes are signified by effects and bipeds stand for men. The proper qualities of spiritual substances are unknown to us, and we can signify neither their specific nor their qualitative differences.

Bear in mind that genus and specific difference do not apply in the same sense to intellectual and to sensible substances. With the latter, the genus is taken from what is material in the thing, the difference from what is formal.[2] (Hence, Avicenna, at the beginning of his first book *de Anima*, says that the form in things com-

[1] *de Anima*, v. 3. The expression is not found in so many words in Avicenna's text.

[2] Thus material thing with the specific difference of vegetative life becomes plant, this in its turn is the material of the specific difference of sensitive life so becoming animal, and this with rationality becomes man.

posed of matter and form is the unmixed differentiation
of that which is constituted from it; not, however, that
form is itself the difference, for it is rather the principle
of the difference, as he says in his *Metaphysics*.[1] The
differentiation is said to be unmixed because it is taken
from what is part of the nature of the thing, namely
from the form.)[2] The position is not the same with
spiritual substances. They are simple natures and the
principle of differentiation cannot be sought in what is
part of their nature. It must be from the whole nature.
Therefore Avicenna says that only those natures have
unmixed differentiations whose essences are composed
of matter and form.

So also the genus of spiritual substances should be
taken from the whole essence, but differently in different
cases. Bodiless substances agree with one another in
spirituality, but they differ in degrees of perfection
according as they draw away from potentiality and
draw nigh to pure actuality. Inasmuch as they are
spiritual a genus can be assumed in them; inasmuch as
they are graded in perfection they take specific differences, but what these are we do not know. Note,
however, that these differences are not of accidents,
differences of more or less that do not diversify the
species. The degree of difference in receiving a form
does not make a difference in kind, as in the case of
white and off-white: a different degree of perfection,
however, within the forms or natures themselves makes
a difference of kind.

The third manner of possessing essence is found in
substances composed of matter and form. In them the
existence is received and limited, and also the nature or
essence is received in dimensional matter. Therefore

[1] *Metaphysics*, v. 5.
[2] Form as such is not mixed, or a composite of matter and form.

they are finite both from above and from below. In their case a multiplication of individuals within the same species is possible, because of the divisions of dimensional matter.

433, 539, 589   Opusc. VII, *de Ente et Essentia ad Fratres Socios*, 6

III. DIVERSITY

437. Multitude and distinction are not fortuitous, but decided and wrought by the divine mind in order that divine goodness might be shadowed forth and shared in many measures. There is beauty in the very diversity.

233   Opusc. XIII, *Compendium Theologiae*, 102

438. The divine ideas are set on the being of things. But singulars are real more truly than are universals, since universals do not abide save in singulars, which, therefore, better deserve to be held in the ideas.

Disputations, III *de Veritate*, 8

439. That the effects of God should achieve his simplicity in their likeness to divine goodness is impossible. Accordingly his simple and unique reality is reflected from creatures by diverse and dissimilar facets. Diversity of things is therefore necessary, so that divine perfection should be imitated.

Opusc. XIII, *Compendium Theologiae*, 72

440. A thing is known the more fully when its differences from others are appreciated. Each thing has its own proper being distinct from all others.

I *Contra Gentes*, 14

441. Nothing but his goodness moves God to produce things.

II *Contra Gentes*, 46

442. Many embarrassments crop up from the conclusion that no creatures take an active part in the production of natural effects. To begin with, if God alone operated, and none of them—bodies especially—were causes, variegation would not be found among their apparent effects, for it is not God who is modified through working in various things. Empirically you do not expect fire to freeze, or anything but a baby to be born from human parents. The causation of lower effects should not be so attributed to divine power as to abolish the causality of lower causes.

361   III *Contra Gentes*, 69

443. From the first unique being proceeds multitude and diversity, neither because of the exigencies of matter nor because of any limitation of power, but because of the order of wisdom.

Disputations, III *de Potentia*, 16

444. How many things there are distinct from one another that cannot be made from pre-existing material. Therefore the first cause of the distinction of things cannot be diversity of matter.

II *Contra Gentes*, 40

445. Forms are not diverse so that they may belong to diverse materials, instead materials are diverse so that they may be charged with diverse forms.

Opusc. XIII, *Compendium Theologiae*, 71

446. Matter acquires actual being by acquiring a form.

Summa Theologica, 1a. lxxv. 6

IV. INDIVIDUATION

447. All plurality is a consequence of division. Now division is twofold. The first is material, through the separation of continuous quantity; number, which is a species of quantity, is the result. This numeration is restricted to material things. The second is formal, by contrasted and diverse forms; the result is a multitude, not as such included in the physical categories, but ranged with the transcendentals[1] as when reality itself is divided into the one and the many. This kind of multitude applies to supra-material things.

197, 1118   *Summa Theologica*, 1a. xxx. 3

448. God should not be called an individual substance, since the principle of individuation is matter.

196, 1119, 1120   *Summa Theologica*, 1a. xxix. 3, *ad* 4

449. There is a double distinction in things: one is material in things numerically distinct; the other is formal in things different in kind.

In things subject to birth and death there are many individuals of the same kind, for the conservation of the species.

436   *Summa Theologica*, 1a. xlvii. 2

450. This flesh and these bones and this complexion are not implicit in the definition of man, nevertheless they are included in a thing called a man. Therefore that thing which is a man has in himself something that humanity does not have, and for this reason a man and humanity are not convertible terms. Humanity signifies the formal part.

305, 307, 539, 658   *Summa Theologica*, 1a. iii. 3

451. Numerically distinct substances do not differ merely by their accidents, but also by matter and form. If one asks why one form differs from another of the same kind, no other explanation can be offered except

---

[1] Realities not confined to a class of things.

that they are in different determinate matters. Nor can it be discovered how matter comes to be earmarked otherwise than because of quantity. Therefore matter as subject to dimensions is indicated as the principle of this diversity.

556   Opusc. xvi, Exposition, *de Trinitate*, iv. 2, *ad* 4

452. Among all other accidents quantity has the peculiarity of being self-individuated, because the position or order of parts in the whole is implied in its very meaning. Wherever there is diversity of parts in the same species there also is individuation implied, for what are of the same kind are not repeated except individually. Because the category of dimensive quantity alone carries this separation of specifically similar units, dimensions would appear to lie at the root of individual multiplication.

iv *Contra Gentes*, 65

453. You misjudge quantity if you regard it as an obstacle, except incidentally, to a form's activity.

iii *Contra Gentes*, 69

V. INEQUALITY

454. When Origen wished to refute the theory that the distinction of things derives from a fundamental dualism of good and evil, he taught that in the beginning all rational creatures were equal, and that inequality sprang from free will, since some turned to God more and others less, and some others turned away more and others less. Those who turned to God were promoted to the different orders of angels according to their different merits, while those who turned away were imprisoned in bodies according to the diversity of their sins: this, he explained, was the cause of the creation and diversity of bodies.

This doctrine, which would have it that the corporeal universe came about as a punishment of sin, not for the communication of divine goodness, does not fit what is said in Genesis;[1] *God saw all the things that he had made, and behold they were very good.*

As causing the distinction of things for the perfection of the whole, the same divine wisdom is also the cause of inequality. The universe would not be perfect were there but one level of goodness.

330, 432, 1098   *Summa Theologica,* 1a. xlvii. 2

455. The inequality of parts in the constitution of things is not from any antecedent inequality either of merit or of material predisposition. Inequality is demanded for the perfection of the whole, as appears in works of art: the roof of a house does not differ from the foundations because made of different material, rather the builder selects different materials in order that the house may be perfect in its different parts, and indeed would manufacture such materials if he could not find them.

516, 565   *Summa Theologica,* 1a. xlvii. 2, *ad* 3

456. All things issuing from God are ordered to one another and to God, and therefore all belong to one world. You can assert that many worlds exist on condition that you do not acknowledge one directing wisdom as their cause. You may fancy that everything comes about by chance. Democritus, for example, thought that this world had happened from a collision of atoms, and that there was an indefinite number of other worlds.[2]

164   *Summa Theologica,* 1a. xlvii. 3

[1] Gen. i. 31.
[2] Cf. Aristotle, *de Caelo,* 303ª4.

457. According to Aristotle two systems can be considered in the universe;[1] by the first the whole is ordered to something outside itself, as an army to its general; by the second the parts are ordered to one another, as the various formations of an army among themselves. The second co-ordination is on account of the first subordination.

1117   1 *Contra Gentes,* 78

[1] *Metaphysics,* 1075ᵃ11.

VII

The Problem of Evil[1]

458. Nothing appears more to impugn divine providence in human affairs than the affliction of the innocent.

341, 1106   Commentary, *in Job*, Prologue

459. Though evil is neither good nor of God, nevertheless to understand it is both good and from God.

313   Commentary, *I Sentences*, XIX, v. 2, *ad* 5

I. NATURE OF EVIL

460. Evil cannot be known simply as evil, for its core is hollow, and can be neither recognized nor defined save by the surrounding good.

Summa Theologica, 1a. xiv. 10, *ad* 4

461. Evil precisely as such is not a reality in things, but a deprivation of some particular good inhering in a particular good.

Disputations, 1 *de Malo*, 1

---

[1] The texts follow the order of the *Summa Theologica*. After defining the nature of evil, they turn to the distinction between physical and moral evil, then to the causes of evil, finally to the effects of evil. The universal causality of goodness and the tension between particular goods are the guiding principles. A theoretical dualism of good and evil is rejected, at least in the sense that two fairly equally matched contestants are here represented. Evil is wholly subordinate—the conclusion is not a piece of wishful thinking, but is reached by rigorous analysis. Yet there is no indifference to the combat in practice, no easy optimism; nor is evil dismissed as a mere negation. The good that goes with it provides at once the specific interest and the tragedy.

462. Let us inquire into evil, and then into its causes. And first as to whether it is a real form. Apparently it is.

First, because every class represents a real nature, and evil is a class of things. As Aristotle says, good and evil are not in a class, but are themselves the classes of things.[1]

Second, a specific difference is a real form, and evil is a determinate difference in human conduct, for a good habit differs in kind from a bad habit, as liberality does from avarice or prodigality.

Third, both extremes of two contraries are real forms. Now good and bad are contrasted, not as possession and deprivation, but as contraries. Aristotle proves this by showing that between them there is an intermediate condition, and that one can return from evil to good.[2]

Fourth, what does not exist does not act. But evil acts, for it corrupts good.

Fifth, nothing else but real beings and real natures conspire to the perfection of the universe. Now evil is part of the perfection of the universe. As Augustine says,[3] the admirable beauty of the world is composed of everything; even what is called evil, well ordered and in its place, accentuates the goodness of things.

On the contrary, Dionysius says that evil is neither an existent nor a good.

I answer by explaining that one opposite is known from the other, as darkness from light. Hence the meaning of evil depends on the meaning of good. Now everything desirable is good, and since every nature loves its own being and perfection, it must be said that the being and perfection of any nature has the force of good. Consequently it cannot be that evil signifies a being, or form, or nature. We are left, therefore, to

[1] *Categories*, 14ª33.   [2] Ibid. 22ª, 22ᵇ, 26.
[3] *Enchiridion* x.

draw the conclusion that evil signifies some absence of good.

To the first objection I reply: Aristotle is speaking according to the opinions of the Pythagoreans, who maintained that evil was a reality and that good and evil were genera; he was in the habit of citing contemporary opinions that seemed plausible, especially in his logical works. Or alternatively, we may say with Aristotle[1] that the primary contrast is that between a positive condition and a privation, and this is verified in every contrast of contraries, for one extreme is always imperfect with respect to the other, as black to white, or bitter to sweet. Hence, good and evil may be termed genera, not absolutely, but relatively to the contraries in question, and thus every due form has the character of good and its absence that of evil.

To the second: good and evil are not constitutive differences except in moral matters, where the end is the specific determinant, because the object of will is that on which morality depends. Good and evil are specific differences in morality; good in itself as an end, and evil as the absence of the required end. Not that the mere absence of a required good of itself constitutes a moral kind, an attachment to an improper end is also needed, by analogy with natural processes, where a privation of a natural form is not caused except by the invasion of another form. The evil that is the constitutive difference in moral matters is a particular good joined to the privation of another good; the end sought by the intemperate man is not the loss of the benefit of reason, but sense-delight involving rational disorder. Hence, evil as evil is not a constitutive difference, but evil as having a good conjoined.

To the third: the above remarks may have cleared up

[1] *Metaphysics*, 1055ᵃ33.

this difficulty. For Aristotle is here referring to good and bad in morality, where an intermediate condition is possible if good be taken for rightly ordered activity and evil for activity that is not only out of right order but injurious to another as well. Hence, he says that a prodigal man is foolish, but not bad.[1] From moral evil there may be a return to good, but not from every sort of evil; from blindness there is no return to sight.

To the fourth: a thing may be said to act in a three-fold sense. First, as a form, as when we say that whiteness makes something white, and in this sense evil as a privative result is supposed to destroy good, for it is that very corruption of good. Second, as an efficient cause, as when a painter is said to whitewash a wall. Third, as a final cause, as when an end is said to cause by moving the efficient cause. In these last two senses, evil when considered precisely as a privation, and not in terms of the good coupled with it, does not cause anything directly. For every action is from some form, and everything desired as an end is somehow a value. Therefore, as Dionysius says,[2] evil does not act, nor is it desired, except in virtue of some good conjoined; of itself it is indefinite and outside our will and intention.

To the fifth: the parts of the universe are complementary and interacting. One may be the purpose and pattern of another. But evil is contracted here only by reason of the good involved. Evil as such does not belong to the perfection of the universe, nor is it comprised in the order of the universe, save accidentally, that is by reason of its incidental conjunction with good.

III, 455, 610   *Summa Theologica*, 1a. xlviii. 1

463. Pure evil, considered in the abstract, is not a specific determinant. Nevertheless, as occurring in a concrete

---

[1] *Ethics*, 1121*25.   [2] *de Divinis Nominibus*, iv. 20.

subject, it is a differentiating characteristic. Moral acts
are diversified by good or bad ends.

Commentary, II Sentences, xxxiv. i. 2, *ad* 3

464. Initially and without qualification something may
be judged to be good or evil, yet this decision may have
to be reversed when additional circumstances are taken
into account. It is good for a man to live, bad for him
to be killed; but if we add that the man is a murderer
and a public danger, then his death may be good and
his living an evil.

170   *Summa Theologica*, 1a. xix. 6, *ad* 1

465. Evil denotes the lack of good. Not every absence
of good is an evil, for absence may be taken either in
a purely negative or in a privative sense. Mere negation
does not display the character of evil, otherwise non-
existents would be evil and, moreover, a thing would be
evil for not possessing the goodness of something else,
which would mean that man is bad for not having the
strength of a lion or the speed of a wild goat. But what
is evil is privation; in this sense blindness means the
privation of sight.

Now the subject alike of a form and of its privation
is identical, namely potential being. This is either
simply potential being, that is bare matter, which is the
subject of a substantial form and of its contrasted
privation, or being which is actual simply speaking,
though potential relatively and from one point of view,
thus a transparent body which can be the subject both
of light and of darkness.

Every being in potentiality as such is good, for to the
extent that it is related to being to that extent is it
related to good. We are left to draw the conclusion that
the material subject of evil is good.

Summa Theologica, 1a. xlviii. 3

466. The material of evil is not, of course, the good which is opposed to it, but some other good; the subject of blindness is not the sight, but the animal.

575   *Summa Theologica*, 1a. xlviii. 3, *ad* 3

467. A thing is called evil for lacking a perfection it ought to have; to lack sight is evil in a man, but not in a stone.

Opusc. xiii, *Compendium Theologiae*, 114

468. The drive to good is essential to every cause, natural and voluntary alike; and therefore evil is not directly purposed.

But not everything besides what is intended is casual or fortuitous. It may be a regular or frequent consequence of what is directly intended.

Evil is a deprivation of good, and a privation is not a nature or real essence, it is a negation in a subject.

Evil cannot be caused except by good, and even then indirectly; this is clear both in physical and moral affairs.

Every evil is based on some good, for it is present in a subject which is good as having some sort of nature. Evil cannot exist but in good; sheer evil is impossible.

iii *Contra Gentes*, 4, 6, 7, 10, 11

469. The subject of evil is good, not precisely the good opposed to evil but the good potential to it. From this it is clear that not any kind of good is the subject of evil, but that alone which is potential to a perfection of which it can be deprived.

Opusc. xiii, *Compendium Theologiae*, 117

470. Evil is a by-product.

Disputations, iii *de Potentia*, 6, *ad* 3

471. Good enters every genus.

208 *Summa Theologica*, 1a. xlviii. 3, *ad* 3

472. No evil as such can be desirable, either by natural appetite or by conscious will. It is sought indirectly, namely because it is the consequence of some good. This is the rule for every type of appetite. A natural force works for a form, not for the absence of form. Yet one form may extrude another. A lion kills for food, that means the death of the deer; a fornicator wants pleasure, and incurs the deformity of sin.

Summa Theologica, 1a. xix. 9

473. The universe is for the best considering the present postulates, but not considering what God could have done.

565 *Disputations*, III *de Potentia*, 16, *ad* 17

474. God and nature and every other cause work for the optimum total effect, and to the completion of each single part, not in isolation but in relation to the entire system. The whole itself, the universe of creatures, is better and the more perfect for the things that can fall short in goodness, and which sometimes do fall short in the event without God preventing them. It happens thus, for, as Dionysius says, the role of Providence is not to regiment but to respect nature. What may fail should fail sometimes. Also, as Augustine says, God is so powerful that he can make good even out of evil.[1] Many good things would be missed if God permitted no evil to exist: fire would not burn unless air were consumed, lion would not thrive unless asses were killed, nor would just retribution be inflicted and long-suffering patience praised but for the iniquity of persecution.

147, 1107 *Summa Theologica*, 1a. xlviii. 2, *ad* 3

[1] *Enchiridion*, xi.

II. DUALISM

475. Under the good the Pythagoreans ranged light, unity, understanding, rest, the straight, male, right, definite, even, and square; and under evil as contraries, darkness, plurality, opinion, movement, the curved, female, left, indefinite, odd, and irregular.

Commentary, I Ethics, lect. 7

476. The goal of purpose is what is good, and to this responds the motion of desire. Government is conducted according to a scheme directed to an end. To this end all means are subordinate. Its purpose, therefore, is what is conceived to be good. There cannot be a ruling sovereignty which seeks evil for its own sake. There is no justification for holding that there are two kingdoms, one of good, the other of evil.

This error seems to result from the habit of lifting departmental considerations into the domain of universal causes. When people experience contrary particular effects proceeding from contrary particular causes, for instance, when they observe how water cools and fire heats, they are prone to believe that these opposed processes are continued back into the first principles of things. Then, because all contraries seem to be comprised under the headings of good and evil in that one of them by comparison is always deficient, they reckon that the primary active principles are the Good and the Evil.

170   Opusc. VII, *de Substantiis Separatis*, 15

477. There is not one first principle of evil as there is of good. In the first place, the original principle of things is essential good. Nothing can be essentially bad. Every being as being is good; evil does not exist except in a good subject.

In the second place, the first principle of good things is supreme and perfect good containing all goodness in itself. Now there cannot be a supreme evil, for though evil lessens good, it can never totally destroy good; while good remains, nothing can be an entire and unmitigated evil. For this reason Aristotle observes that a wholly evil thing would be self-destructive.[1] Were all good entirely destroyed—and this would be required for evil to be complete—evil itself would vanish since its subject, namely good, would no longer be there.

In the third place, the very notion of evil is irreconcilable with the notion of a first principle, because evil is caused by good; also because evil can be a cause only incidentally, and therefore cannot be the first cause, since the accidental is subsequent to the essential.

Some have proclaimed that the two prime rulers are Good and Evil. Here lies a root of error from which other strange doctrines of the ancients have sprouted. In attending to the particular causes of particular effects they failed to consider the universal cause of all being. When they found one thing by its natural force injurious to another, they reckoned that the very nature of the thing was evil; as if one were to say that the nature of fire is evil because it burns down the house of some poor man. The estimate, however, of a thing's goodness does not primarily depend on any particular reference, but on its being and on its relation to the whole universe, wherein every part holds its perfectly appointed place.

Similarly, when they discovered two contrary particular causes of two contrary particular effects they were at a loss how to resolve them into a universal common cause; therefore they pushed back the contrariness of causes into the first principles of things. Since all

[1] *Ethics*, 1126ª12.

contraries have a common ground, we should instead look for one common cause above their proper contrary causes.

121, 206   *Summa Theologica*, 1a. xlix. 3

478. The devil is called the god of this world, not because he created it, but because worldlings serve him. St. Paul uses the same turn of phrase: *Whose god is their belly.*[1]

541   *Summa Theologica*, 1a. lxv. 1

479. To shun evil and seek good are parts of the same process, like movement downwards and upwards.

III *Contra Gentes*, 3

III. PHYSICAL AND MORAL EVIL

480. An evil in natural things is a privation of a due form, and therefore to receive a form which involves the loss of a proper form is an evil; thus to be set on fire. In moral matters, to attach oneself to an end which involves missing the due end is evil, not precisely because of the end desired but because of the coupled deprivation. Two moral acts directed to contrary ends differ from one another as right from wrong.[2] The two corresponding contrary habits are antagonistic, not precisely because of the privation by which one is termed vicious, but because of the end to which the privation is attached.

777, 883, 908   Opusc. XIII, *Compendium Theologiae*, 116

481. Since evil is deprivation and defect, and since defect can occur not only within a thing's natural condition but also in its dynamism as directed to an end, it

[1] Phil. iii. 19.
[2] Morality is a general category of human acts, covering right, wrong, and indifferent.

follows that evil can have this double sense, namely of a deficiency of being, thus blindness is an organic defect, and of a deficiency of activity, thus limping is a functional defect. This evil in an activity, either physical or voluntary, which is not ordered to its appropriate end is called *peccatum*, or sin.[1] So a doctor sins in his action when he does not operate for health, so also does nature sin in begetting a monster.

Opusc. XIII, *Compendium Theologiae*, 119

482. In voluntary activity it is called not only a sin but also a *culpa* or fault, since the doer is responsible and therefore deserves blame and punishment.

780, 781, 891 *Opusc.* XIII, *Compendium Theologiae*, 120

483. Evil is privation of good. Good is actuality, and this is double; primary actuality, which is the form and integrity of a thing, and secondary actuality, which is its operation. The incidence of evil is on both; on the former by a withdrawal of form or of any integral part, thus blindness or the lack of a limb; on the latter by a gap in the proper activity, either by non-performance or failure in execution or direction.

Now since good for its own sake is the proper object of will, the evil of being deprived of it has a special relevance to rational creatures endowed with will. The evil which consists in the impairment of form and integrity has the characteristic of penalty or pain; the evil which consists in bad operations has the characteristic of fault, for it is imputed to someone as a fault when he falls short in his proper and responsible activity.

Summa Theologica, 1a. xlviii. 5

[1] Yet unless otherwise qualified by the context sin means moral disorder or fault, that is misdirection as regards man's ultimate happiness.

484. Guilt and penalty are not the main divisions of evil in general, but of the special evil arising from a moral issue.

Summa Theologica, 1a. xlviii. 5, *ad* 2

485. Fault, more than penalty, has the character of evil, even when penalty is given a meaning broader than that of a physical forfeit. Two reasons can be offered. First, a man is bad by the evil of fault rather than of penalty: as Dionysius says,[1] to be worthy of punishment rather than to be punished is evil. The reflection that God is the author of physical evil but not of moral evil prompts the second reason.

328　　　　　　　　　　*Summa Theologica*, 1a. xlviii. 6

486. Considering the exigencies of the material from which he is made, death and disease are natural to man; but considering his form, immortality is his right, though the principles of nature alone are not sufficient to ensure this: the aptitude is inherent, but the achievement is a gift.

565, 570　　　　　　　　　　Disputations, v *de Malo*, 5

IV. CAUSE OF EVIL

487. We must say that every evil in some way has a cause. For evil is the deficiency of a good that is a thing's birthright. That anything falls short of its due and natural perfection can come about only from some cause dragging it out of its course.

Yet only what is good can cause. If we consider the various kinds of cause, the efficient, final, and formal causes, all spell a certain finish, which is a characteristic note of good; matter also, as being potential to good, verges on the nature of good. That good is the

---

[1] *De Divinis Nominibus*, iv. 22.

material cause of evil has already appeared. As regards the formal cause, evil has none; instead it is rather the privation of form. Similarly, it has no final cause, but is rather the privation of due order to end; good covers not only the end, but also the means. Evil has an efficient cause; this, however, is indirect, not direct.

Let us make this clearer by observing the difference of causation as regards evil in the action and as regards evil in the effect respectively. In the action evil is caused by defect of some active principle, either in the principal or in the instrumental cause; an ungainly walk may result either from a defect of motive power, as in babies, or from a disability of the limb, as in the lame. On the other hand, evil is caused in the effect sometimes by the very energy of the agent—not, however, in the proper effect of the agent—and sometimes by the intractability of the matter. When the privation of one form is a necessary consequence of the form introduced by the agent, as when fire expels the form of air or water, the more energetic the agent the more forcibly it impresses itself and destroys the contrary. Destruction comes then from the very strength of the flames; even so the energy is directly bent on mastering, not on destroying, though in effect it is incidentally destructive. But if there be a defect in the proper effect of fire, if, for instance, it fails to heat, then this is either because of weakness in the action, which throws us back on the defective principle already referred to, or from unsuitableness in the material, which does not receive the action of the flame playing on it.

But the fact that a thing is deficient is incidental to the goodness by which it is active. Hence, it is true to say that evil has naught but an incidental cause; in this sense good is the cause of evil.

III   *Summa Theologica*, 1a. xlix. 1

488. Augustine says that God is not the author of evil because he is not the cause of sagging to nothingness.[1] The evil which consists in a defective action is always caused by some weakness in the agent. God's supreme perfection is flawless. Hence the evil which consists in defective action or which derives from a defect in the agent is not to be reduced to divine causality.

But the evil consisting in the destruction of something falls under divine causality, as appears in natural and voluntary affairs alike. A cause which by its power produces a form is also the cause of the consequent destruction and defect. The form principally intended by God among created things is the well-being of the general scheme, which requires that some can and will fail. And so in causing a good collective arrangement, God consequentially, and as it were indirectly, causes the corruption of things. *The Lord killeth and maketh alive*.[2] When we read, *God made not death*,[3] the sense is that he does not will death for its own sake. Nevertheless, the demands of justice are bound up with the order of the universe, and they require that sinners should be punished. Thus God is the author of the evil of penalty, but not of the evil of fault.

328, 1062   *Summa Theologica*, 1a. xlix. 2

489. We should cast back to the first unfailing cause for all the reality and value present in the effect of a deficient secondary cause, but not for what is missing there. All the motion in the action of limping is caused by the power of walking; that the gait is lopsided does not come from the power but from the malformation of the limb. So, too, whatever being and act there is in an evil action, all must be resolved into God as

[1] *Lib. lxxxiii Quaest.* 21.   [2] 1 Kings ii. 8 (Vulgate).
[3] Wisd. i. 13.

in its cause, but whatever defect is present there is caused, not by him, but by the defective secondary cause.

Summa Theologica, 1a. xlix. 2, *ad* 2

490. In one respect a thing may be actual and causal, and in other respects lacking and deficient. Thus, a blind man has the power of walking, but because of his disability he may undergo the defect of stumbling.

An evil action can have a proper effect by the goodness and being that it possesses. Thus adultery causes human generation inasmuch as it is the mingling of man and woman, not inasmuch as the order of reason is wanting.

Summa Theologica, 1a–2ae. xviii. 1, *ad* 2, 3

V. EFFECTS OF EVIL

491. However greatly multiplied, evils can never consume the whole of good.

III *Contra Gentes*, 12

492. To make this clear we should distinguish three headings of good: the first is precisely that good totally taken away by evil, namely the good attacked by evil; thus the light lost in darkness and the sight in blindness. The second is the good neither totally destroyed nor yet even lessened, namely the good which is the subject of evil; for example, the substance of air undiminished by darkness. The third is the good which is diminished but not destroyed, and this is the ability of the subject to act in the proper fashion.

Now this diminution should be illustrated by comparison with the slackening of qualities and forms, not with the subtraction of quantities. This slackening of ability may be tested by its contrary intensity. Ability grows more intense by dispositions toning the active faculty; the more multiplied the acts, the readier the subject becomes to receive the perfection and form of activity. And conversely, the more weakened the subject becomes by contrary dispositions induced by repeated and strong contrary acts, the slacker grows the power for right activity.

But even were the contrary disposition piled up indefinitely, the aptness for right action would be but indefinitely weakened, not wholly destroyed. The root would always remain, namely the substance of the subject. If you interposed an infinity of opaque screens between the air and the sun you would immeasurably diminish the lucidity of air, but this quality would not be destroyed so long as air remained, which of its nature is transparent. Similarly, even if sins could be piled up infinitely, and the soul's ability for gracious activity thereby infinitely lessened (for sins are like obstacles interposed between us and God, *our sins have separated between us and God*),[1] nevertheless, the aptness for virtue would not be totally destroyed, for it follows from the very nature of the soul.

Summa Theologica, 1a. xlviii. 4

493. The schedule of human nature's good estate can be set out under three heads: first, the very principles, components, and resulting properties of human nature, such as the psychological abilities of the soul and so forth; second, the moral inclination to virtue; third, the original endowment of integrity.

The first are neither destroyed nor diminished by moral evil; the third is entirely taken away, while

[1] Isa. lix. 2.

the second is weakened. Acts set up a tendency to do more of the same sort, and given a bias in one direction the trend to the opposite is correspondingly lessened.

Summa Theologica, 1a–2ae. lxxxv. 1

494. The capital of human nature diminished by sin is the natural inclination to virtue instinctive in man as a rational being; to act aright is to act according to reason. Now sin cannot destroy man's rationality altogether, for then he would no longer be capable of sin.

To illustrate a continuous diminution an example has been drawn from quantity. A given quantity can be infinitely subtracted from and yet never wholly disappear. Aristotle says that if you continuously take away the same quantity from a given amount it will eventually disappear,[1] for instance if you keep on taking away a handsbreadth; but if instead the subtraction is always according to the same proportion, you can go on for ever, for instance if you halve what you start with, then again halve a half, and so on: what is subtracted is always less than what was subtracted just before. But this does not apply to the present case, for a later sin does not less diminish the virtue of nature than does a preceding one, but if anything rather more, especially if it be graver.

Therefore we must illustrate the situation otherwise. The inclination to virtue should be taken as a kind of intermediate reality between two extreme terms; on one side supported by and rooted in rational nature, and on the other side climbing to the achievement of virtue as to its finish and end. Weakening may affect either side. But sin does not strike at the root, since it does not

[1] *Physics*, 206^{b}3.

diminish nature itself: what it does is to block the ability from reaching its end; the disability consists in the interposition of a barrier. Thus there can be an infinite lessening of virtue, for always another layer can be added, as when man piles sin on sin. Yet the instinct for right action always remains radically intact.

905, 906, 907   *Summa Theologica*, 1a–2ae. lxxxv. 2

VIII

Body and Spirit[1]

495. Now we must look at the distinction between spiritual and bodily creatures; and first we take the purely spiritual creatures, then purely bodily things, and finally those composed of spirit and body, namely men.

Summa Theologica, 1a. 1, Prologue

496. Every effect shows some trace of its cause. Sometimes it may manifest the causality but not the form of the cause; there is no smoke without fire. This has been termed a footprint, which notifies that someone has passed, but not what manner of man he was. Other effects represent the form of the cause, as when fire is kindled or a statue carved of Hermes. Such a likeness is termed an image.[2]

There is an image of the Trinity in all conscious and loving creatures so far as they exhibit the analogy of conceiving a word and advancing in love.

But in all creatures there is the footprint of the Trinity, inasmuch as each reveals realities to be re-

---

[1] The principles have been stated in previous chapters. All reality is kin; the division between mind and matter is not that between two utterly opposed worlds. Being is scaled down in degrees, from the sheer actuality of God to the bare potentiality of matter. There is no admission of uncreated and intractable stuff, independent of the first cause; no hint that the limited actuality of a spiritual form is contaminated by contact, or even by union, with body. On the contrary, the beauty of the world demands numerical multiplication within the same kind, possible only in material substances; moreover, there are minds which properly require the assistance of sense.

[2] St. Augustine, *de Trinitate*, vi. 10.

solved necessarily into their causes, namely to the divine Persons.

270   *Summa Theologica*, 1a. xlv. 7

I. THE SCALE OF BEING

497. The higher a nature the more intimate what comes from it, for its inwardness of activity corresponds to its rank in being. Inanimate bodies hold the lowest place of all; from them nothing emanates save by the action of one thing on another.

Plants are higher; already in them there is an issuing from within, for the sap is converted into seed, and this when planted in soil grows into a plant. Here the first degree of life may be discerned, for living things are those that set themselves into activity, whereas things that are in motion only inasmuch as they are acted on from outside are lifeless. This is the index of life in plants, that within them there is a principle of motion. Nevertheless, their life is imperfect, for though the emanation is from within at the beginning, that which comes forth gradually becomes wholly extraneous in the end; the blossoms change into fruit distinct from the boughs on which they grow, and presently these, when ripe, fall to the ground and in due course become other plants. Scrutiny shows that the principle of this process is extrinsic to the plant.

Above plants there is a higher grade of life, that namely of sensitive things. Their proper process, though initiated from without, terminates within; the more developed the process, the more intimate this result. A sensible object impresses a form on the external senses, this goes into the imagination and then deeper into the store of memory. What begins from without is thus worked up within, for the sensitive powers are conscious within themselves. So this vital process is superior to that of vegetating proportionately to its greater immanence; but is not yet wholly perfect, since the emanation is always from one thing to another.

The supreme and perfect grade of life is found in mind, which can reflect on itself and understand itself. But there are different degrees of intelligence. The human intellect, though able to know itself, must start from outside objects and cannot know these without sense-images. A more perfect intellectual life is that of pure spirits, where the mind does not proceed by introspection from outside things to know itself, but knows itself by itself. But not yet is the ultimate perfection of life achieved, for though the concept is wholly intrinsic, nevertheless it is not identical with the substance of their mind, since the being and understanding of spiritual creatures are not the same. The highest perfection of life is in God, where acting is not distinct from being, and where the concept *is* the divine essence.

153, 160, 294, 298   iv *Contra Gentes*, 11

498. Production of one thing spells destruction for another. Consequently in human as in animal evolution, when the more perfect arrives the less perfect departs, yet in such a manner that the supervening form keeps the endowment of the preceding, and has much more besides.

534, 553   *Summa Theologica*, 1a. cxviii. 2, *ad* 2

499. Some of the lowest animal kinds scarcely surpass vegetable life. Mussels, for instance, having only the sense of touch, are stationary and embedded like plants.

ii *Contra Gentes*, 68

500. After the works of the six days of creation, none of the things subsequently made by God is so utterly

new as not to be there anticipated in some way. Some
things pre-exist materially, others causally as well, as the
individuals that are now generated pre-existed in the
first individuals of the species. Fresh kinds that may
emerge are present in forces already at work—as animals
of a new species are sometimes produced from the union
of animals of different species, as a mule from an ass
and a mare.

Summa Theologica, 1a. lxxiii. 1, *ad* 3

II. LIVING SUBSTANCE

501. Life is attributed to things observed to be in
motion from themselves and not from another. When
an outside mover is not perceived, simple folk call a
thing alive—quicksilver, for instance, or the waters of
a gushing spring, but not the water in a cistern or
stagnant pond.

519   1 *Contra Gentes*, 97

502. Life is an abstraction from something alive. The
real aliveness of a living thing is its very being.

1 *Contra Gentes*, 98

503. The term *life* has two usages. It may signify the
very being of the living thing, and in this sense happiness
is not life, for to be human and alive is not necessarily
to be happy; only in God is happiness identical with
being. Life may also signify activity, and in this sense
eternal life is termed our last end: *This is life eternal,
that they might know thee, the only true God.*[1]

207   *Summa Theologica*, 1a–2ae. iii. 2, *ad* 1

504. In treating of bodiless substances we begin from
conjectures that have been made from of old, accepting

[1] John xvii. 3.

them when consonant to Catholic belief, and dismissing them when contrary.

57 Opusc. VII, *de Substantiis Separatis*, Prologue

505. The completeness of the universe requires the existence of intellectual and incorporeal substances.

432 *Summa Theologica*, 1a. l. 1

506. Through failing to free themselves from their imaginations, some have been unable to understand that anything can exist without being situated somewhere.

56 Disputations, III *de Potentia*, 19

507. It seems reasonable that the number of spiritual substances should incomparably exceed that of material substances.

418, 423 *Summa Theologica*, 1a. l. 3

III. BODIES

508. Quite untenable is the position that the visible things of this world are created by an evil principle, not by God.

454, 761 *Summa Theologica*, 1a. lxv. 1

509. As Dionysius teaches, it is more fitting that divine truths should be expounded under the figures of humble and not of sublime bodies.[1] First, because the fancy is thereby preserved from error, especially in the case of those who cannot rise above the thought of bodily loveliness; the comparison will certainly not be mistaken for a literal description. Secondly, such portrayal is better adapted to our present state of knowledge about God, when what he is not is clearer than what he is; therefore comparisons drawn from earthly things farthest away from him convey more truly that he

[1] *De Coelesti Hierarchia*, ii. 1.

is beyond anything we can say or think about him. Thirdly, because they serve to veil divine mysteries from those who care not for them.

69, 264 *Summa Theologica*, 1a. l. 9, *ad* 3

510. Since we know through form, we cannot know bare matter in itself.[1] Matter, to begin with, is taken as the subject of form, but we can know it by analogy or proportion, for instance, when we judge that wood is a reality other than the form of a cabinet or a couch.

Commentary, *I Physics, lect.* 13

511. Matter itself cannot be adequately known except through motion. Its investigation is the physicist's job; the philosopher should accept his findings.

44 Commentary, *VII Metaphysics, lect.* 2

512. Matter by itself is neither existent nor knowable.

Summa Theologica, 1a. xv. 3, *ad* 3

513. In our present life one man's thoughts are hidden from another by two barriers, the grossness of the body and the secrecy of the will. The first will be removed at the resurrection; the second will remain and is present now among pure spirits. Nevertheless, the candour of body will display the quality of mind.

565 *Summa Theologica*, 1a. lvii. 4, *ad* 1

514. In the renewal of things at the end of the world it is certain according to Catholic doctrine that all bodily creation will be improved.

763, 764 Opusc. xxii, *Declaratio xlii Quaestionum ad Magistrum Ordinis*, 36

[1] Bare matter, i.e. primary matter, *materia prima*, the potential substantial substrate of bodies, formless of itself, and therefore as such not discoverable by experiment. Its presence is inferred.

IV. THE UNIVERSAL FRAME

515. Concerning the inquiry whether hell is at or near the centre of the earth, my opinion is that nothing should be rashly asserted, not least because Augustine reckoned that nobody knows where hell is. The lower regions can mean whatever is meant by the term *inferior*.

For myself I do not believe that man can know the position of hell.

Opusc. xxi, *Declaratio xxxvi Quaestionum ad
Lectorem Venetum*, 24, 25

516. *He watereth the high hills from his chambers; the earth is satisfied with the fruit of thy works.*[1]

From eternity the Lord King of Heaven made the law that the gifts of his providence should reach lowly things through intermediate principles, wherefore Dionysius says this to be the holy law of divinity, that they should be led by measured steps to divine light. This law is developed in bodily as well as in spiritual creatures. On this point Augustine remarks, that just as the crasser and weaker bodies are ruled by subtler and more potent bodies according to plan, so are all bodies ruled by the rational spirit of life. And therefore the psalm of our text sings this law, observed in the communication of spiritual truth, through metaphors drawn from things of sense. From the heights of the clouds showers fall and the mountains are watered; thence streams flow down and, drinking them in, the earth is made fruitful. So also from the heights of divine wisdom are watered the minds of teachers, signified by mountains, and through their ministry divine wisdom is shed on the minds of their hearers. Let us consider four points in the text we have cited: the height of spiritual

[1] Ps. ciii. 13. All references are to the Vulgate.

doctrine—the dignity of its teachers—the condition of the hearers—and the method of communication.

(i)

The height is beckoned to by the words, *from his upper rooms*; the Gloss says, *from his higher chambers.* Three comparisons may illustrate how near sacred theology is to the summit of knowledge.

First, by its origin, for this is the wisdom described *as descending from above*;[1] also, *the word of God on high is the fount of wisdom.*[2]

Secondly, because of the rarity of the air. *I dwelt in the highest places.*[3] There are some heights of divine wisdom to which all may climb, though with difficulty; as Damascene says, some knowledge of God's being is naturally inborn. *All men see him, everyone beholdeth him afar off.*[4] There are other heights to be reached only by the skill of experts, guided by their reason; *that which is known to God is manifest to them.*[5] But the highest peaks are beyond all human reasoning; *hidden from the eyes of all living*;[6] and again, *he makes his covert in darkness.*[7] These are the places where wisdom is said to dwell, and they are discovered to dedicated guides; *thy spirit searcheth all things, yea even the deep things of God.*[8]

Thirdly, because of the sublimity of the end, which is the highest of all, namely eternal life. *These are written that you may believe that Jesus is the Christ, the son of God, and that believing you may have life in his name*;[9] and again, *seek the things that are above, where Christ is sitting at the right hand of God; mind the things that are above, not the things that are upon the earth.*[10]

[1] James iii. 17.   [2] Ecclus. i. 5.   [3] Ecclus. xxiv. 7.
[4] Job xxxvi. 25.   [5] Rom. i. 19.
[6] Job xxviii. 21.   [7] Ps. xviii. 11 (Vulg.).
[8] 1 Cor. ii. 10.   [9] John xx. 31.   [10] Col. iii. 1–2.

(ii)

Because this doctrine is awe-inspiring, dignity is demanded of its teachers. They are signified by mountains, *he watereth the high hills*. And this also for three reasons.

First, because of their loftiness, lifted above earth and nigh to heaven. Theologians should spurn earthly things and gaze with longing at the heights above. *Our conversation is in heaven.*[1] And it is said of the teacher of teachers, namely Christ; *he shall be exalted above the hills, and all nations shall flow unto him.*[2]

Secondly, because of their splendour. For hills are the first to reflect the dawn, and similarly holy teachers are the first to catch the light of divine wisdom. *How wonderful was thy dawning over the everlasting hills; dismayed are the rash-hearted,*[3] that is by teachers who are nigh to eternity. *Among whom ye shine as lights in the world.*[4]

Thirdly, because mountains are a bulwark and protect a country from its enemies. So the teachers in the Church should be defenders of the faith against error. The children of Israel relied, not on lances and arrows, but on their hills; and for this they were sometimes taunted: *You have not gone up to face the enemy, nor have you set a wall for the house of Israel, to stand in battle in the day of the Lord.*[5] Accordingly, all teachers of holy writ should stand out in virtue that they may be fitted to preach, for as Gregory says, it must needs be that the teaching will be contemned of those whose life is despised. *But the words of the wise are goads, and nails deeply fastened in.*[6] The pulse cannot beat steadily in the fear of the Lord unless we are trained to heights. Guides

---

[1] Phil. iii. 20.   [2] Isa. ii. 2.   [3] Ps. lxxv. 5 (Vulg.).
[4] Phil. ii. 15.   [5] Ezek. xiii. 5.
[6] Eccles. xii. 11.

must be experienced if they are to be helpful and show us the way. *Unto me, who am less than the least of all the saints, is the grace given, to preach among the gentiles the unsearchable riches of Christ, to make all men see what is the fellowship of the mystery, which hath been hid from the beginning of the world.*[1] So also must they be well equipped to tackle errors. *I will give you mouth and wisdom so that all your adversaries will not be able to gainsay nor resist.*[2] Concerning these three functions, namely preaching, studying, and disputing, it is said:[3] *that you may be able to exhort*, as regards preaching; *in sound doctrine*, as regards study; and *to convince gainsayers*, as regards disputation.

(iii)

The condition of the hearers is compared to earth, the text saying, *the earth shall be satisfied.* Here again there are three characteristics. The earth is lowest, *the heavens above and the earth beneath.*[4] Secondly, it is stable and firm, *the earth standeth for ever.*[5] Thirdly, it is fruitful, *let the earth bear fresh plants and herbs yielding seeds, and trees bearing fruit after their kind.*[6]

Therefore, like the ground should learners be low according to humility: *where humility is there also is wisdom.*[7] And firm in soundness of sense: *be no more childish.*[8] And fruitful, that the words of wisdom may be taken and yield good fruit: *what fell on good ground, these are they who in a good and honest heart hearing the word keep it and bring forth their fruit in patience.*[9] Modesty is required, for they are instructed through listening: *if thou wilt incline thine ear thou shalt receive*

[1] Eph. iii. 8–9.   [2] Luke xxi. 15.   [3] Tit. i. 9.
[4] Prov. xxv. 3.   [5] Eccles. i. 4.   [6] Gen. i. 11.
[7] Prov. xi. 2.   [8] Eph. iv. 14.   [9] Luke viii. 15.

instruction, and if thou lovest to hear thou shalt be wise.[1]
Also judgement of the right sense of what is meant:
doth not our ear try thy words?[2] Finally, fruitfulness of
discovery, for a good listener takes much from the little
he hears: *give occasion to a wise man, and wisdom will be
added.*[3]

(iv)

In conclusion the conditions of communication are
touched on and at three points, the method, the
quantity, and the quality.

As regards the method of delivery, note that the
minds of the teachers cannot grasp the complete plan of
divine wisdom. It is not said that the high truths descend
into the mountains, but that *he watereth the high hills
from his chambers. Lo, these are said in part.*[4] Similarly,
the teacher cannot communicate to his hearers all that
he grasps. *He heard unspeakable words which it is not
lawful for a man to utter.*[5] The text does not say that
the fruit of mountains is given to the earth, but that the
earth is satisfied with its own fruits. In expounding the
text, *he bindeth up the water in his clouds, so that they
break not out and fall down together,*[6] Gregory says that
a teacher should not teach all he knows to unlearned
folk, for he himself cannot know of the divine mysteries
all they be.

Secondly, the manner of possession is here referred
to, for God has wisdom of his nature, and wisdom comes
from his own higher parts. *With him is knowledge and
strength, he has counsel and understanding.*[7] But enough
of this knowledge is bestowed on teachers, therefore they
are said to be watered from on high. *I will water my*

---

[1] Ecclus. vi. 33.   [2] Job xii. 11.   [3] Prov. ix. 9.
[4] Job xxvi. 14.   [5] 2 Cor. xii. 4.   [6] Job. xxvi. 8.
[7] Job xii. 13.

garden of plants, with abundance the fruits of my meadow.[1]
The hearers share in this, signified by the fruitfulness of
earth. *I shall be satisfied when thy glory shall appear.*[2]

Thirdly, as regards the authority for teaching. God
gives wisdom of his own power, therefore he is said
to water the mountains. But human teachers impart
wisdom only as ministers. Therefore, the fruits are not
attributed to the mountains, but to God's activity: *the
earth is satisfied with the fruit of thy works.* For *who then
is Paul, and who is Apollos, but ministers by whom ye
believed, even as the Lord gave to every man?*[3]

But who is sufficient for these things?[4] God demands
upright servants; *he that walketh in a perfect way, he
shall serve me.*[5] They must be intelligent; *a wise servant
is acceptable to the king:*[6] and ardent; *who makest thy
angels spirits and thy ministers a burning fire:*[7] and
disciplined; *you ministers of his that do his will.*[8] Through
and of himself no man is equal to such a ministry, but
we hope for divine help. *Not that we are sufficient to
think anything of ourselves as of ourselves, but our suffi-
ciency is of God.*[9] It should be entreated of him. *If any
of you lack wisdom, let him ask of God, that giveth to all
liberally and upbraideth not; and it shall be granted him.*[10]

Let us pray that Christ may bestow this wisdom on
us: Amen.

> Opusc. XL, *Breve principium fratris Thomae
> de Aquino quando incepit Parisiis ut Magister
> in Theologia*[11]

[1] Ecclus. xxiv. 35.   [2] Ps. xvi. 15 (Vulg.).
[3] 1 Cor. iii. 5.   [4] 2 Cor. ii. 16.   [5] Ps. c. 6.
[6] Prov. xiv. 35.   [7] Ps. ciii. 4.   [8] Ps. cii. 21.
[9] 2 Cor. iii. 5.   [10] James i. 5.
[11] St. Thomas's inaugural lecture as Professor in Paris University.

IX

Human Nature[1]

517. Psychology is part of natural philosophy and physical science.

43, 48   Commentary, *I de Anima, lect.* 2

518. The two notes of motion and sensation mark the difference of animate things from inanimate things. Correspondingly, the early psychologists diverged in following different interests, some stressing motion, others stressing consciousness.

Commentary, *I de Anima, lect.* 3

I. SOULS

519. Let us agree on the meaning of the term. Soul is the first principle of life within living things about us: living things we term animate, things lacking life inanimate.

[1] The *Summa Theologica* follows the order of the first chapter of Genesis. The treatise on man, rather an anthropology than a psychology, comes as a climax to the questions on the different days of creation and should be set against that zoological background: farther back lies the study of spiritual substances. St. Thomas works with two apparently irreconcilable principles; first, that man is a material and animal substance; second, that his single soul, composing a natural unity with his body, is spiritual. The contrasted themes run throughout his teaching: it was this part of it his contemporaries found most contentious. He has a clear scheme of the specific abilities of man, but his faculty-psychology does not lose sight of the single wholeness of the organism: 'actions come from the complete substance', this saying is frequently quoted. The appropriate method of inquiry is introspection, but it is based on, and controlled by, external data.

Now life is chiefly manifested in the two functions of motion and knowledge. According to some of the ancients its principle is bodily: this, however, was because they had not developed far enough to appreciate what lies beyond the range of the imagination; bodies alone were real, they held, and anything else unreal.

That they were at fault in their opinion may be shown in many ways, and we will take but one, confidently and in general terms. Obviously not every principle of vital operation is soul, otherwise the eye would be soul, since it is the principle of sight; and the same applies to other vital organs. The term should be reserved to the first principle of life, for though there may be bodily vital principles, the heart for instance, a body cannot be the first principle of life.

For evidently to be the principle of life, or even to be alive, does not belong to body precisely as such, otherwise every body would be a principle of life or alive. Life is in a body because it is a special kind of body; that body is in fact of such a kind comes from a factor which may be called its actuality. The soul, therefore, is not a body, but the actuality of a body, by analogy with heat where the principle of warmth, which is not itself a body, is a kind of actuality of body.

Summa Theologica, 1a. lxxv. 1

520. Some psychological investigations concentrated solely on the human soul. The Platonic philosophers held that bodiless universal forms and ideas were the causes both of the being and of the being known of particular things, and they sought the pure and essential soul, the cause and idea of all that is in particular souls. The physical philosophers, on the other hand, felt no hankering for universal substances and kept to facts. From these two conflicting opinions rises the issue

whether we should investigate soul as such or keep to
this or that soul, of horses, men, and the heavenly
bodies. Aristotle sought to keep the balance between
the Platonist and the physical philosophers, between
the general nature of soul and the specific characteristics
of each type.

44, 652   Commentary, *I de Anima, lect.* 1

521. We should deal first with food, which is the
burden, and of generation, which is the act, of vegetable
soul. This part of the soul is primitive; it is, as it were,
the foundation of the sensitive and intellective souls,
for natural being is basic to sensible and intelligible
being.

498   Commentary, *II de Anima, lect.* 7

522. To inquire into the meaning of animal is one
business, to inquire into the meaning of human animal
quite another.

Summa Theologica, 1a. xxix. 4

523. Some have barbarously spoken of the soul as
though it were blood.

Commentary, *I de Anima, lect.* 5

524. Human souls and pure spirits are different kinds
of things.

Summa Theologica, 1a. lxxv. 7

525. Sensation is not an activity of pure soul. Though
not peculiar to man, it is truly human. It follows that
man is not just soul, but a compound of body and soul.

624   *Summa Theologica,* 1a. lxxv. 4

526. The sensitive soul has no operation proper to
itself in isolation. Sensitive activity is always that of soul

and body conjoined. We are bound to infer that animal souls are not completely substantial, since they are not independently active.

Summa Theologica, 1a. lxxv. 3

527. The principle of intellectual activity, which we term the human soul, is a bodiless and completely substantial principle.

This principle, also termed the mind or intellect, can act without the body having an intrinsic part in the activity. Nothing can act independently unless it be independent.

Summa Theologica, 1a. lxxv. 2

528. Even though it be part of a substance, a thing may be called completely substantial[1] so long as it neither is bound up with matter, like a material form, nor inheres in a substance, like an accident. We can pass the statement that the human soul understands, though it would be more accurate to say that the man understands through his soul.

563   *Summa Theologica*, 1a. lxxv. 2, *ad* 2

529. Were the principle of intelligence inwardly a bodily principle, it would not be able to range over all bodies, for a bodily substance is pinned down to one determinate kind of body.

586   *Summa Theologica*, 1a. lxxv. 2

530. Intellectual activity requires a body, not as an organ through which it operates, but in order that an object may be provided.

Summa Theologica, 1a. lxxv. 2, *ad* 3

[1] That is, it is able to exist alone, though specifically incomplete, e.g. a disembodied human soul.

531. The soul is part of time existing above time in eternity: it contains nature, but surpasses the physical principle of motion measured by time.

239   Opusc. x, Exposition, *de Causis, lect.* 9

II. PSYCHO-PHYSICAL UNITY

532. Aristotle's doctrine, rather than Plato's, is corroborated by experience.

Summa Theologica, 1a. lxxxviii. 1

533. Having shown that an intellective substance is neither a body nor a power dependent on the body, we now have to investigate whether it can be united to a body.

In the first place the union obviously cannot come about in the manner of a mixture nor by touching properly so called, for contact is between bodies. Neither by merging nor by being fastened together can one perfectly single thing be constituted from intellectual and from bodily substance. There is, nevertheless, a mode of contact by which spirit can be joined to body, not by a mutual joining of quantities, but by the touching implied in the action of one thing on another: thus we say that we are touched by another's grief. This is the touch of power, not of quantity; it is feasible between spirits and bodies: intellectual substances can act on bodies and set them in motion. Yet though spirit and body are united as regards action and reaction, they do not thereby make up one thing simply so called.[1]

Consequently we find ourselves inquiring whether one thing simply speaking can be constituted from spirit and body. Now a natural unity cannot be constituted from two permanent realities unless they be related as

[1] However pervasive and subtle the interaction of two things, they never compose one substance.

substantial form and matter. Hence, we are faced with the problem how an intellective substance can be the substantial form of a body.

To some serious inquirers this seemed quite out of the question. Supported on several sides, they felt emboldened to declare that no intellectual substance can be the form of a body. At the same time they were well aware that such a statement appears to run counter to the simultaneously spiritual and material nature of man, and that the onus lies on them of devising how this psycho-physical unity can be salvaged. Plato and his followers laid down that the intellectual soul is united to the body as mover to thing moved; the soul is in the body as the sailor in the ship; the union of soul with body is by contact of power.

But this is not without embarrassment, for man, made up from such a union of soul and body, would not be one thing simply speaking, or a substantial whole, but an accidental whole.[1] To avoid this consequence, Plato held that man was not a thing composed of soul and body, but that he was a soul, using the body.

But this is impossible, for animals and men are natural and sensible things, which would not be the case were bodies and bodily organs not part of their essence, in other words, were they wholly souls. Moreover, it is impossible to have one single operation issuing from things which are diverse in being—I say one single operation, not as regards the term or effect, but as regards the going out from the principle, for when many haul at a boat, though one effect is produced, there are many efforts and different heaves from the haulers. Now there are actions common to soul and body; for sensing and feeling are functions of soul and body simultaneously, which are here at one, and not diverse in their being.

[1] i.e. a close arrangement (an accident) of different substances.

To obviate this reasoning, Plato agreed that these operations were common to soul and body, but to the soul as mover and the body as moved.

But this will not do either, for, as Aristotle proved, sensation results from motion from sense objects;[1] at this point the sensitive soul is like a receptive, not an active, principle. Furthermore, were the sensitive soul the active principle and the body the passive principle, the operation of the soul would be other than the operation of the body. The sensitive soul would then have its own proper activity, and therefore its own proper subsistence. It would not cease with the body, and the souls of animals would be immortal. Such a conclusion, though improbable, does not conflict with Plato's statements.

Furthermore, after the departure of the soul, the body and its parts would remain specifically the same. Nor would the very being of the human body be quickened by the soul. Moreover, death, which consists in the separation of soul and body, would not be the dissolution of the animal.

554, 761, 1081   II *Contra Gentes*, 56, 57

534. We should assert that the mind, the principle of intellectual activity, is the form of the human body. The body's first animating principle is the soul. And since life is manifested by various activities in the various grades of living things, that which is the first principle of these vital activities is the soul. For by soul primarily we take nourishment, feel, walk about, and also understand. Call it mind or intellective soul, this principle is the form of body.[2] If anyone wishes to deny this, let him explain how otherwise he can attribute the activity of

[1] *de Anima*, 417ª18.
[2] Ibid. 413ª10.

understanding to the individual man. Everybody experiences in himself that it is veritably himself who understands.

554, 634   *Summa Theologica*, 1a. lxxvi. 1

535. Physical pain, more than sadness, prevents contemplation which demands quiet. Nevertheless, mental suffering, if protracted, so drains our interest that we can discover nothing further fresh. It was from sadness that Gregory broke off his commentary on Ezekiel.

Summa Theologica, 1a–2ae. xxxvii. 1, *ad* 3

536. The soul's power is non-material though it be the cause of matter, spiritual though the cause of bodies, and dimensionless though the cause of quantities.

Opusc. x, Exposition, *de Causis, lect.* 14

537. Consider that the nobler a form the greater its domination over matter, the less imprisoned it is in body, and the more its virtue and activity transcend bodily functions. As we climb in the scale of forms the more we find their power exceeding elementary matter; a plant-form is more than mineral, an animal-form more than plant. The human soul is the last word in forms, exceeding bodily matter because its inward virtue and activity is free from matter.

292, 305   *Summa Theologica*, 1a. lxxvi. 1

538. Of factors that can change man, some are physiological and others psychological. The latter may be sensible or intelligible, and the former again may be practical or theoretical. Of the first, the strongest is wine; of the second, women; of the third, the power of the government; of the fourth, truth.[1] They should be subordinate to one another in the reverse order.

XII *Quodlibet*, 20

[1] Cf. 3 Esdras iii–iv.

539. The proposition, *souls are individuated by the matters of bodies, and they keep their individuality when disembodied, as wax the impression of a seal,* can be understood aright though it is also open to misconception. If taken in the sense that bodies are the total cause of the individuation of soul, then the proposition is false; but if the sense is that they are the partial causes, then it is true. The body is not the total cause of the being of soul, though the very being of soul is in relationship to body. Similarly, the body is not the total cause of the individuality of this soul, though it is this soul's nature to be joinable to this body, which relationship remains in the soul after the body's death.

436, 447   Opusc. xxiii, *Declaratio cviii Dubiorum ex commentario fr. Petri de Tarentasia super Sententiis ad Magistrum Generalem,* 108

540. Though generically the same, sensitive life is not specifically the same in beasts and men. In men it is much higher, as appears in the senses of touch and internal perception.

623   *Disputations,* iii *de Potentia,* 11, *ad* 1

541. Our body's substance is not from an evil principle, as the Manichees imagine, but from God. And therefore by the friendship of charity, by which we love God, should we cherish the body.

475, 904   *Summa Theologica,* 2a–2ae. xxv. 5

542. *The flesh rejoices in the living God,*[1] not by carnal activity reaching up to God, but by the overflowing of the heart, as when feeling follows willing.

Summa Theologica, 3a. xxi. 2, *ad* 1

543. To be united to body is not to the detriment of soul, but for its enrichment. There is the substantial

[1] Ps. lxxxiii. 2 (Vulgate).

benefit of completing human nature, and the accidental benefit of achieving knowledge that can only be acquired through the senses.

630   Disputations, *de Anima*, 1 *ad* 7; 2 *ad* 14

544. Neither the human soul nor the human body falls into a species or genus except indirectly, as parts are virtually classed with the species or genus of the whole.

Disputations, *de Anima*, 1, *ad* 13

545. Soul moves the body it vivifies; if any member of the body decays it does not obey the soul as to local motion. A disembodied soul does not quicken body, and therefore—though a miraculous exception may be made—it has no control over the local motions of bodies by its natural power.

Summa Theologica, 1a. cxvii. 4

III. PHYSIQUE AND TEMPERAMENT

546. The soul is the completion of an organic body. Such a body is not receptive of soul without biological predispositions.

Disputations, III *de Potentia*, 12

547. Two sorts of material conditions can be recognized. By one, matter is adapted to form, but the other follows as a necessary result of previous dispositions. The toolmaker selects steel to make a saw from, because it is tough and able to cut hard objects; but that the teeth can become blunt and the metal rusty follows from the necessity of the material. Similarly, a well-balanced organism fits the intellective soul; all the same it is corruptible from the necessity of the matter.

455   *Summa Theologica*, 1a. lxxvi. 5, *ad* 1

548. A man is rendered apt of intelligence by the healthy disposition of the internal powers of the organism, in which the good condition of the body has a part. Consequently intellectual endowments can be in the powers of sense, though primarily they are in the mind.

852 *Summa Theologica*, 1a–2ae. l. 4, *ad* 3

549. Because some people have more finely tempered bodies their souls have greater strength of understanding.[1]

996 *Summa Theologica*, 1a. lxxxv. 7

550. There are animals with better eyesight, hearing, and sense of smell than man, but his sense of touch has greater assurance than theirs. Because he has the finest touch he is the most prudent of the animals. And among men themselves it is because of the sense of touch, rather than the other senses, that some are more ingenious than others. Rough-skinned and coarse-textured people are mentally rather inept, unlike those with a sensitive skin and delicate touch.

Touch is the foundation of all the other senses. A good touch results from a good complexion or temperament. Excellence of mind follows from bodily complexion, for every form is proportioned to its matter. People with a good sense of touch are therefore of a higher soul and clearer mind.

621, 622 Commentary, *II de Anima, lect.* 19

551. The intellective soul ranks lowest in the scale of intellectual substances in that it lacks the natural inborn knowledge of truth with which pure spirits are endowed, but must piece together the fragments of truth perceived through the senses. Nature does not fail in necessaries, and therefore the intellective soul has to

[1] *de Anima*, 421ª25.

possess the power of sensing as well as of understanding. Now the activity of the senses is not performed without physical organs. Therefore, the soul must be united to that kind of body which can be the instrument adapted to sense. All the senses are based on touch. Among all the animals man has the best-developed sense of touch, and among men those have the finer minds who have the more delicate sense of touch. A rare mind goes with bodily refinement.

666   *Summa Theologica*, 1a. lxxvi. 5

552. Man excels the other animals in the internal senses, but in some of the external senses he does not compare; thus his is the weakest sense of smell.

582   *Summa Theologica*, 1a. xci. 3, *ad* 1

IV. THE SINGLE SOUL

553. The intellective soul confers on the human body all that the sensitive soul confers on animals, and likewise the sensitive soul confers on animals whatever the nutritive principles confer on plants, and more. Any soul in man additional to his intellective soul would therefore be superfluous, for it contains the sensitive soul and with something to spare.

533   1 *Quodlibet*, 6

554. If we hold that the soul is united to the body as its substantial form, then the co-existence of several essentially different souls in the same body cannot be entertained. To begin with, an animal having several souls would not compose an essential unity, for nothing is simply one except by one form. Form gives being and unity. Were man alive by one form, namely by vegetable soul, and animal by another, namely by sensitive

soul, and human by a third, namely by rational soul, he would not be one thing simply speaking.[1]

Moreover, when one psychological activity is intense another is held up, which would not be the case were the principle of activity not essentially identical. Therefore the nutritive or vegetable, the sensitive, and the rational souls are numerically one in man.

577 *Summa Theologica*, 1a. lxxvi. 3

555. The rational soul is the unique substantial form in man, virtually containing the plant and animal souls, and all inferior forms as well, doing whatever these do in other things. The same can be said in general of all higher forms with respect to lower forms.

Summa Theologica, 1a. lxxvi. 4

556. The human soul communicates to bodily matter its own existence. Both make up one thing, so much so that the existence of the whole compound is also the existence of the soul. This is not the case with other substantial forms which are not subsistent. The human soul keeps its existence when the body breaks up.

433 *Summa Theologica*, 1a. lxxvi. 1, *ad* 5

557. Because united to body as form, the soul is in each part of the body and throughout the whole organism. It is not an accidental form of the body, but the substantial form, which is the form and actuality, not merely of the whole, but also of each part. When a whole is just an assemblage of parts, the form of the whole does not give being to the parts, but consists in the pattern or shape of the whole, and is an accidental form.

Therefore when the soul has departed, just as we do not speak of what remains as an animal—unless in a pickwickian sense, as we might of an animal in a painting or

[1] *Metaphysics*, 1045^{b}16.

a piece of sculpture—so it is with the hand, the eye, the flesh, the bones.[1] One indication is that no part of the body keeps its proper working when the soul has gone; whereas anything that retains a specific nature retains the specific activity of that nature. Actuality is in that of which it is the actuality, and therefore the soul must be in the whole body and in each and every member.

The soul is entire in each part of the body according to its wholeness of perfection and being, not of power; for it is not in each part by each of its powers, but by sight it is in the eye, by hearing in the ear, and so forth.

Summa Theologica, 1a. lxxvi. 8

V. PERSONAL MIND

558. Since all men naturally desire to know the truth, there is a natural desire to avoid error and, given the ability, to confute it. Of all errors the most indecent attack our heritage of mind. One such has sprung from the words of Averroes, who announced that there is a universal and unique mind for all men. We have already argued against this doctrine elsewhere, but our purpose is to write again and at length in refutation, because of the continued impudence of those who gainsay the truth on this head.

Not that we shall be at pains to show that it is contrary to the Christian faith, for this is sufficiently apparent to all. Since mind is the only deathless part of the soul, were the diversity of minds to be fused, the upshot would be that a unique mind alone remained after death, and so there would be no prospect of rewards and punishments. What we intend to do is to show that this error is no less opposed to the principles of philo-

[1] *de Anima*, 412^{b}10.

sophy. Because some of the advocates of this doctrine do not hold with the statements of Latin authorities, but base themselves on the positions of the Peripatetics, whose writings, except for those of Aristotle, they have never seen, we shall show that their teaching is clean contrary to his statements. . . .

These,[1] then, are the points we have made to destroy this error, not by the documents of faith, but in the light of Aristotle. If anyone who falsely glories in the name of philosopher still wishes to oppose what we have written, let him not mutter in corners with adolescents who lack discrimination in such arduous questions, but let him come out into the open, and write if he dares. I am the least, but he will find others besides myself who are servants of truth and who will resist his errors and instruct his ignorance.

645   Opusc. VI, *de Unitate Intellectus contra Averroistas Parisienses*

559. That a unique mind should be shared by all men is quite out of the question. If Plato's doctrine be adopted, namely, that man is his mind,[2] then it would follow that, if there were one mind for Socrates and for Plato, there would be one man there, and they would not be distinct from one another except by something outside their essence: the difference between them would be no more than that between the man in a tunic and the same man in a cloak.

The thesis is also impossible on Aristotle's doctrine that the mind is a part or power of the soul, which soul is man's substantial form.[3] For there cannot be a unique

---

[1] The argument is summarized in the next extract from the *Summa Theologica*, where, as in the *de Unitate Intellectus*, St. Thomas writes with unwonted informality and vigour.

[2] *Alcibiades I*, 25. The authenticity of this dialogue is disputed.

[3] *de Anima*, 414ᵃ13.

form of several things numerically diverse, as it is impossible for them to possess one being.

Indeed, it is an unworkable thesis howsoever the union of mind with this or that man be stated. For obviously, if there be one principal cause and two instruments, you can talk about one agent and many actions; as when a man touches different things with his two hands, there is one toucher, but two touches. Conversely, if there be one instrument and many principal causes, you can talk about one action but many agents; as when a ship is towed by the same cable, despite many towing there is but one pull. If, however, the principal and the instrument are identical, there is then one agent and one action; when the smith smites with one hammer there is one smiter and one smiting. Now it is clear that howsoever and in whatever fashion the mind is united to this or that man, mind is his chief part and the sensitive powers are subservient. If, therefore, you imagined that there were different minds but one sensorium for two men, for instance if two men had one eye in common, there would be one vision, but two people seeing. But if the mind be one, no matter how the other powers used by the mind as instruments were diversified, in no sense could Socrates and Plato be called anything but one intelligence. And if we add that the activity of understanding comes from no other instrument than the power of the mind, it would follow further that there would be one agent and one action—in other words, all men would be one intelligence producing one act of understanding, providing, of course, it was about the same intelligible object.

You might be able to diversify my intellectual action from yours by the diversity of images, namely, because my picture of a stone was different from yours, but only on condition that the image were the form of the vital intellect, which it is not. The mental form is not a sense-image, but a meaning abstracted from it. The same meaning may be abstracted by the same mind from diverse images; a man may have different images of stone and yet abstract from all of them but one meaning. Were there one mind for all men, a diversity of intellectual activity in this man and that man would not be caused just because there were two sets of images. We dismiss this fiction of the great commentator[1] and are left, therefore, with the conclusion that it is quite impossible and highly inconvenient to postulate one mind for all men.

81, 534, 1091   *Summa Theologica*, 1a. lxxvi. 2

560. Though they concede that the receptive mind is diversified among men, some hold that the factive intellect[2] is one and the same for all. This opinion, while more tolerable than the other, can be confuted by similar reasonings.

644, 650   Opusc. xiii, *Compendium Theologiae*, 86

VI. BIRTH, DECAY, AND IMMORTALITY

561. That the soul's being is made of God's substance is demonstrably untrue.

191   *Summa Theologica*, 1a. xc. 1

562. Since the human soul cannot be produced by the transmutation of matter, it cannot but be produced immediately by God.

388   *Summa Theologica*, 1a. xc. 3

563. Since the soul is united to body as form and as a natural component of human nature, its creation does

---

[1] Averroes.

[2] The *intellectus agens*, νοῦς ποιητικός. Cf. *de Anima* 430ª10. St. Thomas, Commentary *III de Anima, lect.* 10. Usually translated, *active intellect*, but *factive intellect* seems a happier rendering.

not precede its union with the body. By creation God constitutes things in the perfection of their nature. Apart from the body the soul lacks its natural perfection, and it would be awkward for it to be created in this condition.

Summa Theologica, 1a. xc. 4

564. The soul continues to be when separated from the body by the failure of body we call death. But the soul should not suffer this dislocation at its origin.

Summa Theologica, 1a. xc. 4, *ad* 3

565. All natural things are produced by divine art, and may be called God's works of art. Now the artist intends to give his work the best dispositions, considered not absolutely but with regard to his proposed end. The artist cares not if this entails some accompanying defect. When a man makes a saw for the purpose of cutting, he tempers it of metal which suits his purpose; he does not choose glass, for this, though the more beautiful material, would defeat his purpose. Now the proximate purpose of the human body is the rational soul and its activities. I say therefore that God fashioned the human body in the disposition best suited to such a form and such activities.

508   *Summa Theologica*, 1a. xci. 3

566. The immortal soul can have a spiritual birth and spiritual maturity; bodily age is no prejudice to its life. It can attain a perfect age when the body is young, and be born again when the body is old.

Summa Theologica, 3a. lxxii. 8

567. Youth and age can be in the soul both at once, though not in the body; the former for alacrity, the latter for gravity.

Summa Theologica, 3a. i. 6, *ad* 1

568. Sense knows existence only as here and now, but mind apprehends it absolutely and as though transcending time. Therefore every intellectual being naturally desires to be always. But natural desire is not in vain. Therefore every intellectual substance is deathless.

244, 744 *Summa Theologica*, 1a. lxxv. 6

569. Man is mortal like the other animals.

Summa Theologica, 1a. lxxvi. 3, *ad* 2

570. The cause of death and other physical defects in human nature is twofold, remote and proximate. The underlying cause results from the material principles of the human body, which is composed of warring elements. Original justice would have counteracted this cause. Therefore the proximate cause of death is sin, which ruined the original integrity.

486 *Summa Theologica*, 3a. xiv. 3, *ad* 2

571. Three reflections about death. First, as regards its natural cause; here from the condition of his nature it is appointed for man once to die, for his components are contrary. Secondly, as regards his gracious endowment; here man was given the gift of original integrity, by which soul so possessed body that it was deathless. Thirdly, as regards the deserving of death; here man lost this benefit through his own fault and so incurred the penalty of death.

Commentary, *in Hebraeos, ix, lect.* 5

572. Death is natural considering our material status, but penal considering how we lost the divine endowment of deathlessness.

Summa Theologica, 2a–2ae. clxiv. 1, *ad* 1

573. Nothing unnatural can be perpetual, and therefore the soul will not be without the body for ever.

Since the soul is immortal the body should be joined to it again. This is to rise again. The immortality of the soul, then, would seem to demand the future resurrection of the body.

IV *Contra Gentes*, 79

574. When the body is resumed, bliss will grow, not in depth, but in extent.

745   *Summa Theologica*, 1a–2ae. iv. 5

VII. FACULTIES

575. Soul does not act; this man acts through the soul.

554, 829   *Commentary, X Ethics, lect.* 6

576. The habits of building and weaving and making music are in the soul and from the soul. But it is more accurate to say that the builder builds, and not that his art builds, though he builds through his art. So also it is better to say, not that the soul understands or feels pity, but that the man so acts through the soul.

Commentary, I de Anima, lect. 10

577. Though a simple form, the soul is multiple in power. From its substance result diverse abilities, and therefore the soul correspondingly must have distinct parts. For it is the actuality organizing a body with different though interdependent parts.

532   *Commentary, I Sentences,* VIII. v. 3, *ad* 2

578. A psychological faculty is merely the proximate principle of vital activity.[1]

Summa Theologica, 1a. lxxviii. 4

579. The substance of the soul cannot be identified with any of its abilities, though some have maintained

[1] Not a 'thing'.

this.[1] For our present purpose two arguments will serve.

First, a potentiality and its actuality are in the same category, so that if the actuality is not a substance then neither is the relevant potentiality. Now the activity of the soul is not a substance, for this belongs to God alone.

Secondly, the soul by its essence is an actuality. Were its essential substance the immediate principle of activity, it would follow that an actually living thing would always be an actually acting thing. Now we observe that what has a soul is not always actual with respect to its vital activities.

Summa Theologica, 1a. lxxvii. 1

580. The substantial form is the first, but not the proximate, principle of activity; from it derive those accidental forms which are the proximate principles of activity.

Summa Theologica, 1a. lxxvii. 1, *ad* 4

581. Then only is the immediate principle of activity the very substance of the things when its activity is its existence.

Summa Theologica, lxxix. 1

582. Many faculties of the soul should be postulated. To make this evident let us reflect on Aristotle's remark[2] that the lowest things do not lay hold of full goodness, but reach limited goods by a few movements. Those that are higher reach full goodness by many movements. Still higher things hold perfect good by fewer movements. Highest of all is the possession of perfection without movement at all. Thus he is least disposed to health who can acquire imperfect health by a few remedies, better

[1] Peter Lombard and William of Auvergne.
[2] *De Caelo*, 292ª22.

disposed is he who can acquire health by many remedies, better still is he who needs only a few remedies, and best of all is he who has perfect health without need of any remedies at all.

It is said, therefore, that things below man acquire a certain limited goodness, and so have a few determinate abilities and activities, but man can acquire universal and perfect goodness, that is happiness without restriction. Nevertheless, he is at the lowest stage of those to which this is open, and therefore many diverse abilities and activities have to be brought into play. Less variety is required in pure spirits, and in God there is no ability or activity distinct from his substance.[1]

298, 621   *Summa Theologica*, 1a. lxxvii. 2

[1] The psychological faculties are classified according to the following scheme:

```
 ⎧ of cognition
 ⎪        ⎧ in the body-soul compound
 ⎪        ⎪        ⎧ external senses (the five senses traditionally enumer-
 ⎪        ⎪        ⎨    ated, sight, hearing, taste, smell, touch)
 ⎪        ⎨        ⎩ internal senses (imagination, memory, sense of what
 ⎪        ⎪             is beneficial and harmful, communal sense)
 ⎪        ⎩ in the spiritual soul
 ⎪             the mind, intellect, or reason (to which may be attached
 ⎨                 the intellectus agens)
 ⎪
 ⎪ of appetition
 ⎪        ⎧ in the body-soul compound
 ⎪        ⎪    the sensuality or sensitive appetite
 ⎪        ⎨    ⎧ concupiscible
 ⎪        ⎪    ⎩ irascible
 ⎩        ⎩ in the spiritual soul
              the will, with its functions of volition and choice.
```

(Note: the natural appetite is not limited to any one faculty but covers them all and the substance.)

X

Consciousness[1]

583. All conscious things implicitly know God in everything they know.

161, 744   Disputations, XXII *de Veritate*, 2, *ad* 1

584. Knower and known are not agent and patient to one another, they are two things from which one principle of knowledge results.

291, 731   Disputations, VIII *de Veritate*, 7, *ad* 2

---

[1] St. Thomas is sometimes called an intellectualist and, less often, a rationalist. Both epithets are fair enough, the former because of his insistence that the mind is sovereign to will, the latter because of his severely scientific method. In comparison with other religious philosophers his tone may seem dispassionate; it is certainly impersonal. His criticism of knowledge, however, is not the indirect realism of the seventeenth century and after; nor a correspondence theory of concepts requiring the inspection of allegedly faithful reproductions of reality. His position may be outlined as follows. The mind is not a marginal commentator on an outside world, still less an actor in a parallel order; it is the highest actuality within being. He speaks gently of the early Ionians who treated knowledge as a physical assimilation. He studies the implications of pure knowledge in God and spiritual substances before turning to the sensibilities and distractions of knowledge meshed in a physical process. Knowing is a manner of being; in our case a manner of becoming. Yet knowledge as such is immune from the fatal consequences of natural generation: there is no loss, but only gain; the knower becomes the known without ceasing to be himself. It is at once an act of nature and an intimation of immortality. One might say that the problem of knowledge is not solved because it is not allowed to arise, except at the relatively superficial levels of judgement and inference.

I. THE PROBLEM OF KNOWLEDGE[1]

585. Some of the ancients, divining the truth yet from far away, reckoned that the soul knows things because it is composed of them.[2]

Commentary, I de Anima, lect. 12

586. Assuming that they were bodily, the ancient physicists thought objects of knowledge existed materially in the soul that knew them, which, they said, has a nature common to all of them. This explanation, however, can be disproved by the analysis of knowledge. When material objects are known they exist in the knower in some immaterial manner, and for the following reason: since knowledge lights on what is outside the knower, while matter constricts a thing within its own one nature, the conditions of materiality conflict with those of knowledge. When a form is received into

[1] Three lines of approach to the topic of knowledge may be marked, though they are not neatly exclusive, namely the logical, the epistemological, and the psychological. The logic of knowledge, the divisions and correct arrangements of terms, judgements, and arguments, has already been touched on (34–41). Epistemology is engaged with the real existence of truth; its critique of knowledge eventually resolves itself into a metaphysical discussion (585–616). The psychology of knowledge is the natural science of the process at work. After noting the distinction of the faculties (582), this process may be roughly outlined as follows: an object in our environment, an existing individual material nature, through its sensible properties affects the senses of the subject knowing (617–23): an image is produced in the internal senses which, having been heightened and made actually intelligible by the factive intellect, *intellectus agens*, is impressed on the mind, *intellectus possibilis*, and vitally expressed as a concept (624–57). The impression and expression are covered by the term *species intelligibilis*: psychologically this is a quality of the knower, epistemologically it is the spiritual form of the thing known.

[2] The reference is to the early Ionian philosophers.

the material texture, as in the case of plants, it is not known.

291   *Summa Theologica*, 1a. lxxxiv. 2

587. To grasp a thing formally, not materially, is the noblest mode of holding and possessing; similarly, to set oneself into activity is the noblest mode of movement and the heart of life.

231, 617   Opusc. x, Exposition, *de Causis*, *lect.* 18

588. Knower and known are one principle of activity inasmuch as one reality results from them both, namely the mind in act. I say that one reality results, for herein mind is conjoined to thing understood, whether immediately or through a likeness. The knower as such is not an efficient or material cause, except on account of special conditions when knowledge may require action or passion.[1]

731   Disputations, viii *de Veritate*, 6

589. What is first precipitated in the mind's conception is being. A thing is knowable because existence is pointed to. Therefore being is the proper object of mind; it is the primary intelligible as sound is the primary audible.

396   *Summa Theologica*, 1a. v. 2

590. Of its very nature our mind knows being and its essential attributes as such. Hereon is grounded the knowledge of first principles.

                                  ii *Contra Gentes*, 83

591. Of all realities existence is most form.

175, 433   *Summa Theologica*, 1a. vii. 1

---

[1] As when knowledge works through an organic process.

592. Existence is innermost in each and deepest in all, since it is formal with respect to all reality.

Summa Theologica, 1a. viii. 1

593. Existence is the most perfect of realities, related to all others as their actuality.

Summa Theologica, 1a. iv. 1, *ad* 3

594. The being of a thing, rather than its truth, causes truth in the mind.

Summa Theologica, 1a. xvi. 1, *ad* 3

595. Some have held that our cognitive powers know only the impressions made on them, for instance, that sense knows only the alteration of its organ. According to this reading, mental states are the objects of knowledge.

This opinion seems to be false for two reasons. First, if the objects of intelligence and science are merely psychic conditions, it would follow that science does not deal with non-mental things, but merely with impressions in consciousness.

Secondly, it would revive the ancient error of maintaining that whatever seems so is truly so,[1] and that contradictories are simultaneously tenable. Were a cognitive power able to perceive no more than its own proper states, then it could judge only about those. Now an object appears according to the manner the faculty is affected, and were modes of consciousness the only data, a faculty could judge merely its own proper impressions, and every judgement would be true; when a clean tongue judges honey to be sweet then it would judge truly, and when a dirty tongue judges it to be bitter then also would it judge truly, in each case going on its impressions. Every opinion would be equally valid; so also in general would be whatever was fancied.

[1] *Metaphysics*, 1009ª8.

This conclusion should be offset by explaining how a conscious impression is related to a cognitive power as a medium; it is a form by which the faculty knows. That in which the sight sees a thing is the likeness of the visible thing; that in which the intellect understands, namely the intelligible species, is the likeness of the thing understood. Admittedly the mind can reflect upon itself, and therefore can understand its own act of understanding together with the form through which it understands: thus the mental species can be a secondary object of knowledge. Nevertheless the primary object is the thing of which the species is a likeness.

This theory is suggested by the ancient opinion that like is known by like. It was thought that the soul knows earth outside because of its own earthiness, and so also with the other elements. But if we take the concept of earth instead of physical earth, in agreement with Aristotle who says that what is in the soul is not stone but likeness of stone,[1] we shall recognize how the soul knows things outside through the medium of an intelligible likeness.

1117   *Summa Theologica*, 1a. lxxxv. 2

596. The intelligible species is the likeness of a thing's essence, and is, in some manner, the very essence and nature of that thing existing consciously, not physically.

VIII *Quodlibet*, 4

597. The known is in the knower through its likeness. This is the meaning of the remark that the actually known is the knower as actual. It does not follow that the abstracted idea is the thing actually understood, but that it is the likeness of the thing.

244   *Summa Theologica*, 1a. lxxxv. 2, *ad* 1

[1] *de Anima*, 431[b]29.

598. In speaking of the known as actual we imply a distinction between the thing known and its being known. Similarly, in speaking of an abstract universal meaning we imply a distinction between the very nature of the thing meant and its abstractness or universality. The nature itself, of which being understood is a circumstance, exists only in singular things; but its being understood or abstracted, in other words its character of universality, exists in the mind.

653, 655   *Summa Theologica*, 1a. lxxxv. 2, *ad* 2

599. Something is said to be conceived by a bodily process when it is formed in the living womb by the quickening power and action and passion of male and female, and when it is like in kind to both. What the mind conceives is formed in the mind; from the thing is the action, as it were, and from the mind the passion; while the concept is like in kind to object and subject.

639   Opusc. xiii, *Compendium Theologiae*, 38

600. I call the idea or mental image that which the mind conceives within itself of the thing understood. With us this is neither the thing itself nor the substance of the mind, but a certain likeness conceived in the mind from the thing understood and signified by external speech, whence it is called the inner word. That this concept is not the thing understood appears from the fact that one activity is required to understand the thing and another to understand the concept, as happens when the mind reflects on its processes. On this account the sciences that treat of things are distinct from the sciences that treat of concepts. That the concept is not the mind itself appears from this consideration, that the being of a concept consists in being understood, which is not the case with the being of the mind.

37   iv *Contra Gentes*, 11

601. Whenever we understand, by the very fact of understanding, there proceeds something within us, a concept of the thing understood, issuing from the mind and proceeding from our knowledge of the thing. It is called the word of the heart, and is signified by the spoken word.

Summa Theologica, 1a. xxvii. 1

602. Conceptions of heart and mind come forth in silence and without sound, but by audible words the silence of the heart is manifested.

Opusc. xiv, Exposition, *de Divinis Nominibus*, iv, *lect.* 1

603. A thing is known in two ways, either by its proper form, as when eye sees stone through image of stone, or through the form of something else similar, as when cause is seen through the likeness in its effect, or man through the likeness of his image.

Through its own form a thing is known in two ways, either by the form which is the thing itself, and so God knows himself always in his essence, or by a form which is abstracted from the thing.

Opusc. xvi, Exposition, *de Trinitate*, i. 2

II. THE PROBLEM OF ERROR

604. Of the two phases of mental activity, the first is the understanding of essential meanings, while the second is a judgement, either affirmative or negative. A dual reality corresponds to these activities: to the former corresponds the nature of a thing, according to its state of being, complete or incomplete, part or accident, as the case may be; to the latter corresponds the existence of the thing.

39   Opusc. xvi, Exposition, *de Trinitate*, v. 3

605. Concerning pure meaning the mind is not deceived, any more than the senses are about their proper objects. But in passing a judgement the mind can be at fault when it attributes to a thing, whose meaning it apprehends, a predicate neither concordant nor entailed. In this situation the mind is like the senses when they judge common or indirect sense-objects.

However, error can be present accidentally even in simple apprehension, when it is mingled with complexity. This can come about in two ways: first, when a definition is misapplied, thus when a definition of circle is misapplied to man; secondly, when mutually repugnant parts are combined in a definition, which is false both in application and in content, thus the notion *rational quadruped*.

Summa Theologica, 1a. xvii. 3

606. The first operation of the mind responds to the essence of a thing, the second to its existence. Now because existence rather than essence lies at the heart of truth, we say that truth properly speaking—and error in attendance—enters with the judgement and its expression in a statement, rather than with simple apprehension and its manifestation in definition.

38, 49   Commentary, *I Sentences*, xix. v. 1, *ad* 7

607. Expect to find error in the senses to no greater extent than truth. Truth is in the senses not because they can know what truth is, but because they have a true perception of sensible objects. Similarly error enters when the senses apprehend and judge things to be other than what they are.

Sense knows things from being impressed with their likeness. Now this likeness can be taken at three stages. First, immediately and directly, as when the likeness of colour is in the sight; so also with other proper sense-objects in their appropriate senses. Secondly, directly but not immediately, as when the likeness of bodily shape or size is in the sight; so also with sense-objects shared through several senses. Thirdly, neither immediately nor directly but indirectly, as when the likeness of man is in the sight; he is not there because he is a man, but because he is a coloured object.

So then to apply this distinction: we say that the senses are not deceived regarding their proper sense-objects, except by interference and in abnormal cases and when the sense-organ is impaired. Regarding common and indirect sense-objects, there can be erroneous sensations even in a healthy sense, for the sense is not immediately related to them, but only incidentally, namely in consequence of their being involved in its primary datum.

660   *Summa Theologica*, 1a. xvii. 2

608. First, about its proper object a sense is always true or only slightly false. Natural powers are not unable to perform their proper activities, except in the minority of cases on account of illness or injury. So the senses are not deficient in judging their proper objects, except sometimes because of impaired organs, as when the dirty tongue of a feverish patient makes sweet taste bitter.

Secondly, a sense has to deal also with what is indirectly sensible, and here it may be deceived. In seeing white the sense may be deceived as to whether it be snow or flour or something of the sort. Mistakes are especially easy with regard to strange or distant objects.

Thirdly, a sense also has to deal with common objects of sense and with inferences about the thing which displays the proper object; size, for instance, and motion are common sensible properties of bodies. The judgement must vary according to the differences of distance, and misjudgement is easy.

Commentary, III de Anima, lect. 6

609. Truth is defined by the conformity of mind and thing. Hence to know this conformity is to know truth. Sense cannot know truth as such—take sight, for instance, it has the likeness of a visible thing, but does not see the correspondence between the perception and the thing perceived. The mind, on the other hand, can know its own conformity with an intelligible thing, not by staying at the apprehension of a meaning but by going on to elicit an affirmation or denial, for only when the mind judges that a thing corresponds to the form apprehended is human truth first known and articulated.

The matter is put well by saying that sense and mind in their simple apprehending may be true but do not thereby know truth. Truth, of course, is present in sensation or simple apprehension as in any true object, but not—and this is its essential point—as in subject knowing object known. Truth is the achievement of mind, and therefore, properly speaking, is reached by judgement, not by simple sensation or intellectual perception of a meaning.

Summa Theologica, 1a. xvi. 2

610. What is true and what is false are opposed as contraries, and not, as some have thought, as affirmation and negation.[1]

462   *Summa Theologica,* 1a. xvii. 4

---

[1] A contrary opposition—black and white—supposes a common subject: a contradictory opposition—the affirmation black and the negation non-black—entails no real relationship.

611. Since true and false are contrasts affecting the same subject, we must needs seek falsity where truth can live, that is to say, in the mind. In things there is neither truth nor error except in relation to mind.

Artificial things are called false simply and in themselves in so far as they fall short of the artist's idea. In things dependent on God there is no falseness with regard to the divine mind, unless perhaps the term be allowed in the case of voluntary mistakes, or sins. Natural things may be called false in relation to our mind on two grounds: first, when an expected quality is lacking; secondly, by way of cause, when its nature is misleading, thus tin may be reckoned false silver.

859 *Summa Theologica*, 1a. xvii. 1

612. The practical mind causes things, and therefore is their measure. But the theoretical mind is receptive; it is, as it were, modulated and measured by things. Hence it is clear that natural things, from which the mind takes its knowledge, measure our mind, but are themselves measured by the divine mind, in which all things are as the works of art in the mind of the maker. So then the divine mind is a measure, but not measured; a natural thing is both measured and measuring; and our mind is measured and measures artificial things, not natural things.

5 *Disputations*, 1 *de Veritate*, 2

613. The truth caused in our mind by things does not come from the mind's own ingenuity, but from the existence of things.

Disputations, 1 *de Veritate*, 2, *ad* 3

614. Truth is simply one in the divine mind, but many truths flow thence into the human mind, as one face may be mirrored with variety.

189, 291 *Disputations*, 1 *de Veritate*, 4

615. A particular science studies truth in special departments. But prime philosophy must envisage the universal truth of things, and therefore must discuss our relation to the problem of knowledge itself.

56   Commentary, *II Metaphysics, lect.* 1

616. The proposition, that the mind is mistaken when it understands a thing otherwise than it really is, can have two meanings, for the adverb *otherwise* can qualify the verb *understands* as regards either the object known or the subject knowing. In the first sense the proposition is true, but not in the second sense. For mode of mind in understanding is different from mode of thing in reality. The mind spiritually understands material things below it in the scale of being, not that it thinks they are spiritual because it conceives them spiritually. Similarly, as regards higher simple substances, it knows them according to its own manner of composition but does not think that they are composite.

190, 647   *Summa Theologica,* 1a. xiii. 12, *ad* 3

III. SENSATION

617. Some wish to base the distinction and number of the external senses on the difference of their organs; others on the diverse natures of sensible qualities in the medium of sensation.[1] But neither attempt really meets the bill. For faculties are not for organs, but conversely; there are not diverse senses because there are different organs, instead nature provides diverse organs to match the diversity of powers. Similarly as regards the media of sensation. Moreover, it is for the mind to judge about the nature of sensible qualities.

The basis for the distinction and number of the

[1] The reference is possibly to Albert the Great and Alexander of Hales.

external senses should be grounded on what is direct and proper to sense. Sense is a receptive power, the subject of change by an external sensible object. This external principle of action is what is directly perceived by sense, and the senses are diversified according to the diversity found here.

There are two sorts of immutation, physiological and psychological. The former comes about by the physical reception of the agent in the patient, the latter according to a certain spiritual reception. Sensation requires this latter process, the entrance into the sense organ of a likeness of, or relation to, the sensible thing. If physiological immutation alone sufficed, all natural bodies would have sensations when they underwent alteration.

575   *Summa Theologica*, 1a. lxxviii. 3

618. The sense of touch is generically one, though specialized in many senses whose distinctness is not obvious, because they are not clearly separated in their organs, but diffused throughout the whole body.

Summa Theologica, 1a. lxxviii. 3, *ad* 3

619. Taste is not separable from general touch, but only from the various other specific powers of touch distributed throughout the body.

Summa Theologica, 1a. lxxviii. 3, *ad* 4

620. Seeing and hearing, although they demand effort and induce strain on their physiological organs, induce psychological rest.

Commentary, *VII Ethics*, *lect.* 14

621. Since nature does not fail to provide necessaries, one would expect as many actions of the sensitive soul as suffice for the proper functions of sensitive life. Diverse principles must be postulated for those actions that cannot be referred back to one and the same immediate principle. We should next take into account that the activity of complete animals requires the apprehension of sensible objects in the absence as well as at the presence of these objects, otherwise animals would act only for what was immediately in front of them. But they exhibit anticipatory action, especially the higher animals which move by progressive stages. Therefore an animal should have the power of retaining and preserving perceptions.

Then again we should consider that were an animal to be moved by pleasure and pain from impressions merely in the external senses, there would be no need to suppose that it has any other faculties besides the external senses, in which are conveyed the forms at which it takes immediate pleasure or fright. But an animal must be able also to seek or avoid things, not just because they are congenial or otherwise to the external senses, but also because of the benefits they offer or the harm they threaten: sheep stampede at the sight of a wolf, not because of any ugliness of odour or shape but because of the menace; birds likewise collect twigs, not because this is a pleasurable occupation to the senses, but because it serves for building a nest. An animal then perceives purposes not immediately apparent to the external senses, and therefore requires also the appropriate faculties.

The proper external senses are appointed to receive sensible forms, and so also is a common internal sense, which is like a joint root and principle for the external senses. The proper senses judge of their proper sensible objects, discerning one object from another within their proper field; for instance the sight distinguishes white from black or green. But to tell white from sweet cannot be done by the sight or taste, for to discern between two things implies knowing them both. This discrimination is the work of a common sense, to which are referred as in a joint clearing-house the perceptions of the other senses. This sense is also able to sense sensation itself, as when somebody sees that he is seeing. This cannot be done by the proper senses, which merely know the sensible forms that alter them.

Then to hold and keep these images, the phantasy or sense-imagination is appointed; it may be described as the storehouse of sense-impressions. In addition, and in order to perceive connexions that are not apparent in the immediate environment perceived by the external senses, there is appointed the estimative sense. Lastly, to retain what has been discovered the memory is appointed—that animals remember what has been beneficial or harmful is a sign of this faculty, to which any sense of the past also belongs.

As regards sensible forms there is little difference between men and animals, for they are similarly worked on by external sense-objects. But there is a difference as regards the implications in the sense situation. For while animals perceive these purposes by a kind of natural instinct, men need to make comparisons. What is called the natural estimative power in animals is called the cogitative power in men, for these purposes are discovered by drawing comparisons: it is also called the particular reason. Then, as regards memory, man does not merely have the sudden recognition of the past, as in the sense-memory of animals, but also the power of reminiscence, which reproduces preceding individual consequences by an effort of recollection.

Midway between the estimative power and the imagination, Avicenna assigns a fifth internal sense, which arranges imaginary forms, as when we assemble gold and mountain into an eldorado we have never seen. There is no evidence for it in the other animals, and in man the power of the imagination seems enough. So there is no need to postulate more than four internal senses, namely the communal sense, the imagination, the estimative power, and the memory.[1]

575, 658, 659　　　*Summa Theologica*, 1a. lxxviii. 4, *c.* & *ad* 2

622. Wonderful instances of sagacity are manifested in the behaviour of animals such as bees, spiders, and dogs. On coming to a crossing, a hound hunting a stag will cast about to discover whether the quarry has taken the first or second trail, and if he does not pick up the scent on either, being thus assured, he takes the third without sniffing about, as though arguing by the principle of exclusion.

Animals act like this because they are naturally adjusted to complicated processes. We call them keen and clever, but this does not imply that they have reason and choice, as appears from the fact that animals of the same breed behave in a similar fashion.

Summa Theologica, 1a–2ae. xiii. 2, *obj.* & *ad* 3

623. Man's superiority to beasts in animal shrewdness and memory does not result from anything proper to the sensitive part, but from an affinity and closeness to intelligence which, so to speak, flows into them. These powers in man are not so very different from those in animals, only they are heightened.

550, 965, 1083　　　*Summa Theologica*, 1a. lxxviii. 4, *ad* 5

---

[1] Of the four internal senses enumerated, namely the imagination or phantasy, the memory, the *sensus communis*, and the 'estimative', the third and fourth call for remark. Note that the *sensus communis* is not at all what is called *common sense* in English: it is a communal sense for the other senses, a clearing-house in which their impressions are sorted and arranged. The 'estimative' is a kind of sense-prudence: its difference in animals and man is similar to that between horse-sense and common sense.

IV. SENSE AND INTELLIGENCE

624. The senses are bodily powers and know singular objects tied down by matter, whereas mind is free from matter and knows universals, which are abstract from matter and contain limitless instances.

836   *Summa Theologica*, 1a–2ae. ii. 6

625. For man to understand he must also have sense, a sign of this being that he who lacks a sense is without the corresponding scientific knowledge of sense-objects, as a man born blind has no scientific knowledge of colours.

44   Opusc. XIII, *Compendium Theologiae*, 82

626. Were man naturally a solitary animal, individual impressions would suffice for him to be aware of, and adapted to, his environment. But he is naturally a social animal, and therefore one man's thoughts should be made known to another through language. There must be significant speech if men are to dwell together. People of different tongues cannot settle down happily together. Furthermore, if men were restricted to sense knowledge, which deals with the here and now, it would be enough for them to emit such sounds as the animals use. But man can dominate his immediate environment; he is aware not merely of the present, but also of the future in time and the distant in place. To express this knowledge the use of writing is required.

1083   Commentary, *I Perihermenias, lect.* 2

627. Some have held that science takes its rise from an outside cause entirely apart from matter. They are divided into two schools. Some are like the Platonists; they hold that the forms of sensible things are separate from matter and hence are actually intelligible, and that the human mind has scientific knowledge by intercourse with these forms. This position is attacked by Aristotle,[1] who insists that the forms of sensible things can neither exist nor be understood apart from sensible matter, any more than snubness can be separated from nose. And therefore others postulate at the origin of science, not separate forms, but bodiless intelligences, which we call angels. Thus Avicenna proposed that intelligible forms are imprinted on the human mind by a bodiless substance, not through our active psychological power, and that the role of our senses is just to stimulate and modify the ensuing knowledge.

But this opinion does not appear reasonable, especially when we take into account the mutual dependence of intellective and sensitive knowledge.

At the other extreme others held that the origin of scientific knowledge is entirely from an interior cause. They are grouped in two schools. Some held that the human soul contains all knowledge within itself, but that this has been darkened by going into a body. Disciplined study removes the black-out; learning is really remembering. But this opinion, which is consonant with the doctrine that souls are created before their union with bodies, does not appear reasonable. For if the union of soul and body be really natural it would not be an impediment to natural knowledge. Others again say that the soul is the cause of its own knowledge, which it evokes at the presence of sense-objects, but does not acquire from them. But this opinion is not entirely acceptable, for it comes back to the doctrine of innate ideas.

Therefore in comparison the teaching of Aristotle appears preferable. He held that scientific knowledge is partly from within[2] and partly from without our mind,

[1] *Metaphysics*, 987ᵃ29.   [2] By the spiritual power of the factive intellect lighting up the data of sense.

and from without, not only because a higher bodiless principle is at work, but also because sense-objects themselves are external.

44, 50, 55, 645, 1091   Disputations, x *de Veritate*, 6

628. Senses are appointed to men not only for procuring the necessities of life, as in the other animals, but also for the sake of knowledge itself. Other animals take no pleasure in sense-objects unless they be related to food or sex, but man can delight in their very beauty.

227   *Summa Theologica*, 1a. xci. 3, *ad* 3

629. Through smell man enjoys the scent of lilies and roses; he finds them pleasing to him in themselves; whereas other animals take pleasure in smells—dogs, for instance—and colours only because they point to something else.

757, 998   Commentary, *II de Coelo et Mundo, lect.* 14

630. Avicenna agrees with Plato that ideas are derived from bodiless forms, which Plato held to subsist in themselves, while Avicenna placed them in a world-mind. But neither hypothesis can show why our soul should be united to a body. Though the soul's intrinsic existence does not depend on the body, this union appears most necessary for the sake of its proper activity, which is to understand. Were it of the soul's nature to receive ideas from the influence of bodiless principles and not to acquire them through the senses, there would be no need of the body; for the soul to be united to body would serve no purpose. And if it be said that senses are necessary in order to awaken the soul to the ideas it has received from elsewhere the same difficulty remains: the need of such rousing would only arise because the soul is overcome by sleep, as the Platonists expressed it, or forgetfulness, both of which states would result from its union with the body. So senses would not profit the mind except to remove obstacles arising from its union with the body, the reason for which would still remain unexplained.

532, 647   *Summa Theologica*, 1a. lxxxiv. 4

631. Imagining goes with thinking so long as we are in this present life, however spiritual the knowledge. Even God is known through the images of his effects.

262   *Disputations*, xvi *de Malo*, 8, *ad* 3

632. Human contemplation at present cannot function without images, for to see meaning in the play of fancy is connatural to us. The purity of intelligible being is contemplated there, though intellectual knowledge does not consist in these images. This applies to the truths of revelation as well as to those of natural knowledge.

270, 279, 822   *Summa Theologica*, 2a–2ae. clxxx. 5, *ad* 2

633. The image is a principle of our knowledge. It is that from which our intellectual activity begins, not as a passing stimulus, but as an enduring foundation. When the imagination is choked, so also is our theological knowledge.

Opusc. xvi, Exposition, *de Trinitate*, vi. 2, *ad* 5

634. In its present condition the mind cannot actually understand anything except by reference to images. There are two indications of this state of affairs. First, the mind is a power which does not operate as part of a bodily organ, and so, were there no dependence on sense and imagination and faculties within bodily organs, its activity would be unimpaired by a bodily lesion. Yet in understanding, either freshly or summoning knowledge already gained, the mind's activity must be accompanied by activity of imagination and of other sense-powers. When the imagination is warped, as in madness, or the memory is lost, as in amnesia—either condition may result from bodily injury—a man is prevented from understanding even those things he previously knew. Secondly, each man experiences in himself that when he attempts to understand a subject he must picture it and use images as examples to hold his attention.

The reason is this: the proper objects of man's mind are the meanings existing in his material environment. These exist only in individuals, and cannot therefore be known completely and truly except as there embodied. Now the individual is perceived through sense and imagination. In order that it may actually understand its proper object, the mind must needs turn to the images of sense. This reference would be uncalled for were its proper object a bodiless form, or, as the Platonists say, a type existing apart from the individual.

533   *Summa Theologica*, 1a. lxxxiv. 7

635. Scientific knowledge in the reason for the present has to go with images formed in our sensitive part. By repeated acts the mind grows in the ability of considering meanings, and the sensitive powers correspondingly improve and more readily promote speculation. Such intellectual knowledge is chiefly and formally in the mind, dispositively and materially in the lower powers of sense.

56   *Summa Theologica*, 1a. lxxxix. 5

636. Irrelevant daydreamings, which flourish when a man ceases to exercise intellectual habits, will distract him to contraries, so much so that unless the imagination be refined, by frequent use of intellectual habits, a man will get out of practice in making right judgements, indeed sometimes will become quite impotent.

Summma Theologica, 1a–2ae. 'liii. 3

637. There is no free play of mind except when the senses are fit and vigorous.

Commentary, *II ad Corinthios, xii, lect.* 1

V. REASONING FROM EXPERIENCE

638. Reason in man is rather like God in the world.

Opusc. xi, 1 *de Regno*, 12

639. To be passive may be applied in the loosest sense to describe the condition of a potentiality receiving its actuality without being deprived of anything. Whatever passes from potentiality to actuality may be termed passive, even when it is perfected in the process. In this sense to understand is to be passive.

The divine intelligence is not in potentiality but is pure act, whereas no created intelligence is actual with regard to every intelligible, but is potential to their actuality. Now there are two conditions of potentiality: one is that of potentiality which is always perfected, and another is that of potentiality which is not always actual but successively actuated. The angelic intelligence is always in act with regard to the things it can understand. The human intelligence, however, lowest in the scale of minds and most remote from the perfection of the divine mind, is in potentiality with regard to things intelligible. To start with it is like a blank page on which nothing is written.

293,774   *Summa Theologica*, 1a. lxxix. 2

640. There is nothing that the divine mind does not understand actually, nor the human mind potentially.

Disputations, 1 *de Veritate*, 2, *ad* 4

641. Substance is intellectual when able to embrace the whole of being.

231   II *Contra Gentes*, 98

642. In Plato's opinion there is no need to postulate a factive intellect in order to make things actually intelligible, though perhaps the knower has still to be enlightened. For he supposed that the forms of natural things, called species or ideas, subsisted apart from matter and consequently were intelligible, for a thing is actually intelligible in that it is immaterial.

Since we agree with Aristotle in not allowing that forms of natural things exist apart from matter, and since forms existing in matter are not actually intelligible, we infer that the natures or forms of the sensible things we understand are not actually intelligible. Now no potentiality is actualized save by something in act. Therefore we should assign some power on the part of the intellect which can make things actually intelligible by the abstraction of the species from material conditions: this is why we postulate the active intellect.

160   *Summa Theologica*, 1a. lxxix. 3

643. The only difference of powers in the human intellect is that between the possible intellect and the factive intellect.[1]

585   *Summa Theologica*, 1a. lxxix. 7

[1] The *intellectus agens* has here been rendered 'factive intellect'. The translation 'active intellect' is misleading, since it suggests a knowing faculty, whereas the role of the factive intellect is to 'make knowable' by raising the sensible to the intelligible, which is then received and conceived by the *intellectus possibilis*. This is not, as sometimes translated, the 'passive intellect', but the intellect-able-to-become all things. Cf. *de Anima*, 429ª22.

644. The intelligence which is potential to all things intelligible we term, following Aristotle, the possible intellect.

Summa Theologica, 1a. lxxix. 2, *ad* 2

645. The human soul is termed intellectual because it shares in intellectual power. One sign that its power is derived is that the soul is not entirely intellectual, but only partially so. Moreover, it reaches the understanding of truth discursively and by a process of reasoning. Furthermore, its imperfect understanding is betrayed, first because it does not understand everything, and secondly because when it does understand a passage from potentiality has been taken. Therefore there must needs be a higher intellect helping the soul to understand.

For these reasons some[1] have held that this substantially separate intellect is in fact the factive intellect. But even on the supposition that such a disembodied active intellect exists, it would still be necessary to appoint to the human soul a special power which shared in the virtue of that superior mind, and served to make things actually intelligible to us. Consequently we should still postulate in the soul a power derived from a higher mind able to light up sense-images. Its function is experienced, since we perceive that we abstract universal meanings from particular conditions, in other words that we make things actually intelligible.

91, 558, 582, 627, 1091   *Summa Theologica*, 1a. lxxix. 4

646. Consequently there are as many factive intellects as there are men, and they are numerically multiplied according to the number of men. The same power numerically one cannot exist in diverse subjects.

558, 559, 660   *Summa Theologica*, 1a. lxxix. 5

[1] Averroes, Avicenna.

647. Can the soul know bodies through the mind?
Seemingly it does not, for the intellect is engaged with
necessary and constant truths, while bodies are variable
and subject to change.

But on the contrary, scientific knowledge is in the
intellect, and if the intellect did not know bodies there
would be no scientific knowledge about them; in that
case natural science, which is occupied with changing
bodies, would have no standing.

To clear up this question, I answer by saying that the
first philosophers who inquired into the natures of
things imagined that there was nothing in the world
but bodies. And because they observed that all bodies
are changing, they were persuaded that everything was
in a continuous process of flux, and concluded that we
could enjoy no certain knowledge about the truth of
things. Truth cannot be fixed with certitude, they
thought, but slips away before the mind can judge it; as
Heraclitus said, it is impossible to touch twice the water
of a flowing stream.

After them came Plato, a greater authority. Wishing
to safeguard the certainty of truth accessible to our
intellect, he postulated besides bodies another class
of things, aloof from matter and motion, which he
called the species or ideas. It is by sharing in these ideas
that a singular and sensible thing is called a horse or
a man, as the case may be. So then, he said, scientific
and exact knowledge and whatever pertains to the
activity of mind does not bear on these sensible bodies
themselves, but on these other spiritual and separate
substances; in other words, the soul does not understand material things, but their bodiless ideas.

But this appears unwarranted for two reasons. Since
these ideas are spiritual and changeless, the knowledge
of matter and motion, proper to natural science, would

be excluded from science. So also would demonstrations through efficient and material causes. Secondly, it would seem ironic that in seeking knowledge about what is fairly manifest we should have to treat of other things instead. Knowing about these other substances would put us in no sort of position for judging sensible things.

Plato seems to have gone astray here. He held that knowledge is through a likeness, but he also held that the form of the thing known must be in the knower in that same manner as it is in itself. Observing how the form of a thing understood is in the mind universally, spiritually, and unvaryingly—qualities which are revealed in the activity of understanding, for the mode of an activity follows the mode of the form's being—he also assumed that the thing understood in itself existed in the same manner.

But such equivalence is not called for. Even in sensible things we see that the same form exists differently in different objects; in one thing white is more intense than in another, and in one it goes with sweetness and in another it goes without. Similarly the form of a sensible object is in one manner when it is outside and in another manner when it is inside the sensibility, which receives the forms of sense-objects without matter, as golden without gold. So also mind possesses the spiritual and unvarying ideas of bodies which themselves are material and variable. This it does after its own fashion, for a thing is received according to the mode of the recipient. Consequently we conclude that the soul knows bodies through the mind with spiritual, universal, and necessary knowledge.

44, 595, 598, 627   *Summa Theologica*, 1a. lxxxiv. 1

648. Remember that when Aristotle disapproves of Plato's opinions, what he condemns in many cases is the turn of the phrase rather than the main drift of the argument. Plato employed a defective teaching method; he speaks figuratively and symbolically and sometimes intends something other than the plain sense of his words, as when he says that the soul is a circle.

Commentary, *I de Anima, lect.* 8

649. Plato's position, that the human mind is filled with all ideas but is hindered from knowing them because of its union with the body, does not appear altogether well founded, and may be criticized at two points.[1] First, it does not seem possible that the soul could fall into oblivion about such universal natural knowledge were it already really possessed: nobody forgets what he knows naturally, for example that whole is larger than part and so forth. Moreover the embarrassment is increased if we suppose that the soul is naturally united with the body, for that a natural activity should be completely choked by its natural condition is most unlikely. Secondly the weakness of the position appears from the fact that if one sense be deficient, then the knowledge of things that can be gathered through that sense is wanting; for instance a man born blind is not acquainted with colours. This would not be the case if the soul had innate species of all intelligible things. We should therefore conclude that the soul does not know bodily things through innate ideas.

1091   *Summa Theologica,* 1a. lxxxiv. 3

650. Is intellectual knowledge acquired from sense-objects? No; that seems the answer, since intellectual knowledge transcends the things of sense. But to the contrary we have the teaching of Aristotle[2] that the

[1] Cf. *Metaphysics,* 993ª1.
[2] Ibid., 981ª2. *Posterior Analytics,* 100ª3.

beginning of our knowledge lies in the senses. I begin
my explanation by noting three differing opinions of
philosophers on this question.

Democritus laid down that no other cause for any of
our knowledge is required save the emission of bodily
images from things and their entrance into our souls;
the process of knowledge is an affair of images and dis-
charges. The absence of any distinction between mind
and sense underlies this opinion; the assumption is that
all knowledge is like sensation, where a physiological
change is induced by objects of sense.

At the other extreme Plato held that the intellect
differed from the senses and was a spiritual power making
no use of a bodily organ in its thinking. Now since a
spiritual thing cannot be changed by a bodily thing, he
was convinced that intellectual knowledge does not
come about because the intellect is transmuted by sense-
objects, but because it shares in intelligible and bodiless
ideas. Even the senses, he said, are powers acting apart
from body; they are spiritual powers that are not
transformed by sensible objects: though he allowed that
the organs of sense undergo changes and immutations
by which the soul is somehow stirred, and so formulates
to itself the ideas of sensible things. Augustine touches
on this opinion when he says that the body does not feel,
but that the soul feels through the body, which it uses
like a herald for announcing without what is expressed
within.[1] Plato's own conclusion is that neither intellectual knowledge nor even sensitive knowledge entirely
derives from material things, but that sensible objects
excite the sensitive soul to sensation and the senses likewise excite the intellectual soul to understanding.

Aristotle, however, took a middle path. He agreed
with Plato that intellect differs from sense, but he also

[1] *de Genesi ad litteram*, xii. 24.

maintained that there is no proper activity of sense into which the body does not enter; sensation is not the activity of soul alone, but of the body-soul compound. So also with regard to all the activities of the sensitive part. That sensible things outside the soul cause something in the human organism is as it should be; Aristotle here agrees with Democritus that the activities of the sensitive part are produced by the impressions of sensible objects on the senses—not, however, in the manner of a discharge, as Democritus had said, but in some other way. Democritus, incidentally, had also held that all action is the upshot of atomic changes. Aristotle, however, taught that the intrinsic activity of mind was independent of intercourse with body. No corporeal thing can impress itself on an incorporeal thing. Therefore the mere impression of sensible bodies is not sufficient to cause intellectual activity.

A nobler and higher force is required, for the agent is more honourable than the patient.[1] Not, however, in such a way that intellectual activity is caused in us by the sole influence of some higher being, as Plato held, but that there is a spiritual ability within us, called after Aristotle the factive intellect, which by the process of abstraction renders actually intelligible images taken from sense. As regards these images intellectual knowledge is caused by the senses. Yet because an image alone is not sufficient to transform the receptive mind until it has been heightened and made actually intelligible by an active intellect, we should not say that sense-knowledge is the total and perfect cause of intellectual knowledge. Let us say instead that sense-data are by way of offering the material for the cause.

44, 161, 560, 1091   *Summa Theologica*, 1a. lxxxiv. 6

[1] i.e. an active power is stronger than the receiver as such of its influence.

651. Since sensuous and intellectual being are poles apart, the material form is not immediately accepted, but is first worked up and spiritualized by an elaborate process and so brought to the reason.

683   Disputations, *de Anima*, 20

652. Rational knowledge is in the middle stage between sensation and pure intellection. It is not the activity of an organ, and yet it rises from a faculty of the soul, which is the form of body. Accordingly rational knowledge is properly concerned with forms that in fact exist individually in bodily matter, and yet are not known immediately as existing in such or such individual matter. This implies abstraction of the form from the individual matter represented by sense-images. Through material truths thus considered we can reach some knowledge of immaterial truths.

Attending to the spirituality of mind and not to its union with body, Plato held that the object of mind is a bodiless idea, and that understanding results rather by sharing in ideas apart from phenomena than by making an abstraction from individual experience.

519, 744   *Summa Theologica*, 1a. lxxxv. 1

653. There are two kinds of abstraction. First, by way of composition and division, as when we take one note to be inseparable or separable from another. Second, by way of simplicity, as when we consider one reality without attending to another. When things are not really separate from one another, and abstraction after the first method is performed, then the result is not without error. But no error is implied in the second method of abstraction, even when dealing with realities not really separate from one another. This appears in the case of the senses. For we should make a mistake if we imagined and reckoned that colour is not in, or may be separate from, a coloured body. But there would be no mistake if colour and its properties were considered and stated without reference to the apple which is coloured, for to be in apple is not essential to colour, and colour can be treated independently of apple. I say similarly that the specific notes of a material thing, such as man, horse, stone, can be conceived without the individual principles, which are not essential to the nature. This is what we mean by abstraction of the universal from the particular or the intellectual concept from the sense-image; in other words, the nature of the species is considered apart from the individual principles represented in the senses.

If the intellect is said to be false when it understands a thing otherwise than as it is, the statement may be granted if the term *otherwise* refers to the thing understood, for then the intellect is at fault by understanding a thing to be different from what it is, as would be the case if it abstracted the species of stone from matter so as to think, as Plato did, that the species does not exist in matter. But the criticism does not apply if the term *otherwise* be taken to refer to the knower, for assuredly the mode of understanding in the knower is not the same as the mode of the thing in the concrete, for the former is spiritual and the latter material.

315, 598, 838   *Summa Theologica*, 1a. lxxxv. 1, *ad* 1

654. Some have thought that the species of a natural thing is a pure form, and that matter is not part of the species. If that indeed were the case, then matter would not enter into the definition of natural things. We must disagree, and remark that matter is twofold, common matter, such as flesh and bones, and marked out and individual matter, such as this flesh and these bones.

The mind abstracts the meaning of a natural thing from the individual sensible matter, but not from the common sensible matter: for example, it abstracts the species of man from this flesh and these bones, for since these do not belong to the species as such but as are individual parts, they need not be observed in the species: the species of man, however, cannot be discussed apart from flesh and bones in general.

50   *Summa Theologica*, 1a. lxxxv. 1, *ad* 2

655. Concerning the difference between universal and particular ideas, let it be remembered in the first place that higher minds have more universal, and lower minds less universal, ideas. But such universality and particularity should not be misinterpreted to refer to the things known, nor should it be concluded that God understands only the universal nature of being. As regards other minds, one consequence of this reading would be that the higher the mind the more general the knowledge, and this would be tantamount to saying that a superior intelligence knows merely the nature of substance, an inferior intelligence the nature of body, a still lower intelligence a particular species, and so on down the scale. Obviously this calls for revision. For the knowledge of a thing in a generalization is imperfect by comparison with specific and peculiar knowledge; knowledge of a species includes knowledge of its genus, but not the other way round: the sweeping inference would be that the higher the mind the lower the knowledge.

Consequently the difference between universality and particularity should be set in the medium of knowledge. The higher the mind the more universal its medium, yet in such wise that its knowledge covers the specific notes of an object more thoroughly than does the knowledge enjoyed by a lesser mind. This can be confirmed from our own experience; we notice that people of excellent understanding grasp all the points of a problem from a few hints, whereas those of duller wit have to be shown them in detailed repetition.

19, 307 Opusc. x, Exposition, *de Causis*, lect. 10

656. To theorize about universal ideas without previous induction is not possible.

105 Commentary, *I Posterior Analytics*, lect. 29

657. Mental activity rises from sensation, yet in the very object of sense the mind perceives many notes that escape the senses.

537 *Summa Theologica*, 1a. lxxviii. 4, *ad* 4

VI. KNOWLEDGE OF SINGULARS

658. Rational knowledge lights primarily on the form of natural things, and secondarily on their matter as related to form. Form as such is universal, so the mind's bent to form does not enable it to know matter except in general terms. Matter as so expressed is not the principle of individuation. It is such only when taken in the singular, in other words as matter marked out and existing under determinate dimensions. Obviously then, the reason cannot know singulars directly. They are known by sensitive powers quickening bodily organs, and themselves existing under determinate dimensions. Intellectual knowledge brings the knowledge of universal matter, but sense-knowledge brings the knowledge of determinate matter which is the principle of individuation.

Nevertheless, the mind is indirectly involved with singular facts inasmuch as it merges into the sense-powers, which are engaged with particular things. The process works both ways. First in the direction from things to mind, corresponding to the movement of the sensitive part into the mind to reach its climax there. Thus the mind knows the singular by a sort of reflection, for from knowing its own object, namely some general type, it can bend back and be aware of its own activity, and then continue to the concept which is a principle of the activity, and thence to the image from which the concept is drawn: in this way the mind comes by some knowledge of the singular. The second direction is from soul into things, starting from mind and leading into the sensitive parts. Because the mind governs the lower powers and the particular reason, which is the faculty of individual situations, it comes to entertain the knowledge of singular things.

305, 447, 621   Disputations, x *de Veritate*, 5

659. When a singular thing is perceived, as when I recognize that a coloured object is this man or that animal, the apprehension is elicited by the internal sense that appreciates particular situations, also called the particular reason, for it combines individual meanings in much the same way as the universal reason combines general meanings. This power is in the sensitive part of the soul.

Sense and mind are conjoined in man, and the sensitive powers at their best share in the power of the intelligence. In irrational animals the perception of individual characteristics comes by natural sense-judgement; a ewe knows her lamb by hearing or sight. Here the human sense-judgement is rather different from the merely animal judgement. For the particular reason perceives an individual as being of a certain kind, for the faculty works alongside and in the same subject as the intelligence, and therefore may perceive objects as being this *man* or this *stone*. Purely animal appreciation does not judge the individual to be of a certain kind, but only to be the principle or term of some action or passion; thus a ewe knows this lamb, not as being a lamb, but as something to be suckled, and this grass, not as grass, but as something to be eaten.

18, 621, 662   Commentary, *II de Anima, lect.* 13

660. One and the same power can know flesh and the meaning of flesh, as when the mind relates universal to singular. The difference between *sweet* and *white* would not be perceived unless there were one common clearing-house of sense in which both can be joined together. Similarly universal could not be related to particular unless the mind knew them both, though in different ways.

621   Commentary, *III de Anima, lect.* 8

661. It is singular as material that is incompatible with being understood, not singular as singular.

307   *Summa Theologica,* 1a. lxxxvi. 1, *ad* 3

VII. SELF-KNOWLEDGE

662. Because in its present life the mind is connaturally occupied with material and sensible things, it knows itself through its activation by ideas, abstracted from sensible things by the factive intellect lighting the mind. Therefore the mind knows itself through its activity, not through its essence.

This knowledge is exercised in two ways, in the particular and in the universal. By their own individual awareness Socrates and Plato perceive themselves to possess an intellectual soul, because they perceive that they are actually understanding. But the self can also be considered in universal ideas, as when the nature of the soul is inferred from the nature of its activity scientifically considered.

There is a difference between the two knowledges. The presence of the mind to itself suffices for the former, since the mind itself is the principle of the activity wherein it perceives itself; hence it is said to know itself by its presence.[1] But this does not suffice for the latter, which requires further careful and scientific introspection.

    102, 103, 292, 295   *Summa Theologica,* 1a. lxxxvii. 1

663. Through the soul's consciousness we know that the soul exists, because we perceive its activity; then we go on to explore its nature by a scientific study of its acts and objects. Similarly, as regards psychological qualities, abilities, and habits, we know that they exist because we perceive their activities; but to know their characteristics we must measure them by their scientific types.

                                       III *Contra Gentes,* 46

VIII. FUNCTIONS OF INTELLIGENCE

664. If memory means the power of retaining ideas, then of course it is in the intellect; but if one insists that its object is the past precisely as past, then it is not in the intellective part of the soul, but in the sensitive part which perceives singulars. The past as such signifies existence at a determinate time, and therefore contracts the conditions of particularity.

Pastness, however, can refer either to an object known or to an act of knowing. As regards the former, pastness is incidental, and not essential to an intelligible object: the mind understands man as man; whether this object

---

[1] The doctrine of immediate self-consciousness derives from St. Augustine, *de Trinitate,* ix. x.

happens to be past, present, or future is quite irrelevant. But as regards the latter, the pastness of an act can be essential to intellect, for our act of understanding is a particular activity at a certain time: accordingly we speak of a man knowing yesterday, to-day, or to-morrow. This is not inconsistent with intellectuality, for though particular the reality in question is also immaterial.

244, 621 *Summa Theologica*, 1a. lxxix. 6, *c & ad 2*

665. Past and present can be proper differences to objects of sense, but not to objects of mind.

248 *Summa Theologica*, 1a. lxxix. 7, *ad 2*

666. The intellect and the reason cannot be diverse faculties. This clearly appears when their respective activities are considered. To understand is to apprehend an intelligible truth simply; to reason is to proceed from one understanding to another. Ratiocination is compared to intellection as motion to rest, or as acquiring to having. One is a process; the other an achievement. Human ratiocination proceeds according to the method of inquiry and discovery from certain objects simply understood, namely from first principles; following afterwards the method of judgement by analysis, it returns to its principles, in the light of which it examines what has been found. Now it is clear that to be in motion and to be at rest are not to be referred to different powers, but to one and the same power.

244, 298, 696 *Summa Theologica*, 1a. lxxix. 8

667. As Aristotle says, the theoretical mind by extension becomes practical.[1] But one faculty does not become another. Therefore the speculative and the practical reasons are not different faculties.

5 *Summa Theologica*, 1a. lxxix. 11, *sed contra*

[1] *de Anima*, 433ª14.

XI

Love[1]

668. The powers of appetition are now to be considered, and under the following headings: appetite in general, emotion, will, choice.

318   *Summa Theologica*, 1a. lxxx, Prologue

669. In every good the supreme good is desired.

162, 725   Commentary, *II Sentences*, 1. ii. 3

I. APPETITION

670. Propensity follows form. In the case of things without knowledge, each possesses one form limiting it to one existence or condition of natural being. The resulting propensity is called natural appetite. But forms exist more perfectly in things that can know; they possess the determinate being and inclination we have

---

[1] St. Thomas frequently notes the difference between cognition and affection: both are immanent activities completed within the subject, both are intrinsically non-causal and lifted above the law that the birth of one thing is the death of another; yet with knowledge the object is taken into the knower, while with love the lover goes out to the object. Even in desire working through knowledge the attraction is for a thing more than for a meaning. Hence the importance of the dialectic of love in the mystical and aesthetical theory of St. Thomas. The specialized appetite of will is based on natural desire and cannot disavow its origins; even within the field of its proper activity the area of choice is limited. Human liberty is neither an ultimate value nor the power of producing something entirely new. Yet, except in the final stages of human activity, psychological determinism is avoided in the thesis of the poise of the powers of mind and will before anything less than universal truth and goodness.

mentioned, but in addition they can receive the forms of other things, whereupon they evince propensities above the mode of natural appetite. These come from the appetitive part of the soul, whereby an animal can desire the things it apprehends, not merely the thing which it is by its own natural form.

693, 950   *Summa Theologica*, 1a. lxxx. 1

671. Within each power there is its own natural appetite for a suitable object; but over and above there is a special type of appetite, termed the animal appetite, resulting from perception and going for an object, not merely because it is congruous to this or that power, as seeing for the sight or hearing for the ear, but also because it is wanted by the whole organism.[1]

Summa Theologica, 1a. lxxx. 1, *ad* 3

672. He who desires a good seeks to have it as it really is in nature, not as it is in his consciousness.

732, 912   Disputations, XXII *de Veritate*, 3, *ad* 4

673. The will is taken up with things as they are in themselves, the intellect with things according as they exist spiritually in the soul. Action and movement are

[1] Motions of appetite may be usefully divided as follows:
{ the violent, or forced; movement imposed from without:
{ the natural, or spontaneous; movement from within:
  { unconscious; natural appetite:
  { with knowledge; the voluntary:
    { animal appetite; imperfect knowledge of purpose and imperfect voluntary:
    { rational appetite; knowledge of end as such and perfect voluntary:
      { volition, of ends:
      { choice, of means: a human act implying deliberation:
        { liberty of contradiction; of acting or not acting:
        { liberty of contrariety; of acting thus or thus: the issue
          may or may not be between right and wrong.

excited for things existing as realities in nature, not as thoughts.

323, 698   *Disputations, xxii de Veritate,* 12

674. All other motions of the appetite presuppose love as their first root.

394   *Summa Theologica,* 1a. xx. 1

675. All fear springs from love. Ordered love is included in every virtue, disordered love in every vice.

Summa Theologica, 2a–2ae. cxxv. 2

676. Love is absolutely stronger than hate.

476   *Summa Theologica,* 1a–2ae. xxix. 3

II. EMOTION

677. Sensuality is the name of the sensitive appetite.

815   *Summa Theologica,* 1a. lxxxi. 1

678. The sensitive appetite is one generic power, but is divided into two kinds, namely the concupiscible and the irascible. By the former the soul works according to the pain-pleasure principle, by the latter it deals with emergency reactions.

The irascible is, as it were, the champion of the concupiscible, attacking what hinders pleasure or inflicts harm, which respectively the concupiscible desires and shrinks from. Anger starts from desire and leads to it.

819   *Summa Theologica,* 1a. lxxxi. 2

679. While natural and voluntary activities are spontaneous and from an intrinsic principle, violent and forced motions are from an extrinsic principle. As violence makes an action unnatural in things lacking consciousness, so it makes an action non-voluntary in things with consciousness.

703   *Summa Theologica,* 1a–2ae. vi. 5

680. That rule is termed despotic when master governs slaves who are not able to resist, having nothing of their own.[1] But rule is royal and civilized when the prince rules free citizens who, though under government, have something of their own and are able to resist. The soul is said to govern the body by despotic rule; but the reason governs the emotional life by civil rule, because the sense-appetite has something of its own and thereby can resist the commands of the reason. For of its nature it is swayed, not only by the particular reason guided by the universal reason, but also by the imagination and the senses. We experience a resistance when we imagine something pleasant forbidden by the reason, or something unpleasant commanded by the reason. This does not exclude obedience.

996, 1093   *Summa Theologica*, 1a. lxxxi. 3, *ad* 2

681. Of some motions the principle is outside, as when a stone is thrown up into the air; of others it is within, as when a stone gravitates downward. Among things in motion from within, some have not moved themselves, while others have set themselves in motion. In some cases, although there is an intrinsic principle of action, the principle of acting for a purpose is not within the thing, but in something else directing it. In other cases, however, given some knowledge of an end, things have within themselves the principle, not merely of acting, but also of acting for a purpose. Those motions are termed voluntary where the activity is both from within and purposed by the doer.

703   *Summa Theologica*, 1a–2ae. vi. 1

682. An activity from within with some knowledge of purpose—that is the mark of voluntary action. But there

[1] *Politics*, 1254^{b}2.

is a twofold knowledge of an end, imperfect and perfect. Imperfect knowledge is merely perceiving a goal without understanding of purpose as such or of the adaptation of means to ends; animals enjoy that kind of knowledge through their senses. Perfect knowledge requires more, namely, understanding of the meaning of purpose and of the relation of means to end; it is proper to an intelligence. Hence the complete character of voluntary activity, endowed with deliberation and freedom, is found in rational natures alone. From imperfect appreciation of purpose there follows incomplete voluntary activity, the apprehension and spontaneous desire without deliberation which is typical of animals.

Summma Theologica, 1a–2ae. vi. 2

III. VOLITION

683. Objects of sense and of intelligence are at different levels; in consequence the intellectual appetite[1] or will is a power distinct from the sensitive appetite.

801   *Summa Theologica*, 1a. lxxx. 2

684. The will is contrasted with the merely natural appetite, as man is contrasted with animal. The opposition is formal, not of things in the round—for as mind includes animal, so does the will include natural appetite.

Disputations, xxii *de Veritate*, 5, *ad* 6, *ii*

685. Mind influences will as a final cause, for a good understood is the object of will and acts like an end; but the will moves the mind, and also other psychological powers, as an efficient cause.

211   *Summa Theologica*, 1a. lxxxii. 4

[1] The intellectual appetite, or will, a faculty distinct from the intellect; not to be confused with the natural appetite within the intellect. Cf. 671.

686. A triple comparison may be drawn between intellect and will. First, in the abstract and generally speaking, without respect to this or that object: the intellect thus is higher than the will, for to possess the value of a thing is better than to be related to it. Second, with respect to sensible things: again the intellect thus is higher than the will, for it is better to know a stone than to will it, for the form of stone as understood exists more excellently than does form of stone in actual fact, and as so desired by the will. Third, with respect to divine things, higher than the soul: now thus it is better to love them than to understand them; it is better to love God than to know about him, for the divine goodness is most perfectly in God, which is how it is desired by the will, than it is as shared in us or conceived by the mind.

731, 913   Disputations, xxii *de Veritate*, 11

687. Some have thought that the human will is moved to choice from necessity. However, they do not hold that the will is forced, for not all necessary motions are violent, but only those whose over-riding principles are from without.

Disputations, vi *de Malo*, 1

688. Effects are denominated necessary or contingent, as the case may be, by the condition of their proximate causes.

308   Opusc. xiii, *Compendium Theologiae*, 139

689. The term *necessity* has various usages. One is necessity from force, imposed by an efficient cause; another is necessity from the final cause, when a means is indispensable or convenient for an end; a third is natural or absolute necessity from intrinsic principles, either the formal or the material cause.

Now necessity from force is entirely against the

character of willing, for a violent action is induced against the natural inclination of the thing concerned. The motion of the will is spontaneous. A motion cannot be simultaneously violent and natural, nor similarly simultaneously coerced and voluntary.

Necessity from an end is not inimical to the notion of will when an end cannot be reached except by one means; for example, the will is under the necessity of taking ship from the intention of making a sea-passage.

Natural necessity likewise is not against the nature of the will; indeed just as the mind adheres to first principles of necessity so the will cleaves to happiness of necessity and to the last end. This is the constant foundation and spring of all its activities.

III   *Summa Theologica*, 1a. lxxxii. 1

690. But let us consider the necessity from the end. The will does not will of necessity whatever it wills. To make this clearer, let us remark again that as the mind assents to first principles of necessity so does the will go out to the last end. There are some truths that have no necessary connexion with first principles, for example, contingent propositions which may be denied without a denial of first principles. The mind does not assent to them of necessity. Other propositions have a necessary connexion; such are demonstrated conclusions to which the mind assents of necessity once they have been proved. Now the will is in like case.

Some particular goods are not necessarily bound up with happiness. A man may be happy without them. To these the will is not determined of necessity. But there are others which have a necessary connexion with happiness. They are involved in our cleaving to God, in whom alone true happiness consists. Nevertheless, before this connexion strikes us in the certitude of vision, the will does not cleave to God or to divine things of necessity.

213 *Summa Theologica*, 1a. lxxxii. 2

691. The future disposition of a thing may concern either its constitution, as when an artist decides to design a house; or its use and administration, as when a man decides how to train a horse, and this is where predestination comes in. By its natural constitution a thing is not immediately directed towards an end, and therefore natural meanings do not fall under predestination properly speaking; we do not say that man is predestined to have hands.

339, 342 Commentary, *in Romanos, i, lect.* 3

IV. FREEWILL

692. To be free is not to be obliged to one determinate object: as deriving from the mind's apprehension regarding universal good, the appetite of an intellectual substance is not committed to one determinate good.

242, 655 Opusc. XIII, *Compendium Theologiae*, 76

693. The term *will* has two senses: when it stands for the faculty it covers means and ends, but when it stands for the act of volition it is engaged with ends.

As first principles of the mind are known naturally, so the principle of all motions of the will is something that is naturally, that is not deliberately, willed. This is goodness in general, to which the will tends of necessity as any faculty does to its own appropriate object. Again, it is the last end, and by and large it includes all those parts of the good estate appropriate to the nature of man who wills; they concern not his will alone, but also every power, and indeed the whole man. Knowledge of truth, which responds to mind, to be and to

live, which belong to his natural integrity—all these
are implied in the object of will.[1]

595   *Summa Theologica*, 1a–2ae. viii. 2

694. The will addresses itself differently to ends and to
means; to the former simply and absolutely, as to things
good in themselves; to the latter calculatedly, as to
things useful for something else. Therefore there is
a difference in its manner of address to what is willed
in itself, health for instance, and what is chosen for the
sake of something else, medicine for instance. The first
activity is called *thelesis* by Damascene, and willing-as-
natural in the schools; the second is called *boulesis* by
Damascene, and willing-as-reasoned in the schools.[2]

214, 311, 977   *Summa Theologica*, 3a. xviii. 3

695. Freewill is not a habit, but a faculty.

                                 Summa Theologica, 1a. lxxxiii. 2

696. As understanding and reasoning are from the
same faculty of mind, so also are wishing and choosing
from the same faculty of will. The will and the freewill
are not two powers, but one.

666   *Summa Theologica*, 1a. lxxxiii. 4

697. As in physical things there is a form which is the
principle of activity, and an active propensity consequent on that form, called the natural appetite, so in
man there is an intellective form and a propensity of
will, consequent on this form as apprehended, from

---

[1] Several stages are distinguished in the normal present activity
of the will, *voluntas*: the wishing, *velle*, of an end; the willing,
volitio, of an end; the choice, *electio*, of a means; the execution of
the activity, and the consequent pleasure.

[2] *Expositio Accurata Fidei Orthodoxae*, ii. 22. The scholastic
terms are *voluntas ut natura* and *voluntas ut ratio*. The latter is
freewill, the power of choice.

which follows external activity. But there is a difference
here, for the form of natural things is individuated by
matter, on which account the consequent propensity is
determined to one object. A form as understood, however, is universal and can comprise many things. When
activity is about to be directed on a singular object,
which does not exhaust the power of the universal, the
propensity of will in itself is poised indeterminately to
many objects of action. It is as when the architect conceives the form of a house, but his will is not yet made
up as to its style and what lines it will take, angular or
rounded.

Disputations, VI *de Malo*, 1

698. Motion and action do not spring from a universal
conception, unless that be joined with an individual
apprehension, because motion and action are for the
particular. The human intellect by nature is cognitive
of universals. For motion and action to be stirred,
therefore, a general conception must be applied to a
particular case. Potentially it contains many particulars,
and it can be applied in consequence to many and diverse
things. The judgement of the intellect about what should
be done is not committed to any one course. All intellectual natures, therefore, possess freewill.

316, 903   II *Contra Gentes* 48

699. Man has free choice, otherwise counsels, exhorta-
tions, precepts, prohibitions, rewards, and punishments
would all be pointless.

In explanation note that some things act without
judgement, as when a stone falls; others with judgement, but more from natural instinct than deliberate
adjustment, as when a sheep flees from a wolf. Man,
however, can act from judgement and adaptation in the

reason; a free judgement that leaves intact the power of being able to decide otherwise. The reason keeps an open mind, as appears in dialectical proofs and rhetorical persuasions. Particular lines of conduct are contingent. Concerning any one of them the practical reason is not committed beforehand. A man has free choice to the extent that he is rational.

342, 969, 977   *Summa Theologica*, 1a. lxxxiii. 1

700. The will is actuated in two ways, as regards first the exercise and secondly the specification of its activity. In the first way, no object in a humane situation moves the will of necessity, for a man is always able not to think of an object and consequently not to react to it. But in the second way, some objects move the will of necessity, others not. If an object universally and in every respect good is proposed, then of necessity the will must go out in love if it acts at all. But if the object proposed is not good from every point of view, then the will is not moved of necessity. The lack of any good is equivalent to not-good. Only that good which is complete in itself, and without need of supplement, is the good which the will is not able not to will. This is happiness. Other particular goods, in that they fall short of some goodness, can be regarded as not good; as appreciated in that light they can be approved or rejected by the will, which can conduct itself in the same situation according to different points of view.

204, 1038   *Summa Theologica*, 1a–2ae. x. 2

701. Choice is materially an act of the will, formally an act of the reason.

The decision or judgement, drawn by the reason as a conclusion, is followed by choice in the will.

Summa Theologica, 1a–2ae. xiii. 1, *c & ad* 2

XII

Happiness[1]

702. Having proclaimed God as the exemplar, and having discussed the things issuing from his omnipotent will, it remains now to consider his image, that is man, studied as the principle of his own activity and the master of his own deeds. Here we must discuss the final goal of human life, first in general terms and then with reference to happiness.[2]

Summa Theologica, 1a–2ae. i, Prologue

I. PURPOSE AND END

703. Only acts controlled by man through his reason and will are properly termed human: they proceed from deliberation. Others may be called acts of the man, but they are not human in the specific sense of the term.

164, 682   *Summa Theologica,* 1a–2ae. i. 1

---

[1] St. Thomas's debt to the first and last books of the *Nicomachean Ethics* is clear and acknowledged: happiness or beatitude is taken as man's final and immanent perfection, his highest activity of mind. So much for his subjective well-being. But as regards objective happiness, the thing which gives this joy, the rudimentary natural theology of the Peripatetics is supplemented by ideas derived from Plotinus, Augustine, and especially from Boethius. Ultimately, existing sheer truth and goodness answer human desire. St. Thomas parts company with the Stoics, for he holds that virtue is not its own reward, and also with the Epicureans, for pleasure does not constitute the end of human purpose; yet the temper of both is found in his thought.

[2] *Beatitudo,* a more comprehensive term than happiness, and also stronger: it includes not only the active completion of the subject but also the objective causes and conditions of the state.

704. A thing tends to an end in two ways, either like a man setting himself in motion or like a missile shot off. To be self-acting and self-conducting to an end is proper to human nature. Irrational nature is rather acted on or conducted, whether the goal be apprehended, as in the case of animals, or not, as in the case of things wholly lacking consciousness.

679 *Summa Theologica*, 1a–2ae. i. 2

705. Some acts do not appear to be purposeful, for instance playing and contemplating, also inattentive actions such as stroking your beard. Notice that contemplative activity, though not for an ulterior end, itself contains the end; playful activities are somewhat similar, as when we sport for the pleasure of it, though at other times we take recreation to make ourselves fit for work. Actions without attention, as when we scratch an itch, come from sudden sensations or from natural principles; their purposes lie off the map of deliberation.

1, 694 III *Contra Gentes*, 2

706. An act is voluntary in two ways: as commanded by the will, such as speaking or walking; and as elicited from the will, such as the act of volition itself.

Summa Theologica, 1a–2ae. i. 1, *ad* 2

707. Happiness is the greatest human good, the end to which all others are subordinate. It would be pernicious to a degree were happiness a matter of good luck, for then all other goods would be even more fortuitous, and so any deliberate attempt to lead a good life would go by the board.

Commentary, *I Ethics, lect.* 14

708. A man need not be always preoccupied with his last end, any more than a wayfarer should always be

thinking about the end of his journey with every step
he takes.

Summa Theologica, 1a–2ae. i. 6, *ad* 3

709. The last end so satisfies the entire appetite that
naught outside is left to be desired. For the appetite to
be simultaneously attracted by two ends, both claiming
to be ultimate, is quite impossible.

213   *Summa Theologica*, 1a–2ae. i. 5

II. THE OBJECTIVE GOOD

710. Of the ultimate end we can speak in two senses,
in the abstract and in the concrete. Concerning the
former, which expresses the very concept of finality, all
are of one mind in desiring their completion. Though
as to where this may be found, which is happiness in the
latter sense, there is no general agreement. Some set
their heart on riches, others on pleasure, and so forth.
Deliciousness is delightful to every taste, but some find
it best in wine, others in candy, and so forth.

Summa Theologica, 1a–2ae. i. 7

711. Then again in considering the ultimate end, we
should draw a distinction between the object itself
in which goodness lies and the obtaining and enjoying of it.[1]

727   *Summa Theologica*, 1a–2ae. i. 8

712. Wealth is of two kinds, natural and artificial.
Natural wealth, such as food, drink, clothing, and

---

[1] The term *last end* can have three meanings:
the objective end itself, taken
  1. in the abstract, the formal object, divine truth;
  2. in the concrete, the Thing, God;
3. the subjective end, the activity of possessing the end, the
  vision of God.

shelter, supplies natural needs. Artificial wealth, such as money, does not directly serve nature, but is invented by art to facilitate the exchange of goods. Natural wealth ought to support human nature, and therefore cannot be ultimate since it is subservient to man himself. With much less reason is artificial wealth his last end, for it is but a means to natural wealth.

Summa Theologica, 1a–2ae. ii. 1

713. Silly people think that money commands the bodily goods most worth having.

Summa Theologica, 1a–2ae. ii. 1, *ad* 1

714. The lust for natural wealth is not boundless, because nature works within limits; but there is no end to the avarice for artificial wealth.

145   *Summa Theologica*, 1a–2ae. ii. 1, *ad* 3

715. The good life does not consist in renouncing wealth, though that is one method of finding it. Easier for a camel to go through the eye of a needle than for a rich man to enter heaven—the impossibility is not alleged but the rarity is emphasized.

Opusc. xxix, *de Perfectione Vitae Spiritualis*, 7

716. There can be two virtues in the spending of money: liberality in day-to-day disbursing, magnificence in great expenditures.

Summa Theologica, 2a–2ae. cxxxiv. 3, *ad* 1

717. Four general reasons can be brought forward to show that perfect happiness consists neither in riches, nor in honour or fame, nor in power. Of which the first is that perfect happiness is not compatible with any evil. The second is that happiness is self-sufficient; once obtained no other human prize is wanting, such as good health and wisdom. The third is that no harm results from happiness, whereas sometimes *riches are kept to the hurt of the owner*,[1] and this may also be the case with the other goods we have mentioned. The fourth reason is this; happiness wells up from within, but the goods we have mentioned come from external causes and often from good luck.

Summa Theologica, 1a–2ae. ii. 4

718. The dead can be honoured or disgraced, their descendants may be prosperous or unfortunate. And so happiness lies not even in the grave.

Commentary, I Ethics, lect. 15

719. The overriding consideration of an admiral is not to keep his ships undamaged, for his fleet is meant to serve a purpose outside itself. As that is entrusted to him, so a man is commissioned by his reason and will, and since man is not himself the supreme good, his business is to serve another end. Consequently his own safety is not his ultimate end.

171, 457   *Summa Theologica*, 1a–2ae. ii. 5

720. The desire for joy is inherently stronger than the fear of sadness, though under certain circumstances men's preoccupation may be with avoiding the latter rather than seeking the former.

Summa Theologica, 1a–2ae. xxxv. 6

721. Pleasure is naught but the repose of appetite in a good thing, and so if the phrase *for the sake of* indicates final causality we can admit that pleasure is desired for its own sake, for it is good. But if the phrase indicates the formal cause, or even the efficient cause, then pleasure is desired not on its own account, but because of some-

[1] Eccles. v. 12.

thing else, namely the good thing which is the object
of appetite, and which in consequence is the principle
and form-giver of pleasure.

375, 800, 823   *Summa Theologica*, 1a–2ae. ii. 6, *ad* 1

722. There are two phases in pleasure: the perception of what is congenial, which belongs to cognition,
and the satisfaction in what is offered, which belongs to
the appetite, where delight culminates.

Summa Theologica, 1a–2ae. xi. 1, *ad* 3

723. An essential component is distinct from a resulting
property; *rational mortal* is distinct from *endowed
with a sense of humour*. Always bear in the mind that
delight is a quality consequent on happiness. A man
delights because he possesses the very thing he wants,
if not in fact then in hope, or at least in memory.
The substance of his happiness lies in that objective
good.

Summa Theologica, 1a–2ae. ii. 6

724. Perfect enjoyment demands intelligence.

998   *Summa Theologica*, 1a–2ae. xi. 2

725. The ultimate end of everything is its completion.
A part is for the whole as for its end. The whole universe
of creatures, which is called the macrocosm, is related
to man, who is called the microcosm, as the perfect to
the imperfect. Therefore man's happiness is contained
in the cosmos.

Against this argument we must remark that if a whole
is not itself an ultimate but subordinate to a higher end,
then the ultimate end of a part is not the group itself,
but something else outside. The universe of creatures,
in which man is like a part in the whole, is not an
ultimate end itself; it is ordered to God. Man's last end,

therefore, does not consist in the total and collective good of the universe, but in God.

171, 1111, 1117   *Summa Theologica*, 1a–2ae. ii. 8, *obj. & ad* 2

726. Creaturely good is not less than the happiness of which man is capable, when that is taken subjectively as being part of him. It is less than that happiness, when that is taken objectively, or as regards its object, which is infinite.

Summa Theologica, 1a–2ae. ii. 8, *ad* 3

III. THE ACT OF HAPPINESS

727. End can be viewed under two aspects; the thing itself which we desire to have, thus money to the miser, and the laying hold and enjoyment of it, thus his clutching. Under the first aspect, the ultimate end of man is uncreated good, namely God who alone can perfectly fulfil the will of man because of his infinite goodness. But under the second aspect, the ultimate is a creaturely reality in man. The happiness of man, then, considered in its cause and object is uncreated, but considered in its nature it is created.

711   *Summa Theologica*, 1a–2ae. iii. 1

728. And happiness is an activity in this sense.

291, 447   *Summa Theologica*, 1a–2ae. iii. 2

729. By saying that it was an estate replenished with all good things, Boethius described happiness in general terms.[1] Aristotle lays his finger on the point by indicating its constitutive activity.[2]

371   *Summa Theologica*, 1a–2ae. iii. 2, *ad* 2

730. The factors of happiness may be essential, antecedent, or consequent.

[1] *Consolatio Philosophiae*, iii. 2.   [2] *Ethics*, 1097^{a}15.

Sense-activity is not an essential component of happiness; yet for the incomplete happiness of the present life it is an antecedent requirement, because understanding demands previous sensation. Moreover, it is a consequence of that perfect happiness in heaven to which we look forward: Augustine speaks about the happiness of soul flowing out into the body after the resurrection, and the quickening and perfecting of bodily senses.

629   *Summa Theologica*, 1a–2ae. iii. 3

731. I say that the essential moment cannot consist in activity of will. For happiness is the laying hold on the last end, and this is not an act of will, which equally desires a good when absent and enjoys it when present. Desiring is not the same as laying hold of, but is a movement thereto; enjoyment follows because the good is possessed. The converse is not true, a good is not present because the will delights in it. By an activity other than that of will, therefore, is the object made present to the will. This may be illustrated by a mundane example: if the possession of wealth were an act of will, desiring would be equivalent to having; to begin with, however, wealth is absent, and afterwards when it has been acquired, then is it enjoyed. So also with spiritual good. At the beginning we desire to have it, afterwards it is present to us in an act of mind, and then the will delights in it and is at rest. Therefore the activity of happiness consists in an activity of mind, though the consequent delight is in the will; Augustine calls it joy in the truth.

686   *Summa Theologica*, 1a–2ae. iii. 4

732. Union of lover and beloved is twofold, real union, when the beloved is present, and union by affection.

This last is qualified by the knowledge preceding; love, alike of desire and of friendship, results from a perception of the oneness of the beloved with the lover. When we love a thing by desiring it we apprehend it as demanded by our well-being; when we love another in friendship we wish good to him just as we wish it to ourselves, we apprehend our friend as our other self. Augustine remarks that well did a man say to his friend, 'Thou half of my soul'.[1]

Love is like the efficient cause of real union, because it moves a person to seek and find the company of the beloved, who fits in as part of one's life. Love is the formal cause of union of affection, because love itself is this bond. In describing love as a *uniting*, Augustine refers to the union of affection without which there is no friendship, and in saying that *it seeks to unite* he refers to real union.

Summa Theologica, 1a–2ae. xxviii. 1

733. Knower and known are one—this is universally true.

588   *Summa Theologica*, 1a. lxxxvii. 1, *ad* 3

734. The first mover and author of the universe is Mind, and therefore its ultimate purpose is the good of mind: and this is truth.

122   I *Contra Gentes*, 1

735. Were it truly final the attraction of delight would be based on itself. But this is not the case. What matters is the object that gives delight. Consequently delight has its goodness and attraction from elsewhere, and is not the ultimate end but its attendant.

252, 723, 800   III *Contra Gentes*, 26

[1] *Confessions*, iv. 6. Horace, *Odes*, ii. 7.

736. Delight is the resting of appetite in what is good. If that be unqualified good, then will it be delightful and rightful beyond demur. But if it be good only in a relative sense, then the delight will be qualified and the right conditional, or perhaps only putative.[1]

136, 215, 371   *Summa Theologica*, 1a–2ae. xxxiv. 2

737. The best activity is of the best power about the best object. The best power is the mind, its best object the divine goodness. As to its best activity; contemplation is for its own sake, practical judgement serves some purpose; therefore happiness lies in the theoretical rather than in the practical reason.

1, 371   *Summa Theologica*, 1a–2ae. iii. 5

738. Not that perfect happiness is found in the meditations of speculative science, which cannot go beyond inferences from sense-objects.

263   *Summa Theologica*, 1a–2ae. iii. 6

739. Man's final happiness does not consist in moral activity, for it is ultimate and not subservient to a higher end, whereas moral activity is directed to something above itself. We may draw a comparison: a soldierly effort is subordinate to victory and peace; it is foolish to fight for the sake of fighting.

III *Contra Gentes*, 34

740. From which it follows that final happiness is not an activity of prudence.

740   III *Contra Gentes*, 35

---

[1] The simple Good is ultimate, honourable, and delightful: a particular good is right for the will only when it truly leads to the universal final good; otherwise it only has an appearance of rightness. A like subordination is also required for unambiguous delight.

741. At the sight of God the mind cannot but delight.

253   Opusc. XIII, *Compendium Theologiae*, 165

742. The divine substance is not outside the capacity of created mind so as to be wholly beyond its range, as sound is outside sight or as spiritual substance is past sensation; on the contrary, that divine substance is the first principle and evidence of all intellectual knowledge.

91   III *Contra Gentes*, 54

743. In such a vision the divine essence itself must be both medium and object.

255   III *Contra Gentes*, 51

744. There are two kinds of potentiality, the first is natural, and relates to a thing's actualization by a natural force, the second relates to a further actualization requiring a higher active principle. We observe this in natural things, for it is by natural potentiality that a man grows from a boy or that an animal develops from semen, but that a chest is carved from wood or sight is granted to blindness cannot come by mere natural potentiality. Now the same holds true of the human mind.

Our mind is in natural potentiality to those objects which can be presented by the factive intellect, the inborn principle whereby our minds are made actually understanding. Such rational knowledge cannot comprehend our last end, for it is limited to those things whose acquaintance we make through the senses. However expert our knowledge about these material objects, there would always remain a desire to know more. There are many objects which are scarcely hinted at by sense-knowledge; we may be aware of their existence but not of their nature, because spiritual realities are in a different class from bodily realities and surpass them exceedingly. Even among sensible objects, there are

B 628   T

many whose inner constitution we cannot explain with
any certainty, about others we have an inkling, but
about some we are blankly ignorant. Hence our rest-
lessness and desire for more perfect knowledge. Yet it is
impossible for a natural desire to be pointless. Our last
end can be achieved only if the natural desire of the
mind to know is actualized and stilled by an active
principle nobler than anything that is part of us or of
our sort of world. This desire is such that, when an
effect is perceived, we crave to know its cause. Whatever
the situation may be, whenever we know something of
the circumstances, we shall not rest until we reach the
very heart of the matter.

Our natural desire, therefore, will not be quieted until
we know the first cause, not from reflections, but by its
very essence. The first cause is God. Therefore the
ultimate end of rational creatures is the vision of the
essence of God.

254, 650, 924   Opusc. XIII, *Compendium Theologiae*, 104

IV. INTEGRITY OF HAPPINESS

745. The soul is filled with all good things by seeing
God, and is plunged into the fount of goodness. *I shall
be satisfied when the glory shall appear.*[1] And again, *all
good things came to me together with her*,[2] that is with the
contemplation of wisdom.

1, 261   *Summa Theologica*, 1a–2ae. v. 4

746. A desire that banishes boredom, not the desired
object.

139, 821, 822   *Summa Theologica*, 1a. lviii. 1, *ad* 2

747. These three run together: vision, the perfect
knowledge of an intelligible end; comprehension, the

[1] Ps. xvi. 15 (Vulgate).   [2] Wisd. vii. 11.

presence of that end; delight or enjoyment, the ease of lover with beloved.

Summa Theologica, 1a–2ae. iv. 3

748. Vision reigns over delight.

731 *Summa Theologica*, 1a–2ae. iv. 2.

749. Righteousness of heart is required antecedently and concomitantly. None can reach happiness without goodwill, and the loves of one who sees God inevitably fall in with the divine plan.

Summa Theologica, 1a–2ae. iv. 4

750. A requirement may enter at four stages: as a preamble or preparation, thus discipline for learning; as an essential constituent, thus soul for bodily life; as an outside help, thus friends for a venture; and as a concomitant, thus delight for happiness.

Summa Theologica, 1a–2ae. iv. 1

751. Delight perfects happiness as beauty does youth.

827 Commentary, *in Matthaeum*, v, *lect.* 2

752. No one can live without delight, and that is why a man deprived of spiritual joy goes over to carnal pleasures.

Summa Theologica, 2a–2ae. xxxv. 4, *ad* 2

753. Sense-pleasure attacks the practical judgement of prudence rather than the speculative judgement of understanding.

891, 892 *Summa Theologica*, 1a–2ae. iv. 1, *ad* 3

754. Pleasure follows congenial activity, and therefore the more vehement the pleasure the more natural the activity.

997 *Summa Theologica*, 2a–2ae. cxli. 4

755. The voluptuous life places its end in carnal pleasure which is common to us and brutes; the taste is
slavish, the life all very well for a beast.[1]

Summa Theologica, 2a–2ae. clxxix. 2, *ad* 1

756. In the state of integrity there would have been
no lust unmoderated by reason. Not, as some say, that
the pleasures of sense would have been less; indeed they
would have been so much the greater to the extent that
human nature was finer then, and the body more
sensitive. The power of disorderly desire would not
have swamped this reason-tempered delight. The
measure of reason implies, not weaker pleasure, but less
embarrassed pleasure. A gourmet does not have less
pleasure in his food than a gourmand. The words of
Augustine are here to the point; he says that in the
state of innocence the strength of pleasure would not
have been suppressed, but only the heat of lust and the
anxiety of mind. There would have been fruitfulness
without lechery. Continence would not then have been
laudable in the same way as now—that is for the wild
lust it banishes, not the sterility it incidentally imposes.

990   *Summa Theologica*, 1a. xcviii. 2, *ad* 3

757. Men alone take pleasure in the very beauty itself
of sensible things; their faces uplifted, not downcast.

629   *Summa Theologica*, 1a. xci. 3, *ad* 3

758. No man truly has joy unless he lives in love.

1076   Opusc. xxxv, *de Duobus Praeceptis*[2]

759. A moral virtue enjoins due enjoyment—and
grief.

Commentary, *II Ethics, lect.* 3

[1] *Ethics*, 1095[b]20.
[2] Lenten sermons, reported by Peter d'Andria.

760. The pleasure proper to an activity adds to its force, an extraneous pleasure obstructs it. Bodily pleasure may hinder the use of reason on three counts. First, by distraction; things that give us pleasure hold our attention, and weaken or even entirely take away our interest in other things. Secondly, by antagonism; some strong pleasures are against the order of reason and can destroy the judgement of prudence, as Aristotle notes;[1] though purely theoretical judgements may remain unimpaired, for instance that the angles of a triangle together equal two right angles: such judgements are hindered on the first count. Thirdly, by bondage; the bodily changes resulting from pleasure, greater than the effects of other passions, may bind the use of reason, as appears in alcoholics.

892 *Summa Theologica*, 1a–2ae. xxxiii. 3

761. In speaking of perfect happiness, some have said that no bodily conditions are present, indeed they would have the soul entirely disembodied. Augustine introduces Porphyry's words, that for the soul to be blessed everything bodily must be eschewed.[2] But this is unseemly: it is natural for the soul to be united to the body, and one perfection should not exclude another. Therefore we conclude that integral happiness requires a perfect disposition of body, both antecedently and consequently. Antecedently, because, as Augustine declares, if the flesh, corruptible and a weight upon the soul when the mind is turned away from high heaven, is difficult to manage, nevertheless, he concludes, that very flesh, erstwhile a burden, will then be a glory.[3] Consequently, because from the happiness of the soul there will be an overflow into the body, quickening it

[1] *Ethics*, 1140^{b}15.   [2] *de Civitate Dei*, xii. 26.
[3] *De Genesi ad litteram*, xii. 25.

to perfection; as Augustine also says, the soul is made so powerful of its nature that from its fullness of happiness the vigour of deathlessness pours into the lower nature.

827 *Summa Theologica*, 1a–2ae. iv. 6

762. The body is required for the advantage, not the essence, of happiness; as bodily beauty or swiftness of mind for human perfection.

Summa Theologica, 1a–2ae. iv. 5

763. Complete contentment there cannot be unless natural desire is wholly fulfilled. Everything craves what belongs to its nature, and therefore desires its parts to be reunited. Since the human soul is united by nature to the body there is within it a natural appetite for that union. The will could find no perfect rest until the soul and body are joined again. This is the resurrection of man from the dead.

532 Opusc. xiii, *Compendium Theologiae*, 151

764. The soul does not take an airy or heavenly body, or a body of another organic constitution, but a human body composed of flesh and bones and the same members enjoyed at present.

Opusc. xiii, *Compendium Theologiae*, 153

765. Corpulence will be cured, but not corporeity.

Opusc. xvi, Exposition, *de Trinitate*, iv. 3, *ad* 2

766. Hell is ruled by time, not by true eternity.

245 *Summa Theologica*, 1a. x. 3, *ad* 2

767. In the perfect happiness of heaven nothing more will remain to be desired; in the full enjoyment of God man will obtain whatever he has desired in other things. *Who fills thy desire with good things.*[1] The desire is

---

[1] Ps. cii. 5 (Vulgate).

stilled; the desire not only for God, but also what lies at the heart of all other desires. Therefore the joy of the blessed is perfectly complete, and more than complete, indeed over-full, for there they find more than is enough for desire. *It has not entered into the heart of man what God hath prepared for those that love him.*[1] *Good measure, and flowing over.*[2] Nevertheless, because no creature is capable of joy such as God's, the text says, not that man grasps this joy, but that he enters into it: *Enter thou into the joy of the Lord.*[3]

371   *Summa Theologica*, 2a–2ae. xxviii. 3

[1] 1 Cor. ii. 9.   [2] Luke vi. 38.   [3] Matt. xxv. 21.

XIII

Morality[1]

768. Man has a natural urge towards complete goodness.

Disputations, XXII de Veritate, 7

[1] The subject is not introduced abruptly. Behind the brief
treatise devoted to it in the *Summa Theologica* stretch the questions
on the nature of man and his environment; it is preceded by the
study of happiness and the detailed analysis of the structure of
human activity, and followed by an examination of the emotions
and habits. The arrangement is in keeping with the doctrine that
moral science is not autonomous; there is no special faculty of
right and wrong, duty is not for duty's sake, the right is a special
aspect of the good, and the good is a quality of being. The moral
imperative is not categoric, but conditional; act well if you would
reach happiness. Yet without taking account of Christian ideals of
selfless devotion, the rational theory surpasses utilitarianism, for
it is dominated by the idea of God outside the scheme of the world
and certainly not for our use, and is influenced by a dialectic of
desire for things in themselves, not merely for reactions to them.

The second major feature in the moral theory is the insistence
on the measure of mind, from the eternal ideas through the
demonstrations of reason down to the particular judgements of
conscience. The existence of objective moral-kinds of action is
a connected thesis. Motives and individual circumstances modify
the morality of what we do. There is a large field that is morally
neutral until we enter it, but some types of action are right in
themselves, and others wrong independently of what we read into
the situation. No end, however sublime, can justify means that
are thoroughly inhuman. In this sense moral standards are as firm
and impersonal as the principles of science; on that account they
are no substitute for the flair for singular contingencies. Abstract
theory is supplemented by a sense of the concrete situation
expressed in the judgement of conscience, against which it is never
lawful to act. A fundamental moral science is bound to be about
men as they should be, not as they are; yet, touched alike by
sympathy for sinners and by a sense of history, St. Thomas never
gives the effect of writing a satire instead of a morality.

769. Happiness is secured through virtue; it is a good attained by man's own will.

739, 749   III *Contra Gentes*, 28

I. NATURAL FOUNDATIONS

770. Finished moral science demands a knowledge of psychology.

517   Commentary, *I de Anima*, lect. 1

771. Right and wrong in human acts should be discussed in the same temper as good and bad in things.

480, 667   *Summa Theologica*, 1a–2ae. xviii. 1

772. Though convertible with being, good carries a special accent in things with the power of choice.

483   Commentary, *II Sentences*, xxvii. i. 2, *ad* 2

773. Good and evil should be set in the context of what is proper to man as man. This is his rational life. Therefore a good or bad human act is tested by its agreement or otherwise with reason instructed by the divine law, whose principles may be inborn, acquired, or infused.

1044   Disputations, II *de Malo*, 4

774. In point of fact most men seem to live according to sense rather than reason.

Summa Theologica, 1a. xlix. 3, *ad* 5

775. *The Lord is a great God, and a great King above all gods.* He will not reject his people. *In his hands are the ends of the earth; and the heights of the mountain are his. The sea is his, and he made it; and his hands formed the dry land.*[1] The first being is one, possessing the full perfection of all being, and we call him God. He

[1] Ps. xciv. 3–5 (Vulgate).

bestows reality on all existents from the abundance of his perfection. Therefore he is not merely the first being, but also the first principle of all beings. He gives of his own free-will, not by compulsion of nature. Therefore is he the lord of everything, because dominion is over things subject to will. His mastery is complete, for he needs neither outside assistance nor material to work on, since he is the maker of the whole of reality. Now everything produced by an efficient cause is directed to some end, for the good as end is the proper object of will.

A thing reaches its end by activity, which activity is directed by him who endows the thing with its active principles. God is the ruler of all, and he himself is ruled by none; nothing is exempt, for there is nothing that does not owe its being to him. As he is perfect in being and causing, so is he perfect in ruling. The effects of his rule appear differently in different things according to their differences of nature. For some are produced having minds that reflect his likeness and enjoy his image; these are not just directed, but also direct themselves in their own proper activities to their appointed end. If in so doing they obey the divine ruling they are admitted; if not then they are excluded.

361, 388, 1043, 1047   III *Contra Gentes*, 1

776. The human will is constrained by three orders: its own system of reason; the external law of human government, both spiritual and temporal, political and domestic; the comprehensive scheme of divine rule.

1093   *Summa Theologica*, 1a–2ae. lxxxvii. 1

777. Some[1] have maintained that a pure spirit, though by natural desire seeking to have divine good rather

---

[1] The reference is to William of Auvergne.

than its own good, and by friendship wishing a greater good to God than to itself—for of course it wills God to be himself and itself to have its own proper nature—nevertheless by unqualified natural affection loves itself more than God, because it naturally loves itself before loving God and loves itself more intensely.

How baseless this opinion is plainly appears when we consider what is the object of natural movement in physical things. Unconscious drives provide evidence of the inner workings of volition in the case of intellectual natures. Anything whose nature as such consists in being part of another is bent first and above all on that to which it belongs, rather than on itself. Instinctive manifestations are a pointer to this natural inclination; we observe that a member naturally exposes itself for the safety of the whole, as when without hesitation up goes the arm to ward off a blow.

Now, since reason imitates nature, a similar tendency is displayed in the political virtues, as when the good citizen risks death for the safety of the commonwealth: this is a natural motion if we suppose that man is born to belong to a State.[1] God is the universal good, embracing pure spirits and men and all creatures. Every creature is entirely of God. Consequently angels and men by nature love God before themselves and with greater love. If it were otherwise natural love would be perverse; and it would be destroyed, not heightened, by charity.

942, 1117   *Summa Theologica*, 1a. lx. 5

778. Man is not the founder of nature; by art and virtue he makes use of natural things for his own benefit.

Summa Theologica, 1a. xxii. 2, *ad* 3

[1] A view not shared by most contemporaries of St. Thomas: they saw political organization as a conventional institution.

779. It is foolish to say that somebody deserves what he cannot avoid.

Opusc. xxv, *Epistola ad Bernardum Abbatem Casinensem*

780. Evil is a wider term than sin, as good is wider than right. Any privation of good is termed evil; if we would be precise, however, sin consists in a purposed activity that falls short of its end.

In voluntary activity the proximate measure is the human reason, the supreme measure the eternal law. When a human act goes to its end in harmony with the order of reason and eternal law then the act is right; when it turns away from that rightness it is termed sin.

482   *Summa Theologica*, 1a–2ae. xxi. 1

781. Good or evil in human acts alone merits praise or blame. Hence fault, sin, and guilt there amount to the same.

Summa Theologica, 1a–2ae. xxi. 2

782. Sins are as preposterous in morals as monsters in nature.

387   Commentary, *III de Anima*, lect. 16

783. To disparage the dictate of reason is equivalent to contemning the command of God.

804   *Summa Theologica*, 1a–2ae. xix. 5, *ad* 2

784. Aristotle has noted how in the arts the end is unconfined, but that bounds are set on means to ends. A doctor does not impose any limit to health, but tries to make it as complete as possible; yet he rations his physic, for he does not give as much medicine as he can, but just as much as is proportionate to the case; otherwise were the dose either excessive or deficient it would be immoderate. The love of God is the end of all human activity and desire, and here there are no limits.

By what more ultimate test are we to say it is too much
or too little? The mode is the measure itself; no excess
is possible; and therefore the more we love God the
better.

709, 877   *Summa Theologica*, 2a–2ae. xxvii. 6

785. Our will can reach higher than can our intelligence when we are confronted by things that are
above us. Whereas our notions about moral matters,
which are below man, are enlightened by a cognitive
habit—for prudence informs the other moral virtues—
when it comes to the divine virtues about God, a will-
virtue, namely charity, informs the mind-virtue, namely
faith.

913   Disputations, *de Caritate*, 3, *ad* 13

786. Disquisitions on general morality are not entirely
trustworthy, and the ground becomes more uncertain
when one wishes to descend to individual cases in detail.
The factors are infinitely variable, and cannot be settled
either by art or precedent. Judgement should be left to
the people concerned. Each must set himself to act
according to the immediate situation and the circumstances involved. The decision may be unerring in
the concrete, despite the uneasy debate in the abstract.
Nevertheless, the moralist can provide some help and
direction in such cases.

806, 814, 965, 1069   Commentary, *II Ethics, lect.* 2

II. MORAL KINDS

787. A fourfold good can be considered in any human
act: first, its fundamental goodness considered as an
activity; second, its specific moral goodness which is
taken from its appropriate object; third, its accidental
goodness according to its circumstances; fourth, its

relationship to the cause of goodness which is judged by its end.[1]

Summa Theologica, 1a–2ae. xviii. 4

788. An action is not good, simply speaking, unless it is sound by all these tests. As Dionysius says, the good is from an integral cause, while evil results from any single defect whatsoever.[2]

Summa Theologica, 1a–2ae. xviii. 4, *ad* 3

789. As the primary goodness of things is constituted by their forms, which make them things of a certain kind, so the primary goodness of a moral act derives from a reasonable object, which makes it a good kind of action; for instance, to use what is your own. And as in natural things the primary evil consists in lacking the appropriate specific form, for instance when instead of a man something else is generated, so the primary evil in moral activity comes from the object, for instance, to take what does not belong to you.

480   *Summa Theologica*, 1a–2ae. xviii. 2

790. Proximate end and object are here synonymous: the ulterior motive is reckoned as a circumstance.

Disputations, 11 *de Malo*, 7, *ad* 8

791. A right volition and a wrong volition are specifically different activities in morals.

Summa Theologica, 1a–2ae. xix. 1

792. Conjugal intercourse and adultery are specifically different acts, with specifically different effects, in their setting within the plan of reasonable living.

Summa Theologica, 1a–2ae. xviii. 5, *ad* 3

---

[1] Thus a smile of welcome is physically good; morally good as an expression of friendship; suitable as a greeting to a returning friend; ultimately good when prompted by charity.

[2] *de Divinis Nominibus*, iv. 22.

793. Its moral nature is stamped on a human act by its object taken with reference to the principles of moral activity, that is according to the pattern of life as it should be lived according to the reason. If the object as such implies what is in accord with the reasonable order of conduct, then it will be a good kind of action; for instance, to assist somebody in need. If, on the other hand, it implies what is repugnant to reason, then it will be a bad kind of action; for instance, to appropriate to oneself what belongs to another. But it may happen that the object does not immediately involve the reasonable plan of life one way or the other, and then it is an action morally indifferent of its kind; for instance, to go for a walk or to pick up a straw.

1056   *Summa Theologica*, 1a–2ae. xviii. 8

III. MORAL CIRCUMSTANCES

794. To ensure the full perfection of a natural thing more is required than its essential components, namely the complement of supervening accidents, such as a proper figure and a healthy colour in man. If these are wanting something bad is the result. Human activity is similar: its perfection is not entirely guaranteed by what kind of action it is; additional accidents are also required, namely its due circumstances.

1023   *Summa Theologica*, 1a–2ae. xviii. 3

795. An action may be morally neutral when considered in itself; nevertheless, it may happen to be right or wrong when placed in its individual context. This is because a moral act derives its rightness or wrongness, not only from the specific stamp of its object, but also from its circumstances, which are like its accidents. A person's individual condition calls for qualities that are not required by human nature as such. Similarly an individual action has some circumstance, at least of motive, by which it is drawn into the condition of right or wrong.

It is the office of the reason to set things in order, and so a deliberate act which serves no good purpose is by that very fact unreasonable and flecked by fault. On the other hand, if it is subordinate to a good end, it is then in harmony with the order of reason, and has the character of good. A human act either fits in or not with some good purpose. Therefore every deliberate human act in the individual case is either right or wrong.

575   *Summa Theologica*, 1a–2ae. xviii. 9

796. What is natural to things having an immutable nature always follows the same pattern without exception. But the nature of man is variable, and what is normally natural is not to be expected on every occasion. Natural justice demands that a deposit should be restored. If human nature followed a rigid plan this would have to be inflexibly observed. But a case may crop up when a deposit must be withheld from the owner, for instance when a man in a rage, or a public enemy, demands the return of his weapons.

833, 1067   *Summa Theologica*, 2a–2ae. lvii. 2, *ad* 1

797. Means to ends are not narrowly limited in human affairs. They are multifarious according to the variety of persons and situations. Fixed ends are a matter of natural instincts. The appreciation of means, however, is not instinctive, though one man's temperament may be more practical than another's. Consequently the prudence here called for is not an hereditary trait.

765   *Summa Theologica*, 2a–2ae. xlvii. 15

IV. INTENTION

798. Morality depends on intention.[1]

III *Contra Gentes*, 9

799. A particular willing can be condemned if it springs from an evil intention. When a man wills to give alms in order to show off, he wills to do what is good in itself, but to him the good comes in the guise of bad, and therefore it is bad as willed by him. If, however, this motive occurs to him subsequently, then his will in the first place was good and the motive does not spoil that, but the acts that follow after.

Summa Theologica, 1a–2ae. xix. 7, *ad* 2

800. The rightness or wrongness of will is determined by the end. That is reputed the end in which the will rests. The resting of the will, indeed of any appetite, is pleasure. Therefore a man is judged to be good or evil by what his will takes pleasure in. The pleasures of the sensitive appetite, however, are not good moral tests one way or the other: food, for instance, is appetizing alike to good men and bad; the virtuous man takes pleasure in it according to a reasonable way of life, about which a wicked man simply does not bother.

721   *Summa Theologica*, 1a–2ae. xxxiv. 4

V. THE MEASURE OF MIND

801. The object of will is proposed to it by the reason; for a good as understood, not as sensed or imagined, is

[1] There is some difference of opinion among the Thomist moralists on the relative importance of the natural moral purpose (*finis operis*) and the personal intention (*finis operantis*) in determining the morality of an act. It is useful to distinguish between the dominating or overriding motive of a man's life and an incidental motive which may be reckoned among the moral circumstances.

the object proportionate to will. Therefore the goodness of willing depends on the reason and on its object in the same way.

682, 697, 1044   *Summa Theologica*, 1a–2ae. xix. 3

802. The dictate of will should not be accounted the first rule of conduct, for will is directed by reason and mind, in God as well as in us. To say that justice depends on mere will is to say that the divine will does not act according to the order of wisdom, and is blasphemous.

1038   *Disputations*, xxiii *de Veritate*, 6

803. Everything is measured by comparison with a rule. If a thing escapes this rule then it is unmeasured. The measure for human willing is double: one close and of the same nature, namely the human reason itself; the other, first and transcendent, namely the eternal law which is like the reason of God.

Summa Theologica, 1a–2ae. lxxi. 6

804. The proximate rule is the human reason, the supreme measure is the eternal law.

Summa Theologica, 1a–2ae. xxi. 1

805. It is not of the essence of liberty that what is free should be its own first cause, any more than that a thing's cause has to be its first cause.

692   *Summa Theologica*, 1a. lxxxiii. 1, *ad* 3

806. As the speculative reason discusses the theory of things, so the operative reason debates the problems of practice; and as the principles of thought are inborn in the mind, so also are the principles of conduct. The first principles of thought are not elicited by a special faculty, but by a special habit of mind, called the understanding of principles. Similarly, the first principles of

practice, naturally inborn in us, are not evoked by a
special faculty or moral sense, but by a special natural
habit of mind, called synderesis.

5, 1039, 1047   *Summa Theologica*, 1a. lxxix. 12

807. Strictly speaking, conscience is not a faculty, but
an activity, namely, the actual application of moral
science to conduct.

977   *Summa Theologica*, 1a. lxxix. 13

808. Every judgement of conscience, be it right or
wrong, be it about things evil in themselves or morally
indifferent, is obligatory, in such wise that he who acts
against his conscience always sins.

III *Quodlibet*, 27

809. A man does not make up a law for himself, but by
his very act of recognizing a law enacted for him he
binds himself to its observance.

1041   Disputations, XVII *de Veritate*, 3, *ad* 1

810. What is dictated by a mistaken conscience is not
consonant with the law of God, nevertheless it is con-
strued as the law of God, and therefore, simply speaking,
if a man goes against it he contravenes the law of God.

1042   Disputations, XVII *de Veritate*, 4, *ad* 1

811. Though a prelate[1] be superior to a subject, nevertheless God, in whose figure conscience binds, is higher
still.

1096   Disputations, XVII *de Veritate*, 5, *ad* 3

812. Since conscience is the dictate of reason, the
application of theory to practice, the inquiry, *whether
a will that disobeys an erroneous conscience is right*, is the

---

[1] The word is used of a civil ruler, as well as of a church
dignitary.

same as, *whether a man is obliged to follow a mistaken conscience.*

Now because the object of a volition is that which is proposed by the reason, if the will chooses to do what the reason considers to be wrong, then the will goes out to it in the guise of evil. Therefore it must be said flatly that the will which disobeys the reason, whether true or mistaken, is always in the wrong.

Summa Theologica, 1a–2ae. xix. 5

813. The inquiry, *whether the will that obeys a mistaken conscience is right,* is equivalent to, *whether a mistaken conscience is any excuse.*

If the reason or conscience is mistaken through voluntary error, either directly wished or tolerated by negligence, about what one is bound to know, then such an error does not absolve the will from blame. But it is an excuse if the error causing the non-voluntary wrong follows from ignorance of some circumstance without any negligence. For example, if a mistaken reason bids a man sleep with another man's wife, to do this will be evil if based on ignorance of a divine law he ought to know; but if the misjudgement is occasioned by thinking that the woman is really his own wife, and she wants him and he wants her, then his will is free from fault.

Summa Theologica, 1a–2ae. xix. 6

XIV

Feeling and Training[1]

814. Human qualities may be of two kinds, innate and induced. Innate qualities affect either the intellectual part of the soul or the living body and its powers. A man naturally desires his last end, namely happiness, by a quality modifying the mind. This appetite is so natural as not to be subject to freewill. Human character is also settled by qualities of the body and its powers, that is by temperamental dispositions subject to bodily influences as such not reacting to the bodiless life of the spirit. A man's physique and temperament will colour what he likes, and incline him to choose this or reject that. These inclinations can be controlled by the reason and they are not prejudicial to freewill. Induced qualities are passions and habits, in virtue of which a man has a bias towards one thing rather than towards another. And yet even these come under the reason to the extent that it lies in our power to cause them, or dispose ourselves to them, or reject them.

575, 838   *Summa Theologica*, 1a. lxxxiii. 1, *ad* 5

[1] St. Thomas returns to the psychology of human activity and, in the first place, to the motions of the human animal. The study of the passions or emotions, which incidentally offers the occasion for observations on the various states of affection in general, follows the Aristotelean distinction of the concupiscible and irascible appetites already referred to. The habits are then studied in the spirit of functional psychology, as a preliminary to treating of the virtues. Habits are qualities preparing abilities which are not wholly instinctive to act in one direction or another, either for the benefit or otherwise of the subject.

I. PASSIONS

815. Augustine says that the motions of the soul, called passive conditions by the Greeks, are called disturbances by some of our people, thus Cicero; affections or affects by others; and passions by some, more literally following the Greek.[1] They pertain to the affective part of the soul, not to the cognitive; to love, rather than to knowledge.

677   *Summa Theologica*, 1a–2ae. xxii. 2, *sed contra*

816. An organic change is the material part of the definition of emotion; thus anger includes a rush of blood about the heart.

Summa Theologica, 1a–2ae. xxii. 2, *ad* 3

817. A distinction should be drawn between the material elements, namely the physiological change, and the formal element, namely the psychological appetition.

617   *Summa Theologica*, 1a. xx. 1, *ad* 2

818. Joy and expansion of heart; sorrow and contraction.

Summa Theologica, 3. lxxxiv. 9, *ad* 2

819. The object of the concupiscible faculty is straightforward sensible good or evil, namely what is pleasurable or painful. But conflict and stress arise from time to time about obtaining the one or avoiding the other; the situation is not simple, and good and evil as invested with the qualities of hardness or difficulty are then the objects of the irascible appetite. Some emotions, such as love and hate, desire and aversion, pleasure and sorrow, answer to the former appetite, while others,

[1] *de Civitate Dei*, ix. 4.

such as boldness and fear, hope and despair, and anger
answer to the latter.

Summa Theologica, 1a–2ae. xxiii. 1

820. Some passions imply imperfection, such as desire
which is of an absent good, and sadness which is of
a present evil; so also anger supposes grief. But some,
such as love and joy, imply no imperfection.

275   Summa Theologica, 1a. xx. 1, ad 2

821. Pleasure lies in being, not becoming.

136, 746   Summa Theologica, 1a–2ae. xxxi. 1

822. Why we grow weary of what we hitherto enjoyed
is because the object causes some kind of change in us
by weakening or impairing our power. Fatigue is
incidental to the enjoyment of sensible activities; it
comes from strain on their organs. On the same account
we tire after prolonged and concentrated thought, because the mind cannot work without employing instruments of sense.

624   III Contra Gentes, 62

823. In the sequence of execution, that is prior which
comes first in the process. In seeking an end the first
phase is the aptness or proportion of appetite to an
end, which is love; then the motions towards it of
desire or lust; then the quiet after obtaining it, which is
pleasure or joy. But in the sequence of intention the
order is reversed, for intended pleasure causes desire
and love. Pleasure is the enjoyment of a good, and is, in
its way, final.

721   Summa Theologica, 1a–2ae. xxv. 2

824. The sensitive appetite is at the stage between

natural appetite and the higher rational appetite which is termed will.

677   Disputations, xxv *de Veritate*, 1

825. Considered in themselves as motions of the sensitive and non-rational appetite, passions are neither right nor wrong, for morality depends on the reason. They are covered by morality in so far as they are subject to the sway of reason and will.

980, 988   *Summa Theologica*, 1a–2ae. xxiv. 1

826. On the question of the moral evil of passions, the Stoics differed from the Peripatetics, for they professed that the passions were bad, while the latter maintained that moderated passions were good. The difference, though important in words, is in reality of little or no moment when we reflect on what both parties meant. In consequence of not discerning between sense and mind, the Stoics drew no distinction between the sensitive and intellective appetites; not discriminating between the passions of the soul and the motions of the will, they treated will as equivalent to any reasonable movement and passion as movement breaking the bounds of reason—Cicero called passions diseases of the soul. The Peripatetics on the other hand gave the name of passion to all movements of the sensitive appetite, and they esteemed them as good when controlled by reason and will, and deprecated them as evil when not so controlled. Hence, it is clear that Cicero misses the point in criticizing their theory of the mean in the passions when he stresses that every evil, even though moderate, should be shunned.

Summa Theologica, 1a–2ae. xxiv. 2

827. Hence the Stoics held that emotion diminishes an action's goodness. This is true enough if passion means the disorderly surges of the sensitive appetite. But if it simply means the motion of sensitive appetite, then it is better not merely to will good, but also to feel good about it. It is part of man's moral perfection to be moved thereto by his sensitive part as well as by his will. *My heart and my flesh have rejoiced in the living God.*[1]

761   *Summa Theologica*, 1a–2ae. xxv. 3

828. The worth of virtue shines out when a man readily bears many and grievous blows of misfortune: not that he is insensitive to pain and sadness, as the Stoics urged, but that he remains manly and great-hearted, and upright in his reason.

980   Commentary, *I Ethics, lect.* 16

II. HABITS

829. Habit is a quality.

814   *Summa Theologica*, 1a–2ae. xlix. 1

830. The inner coherence and balance of a subject falls under the first species of quality, which is habit and disposition.

Summa Theologica, 1a–2ae. xlix. 2

831. By a faculty we are able to do something, but by a habit we are expert at acting well or ill according to the faculty, that is the difference between ability and habit.

575   iv *Contra Gentes*, 77

832. A habit is a settled disposition.

Summa Theologica, 1a–2ae. xlix. 2, *ad* 3

833. A habit is required when what is in potentiality can be disposed in several manners or to several objects.

[1] Ps. lxxxiii. 3 (Vulgate).

When many factors are present a form or activity may be disposed well or ill. Health and beauty are called habits also, for they imply a happy adjustment of many factors which can be arranged in diverse manners.

Summa Theologica, 1a–2ae. xlix. 4

834. A habit is not a disposition of the object towards the power, but of the power towards the object.

Summa Theologica, 1a–2ae. l. 4, *ad* 1

835. Active habits are in the soul according to its diverse faculties.

575   *Summa Theologica*, 1a–2ae. l. 2

836. The powers of the sensitive part are bent in one direction in so far as they work from natural instinct: in purely natural drives there are no habits. But in so far as they come under the command of reason, they can be trained to various objects, and so can be the subjects of habits, good or bad as the case may be.

617   *Summa Theologica*, 1a–2ae. l. 3

837. Animals can be trained by the reason to perform in this way or that; to this extent we can credit them with habits.

Summa Theologica, 1a–2ae. l. 3, *ad* 2

838. A quality of a thing may be natural either with respect to its specific nature, thus the ability to laugh is natural to man, or with respect to its individual nature, thus to be prone to sickness or inclined to health according to the respective complexions of Socrates and Plato. Then again, under both respects, a quality may be natural either because it is entirely from nature or because it is partly from nature and partly from an extrinsic principle; a man healed of himself is an

example of the former, a man healed by medicine is an example of the latter.

There are no habits in man entirely from nature. But there are natural habits owing their existence partly to some external principle. In the powers of cognition there are inchoate habits, with regard both to the specific and to the individual nature. Thus the understanding of first principles is termed a natural habit, as though coming from the specific nature of the intellectual soul; having once grasped what is a whole and what is a part, a man immediately perceives that the whole is greater than the part. Yet what is a whole and what a part, this he cannot know except through ideas drawn from images. Hence, the knowledge of principles comes through the senses, and so, with respect to nature in the individual one man may be apter by his organic disposition to understand well. In the powers of appetition, however, with respect to the specific nature of the soul there are no innate inchoate habits; these exist only as regards certain principles of general law, called the seeds of virtues. The clue here is that the inclinations to proper objects that look like inchoate habits are really from the very nature of the faculty concerned. With respect to individual natures, however, on the part of the body there are some inchoate appetitive habits. For some people from their bodily temperament are more disposed than others to chastity or meekness.

539, 546, 814   *Summa Theologica*, 1a–2ae. li. 1

XV

Virtues[1]

839. Love is the form, mover, and root of the virtues.

673   *Disputations, de Caritate*, 3

840. When pressed to its utmost an ability deserves the title and meaning of virtue.

Opusc. 1, *de Operationibus Occultis Naturae*

841. A good object is more to the point than a difficult object.

Summa Theologica, 2a–2ae. cxli. 8, *ad* 2

842. By and large every virtue is magnificent.

Summa Theologica, 2a–2ae. cxxxiv. 2

[1] The detailed moral science of the *Summa Theologica* is developed according to the positive course of the virtues. It does not share the preoccupations of systematic casuistry nor follow the conventional divisions according to the negative precepts; the vices are not cardinal, but treated in appendixes to the various sections. Yet sins are closely observed and differentiated, more however by the specific interest than the degree of depravity. The virtues are not seen as mechanisms of conformity to a code, but as perfections whose value begins even before they are given an ethical reference. The healthy and beautiful balance of a living and supple subject within its own nature, and the consequent adjustment to its end, implies the disposition of acting well, the tonic effect of intense and repeated activity. Hence virtue is the complement of ability. Purely intellectual skill is a virtue, but the term in its fullest sense applies only to those qualities of character that go to make up the good man simply so called. These are the moral virtues, of which more than twenty are enumerated and examined, hinging on the four main virtues of prudence, justice, courage, and temperance.

I. NOTION OF VIRTUE

843. Virtue is a good habit.

829 *Summa Theologica*, 1a–2ae. lv. 3

844. This is a specific definition according to genus and difference, for habit is the proximate genus, and good the difference.

Summa Theologica, 1a–2ae. lv.

845. A virtue is in a faculty.

Summa Theologica, 1a–2ae. lvi. 1

846. It designates the complement of ability and demonstrates consummate mastery.

Disputations, de Virtutibus in Communi, 1

847. Complete characters do not take scandal.

Commentary, in Matthaeum, xviii, *lect.* 1

848. Virtue has three effects; it removes evil, works for good, and disposes to the best.

Commentary, in Matthaeum, v, *lect.* 2

849. It chooses and chooses again. Every virtuous act has these four traits: controlled knowledge, right intention, unwavering purpose, and sense of situation.

Disputations, de Virtutibus Cardinalibus, 1

850. Among objects in themselves lovable, some are loved solely for themselves and never for anything else —thus happiness which is the last end—while others are loved both for their own sake, in that they possess some intrinsic worth, and also because they serve the purpose of conveying us to a more perfect good—thus are the virtues lovable.

375 *Summa Theologica,* 2a–2ae. cxlv. 1, *ad* 1

851. Virtuous habits are needed on three scores. First, for regularity; activity is scarcely more than spasmodic unless stabilized by habitual inclination. Second, for promptness; decisions require a great deal of deliberation unless the faculties are already trained, as a man discovers if he has to make a scientific judgement when he is not scientifically equipped, or if he wishes to act virtuously but lacks the habit of virtue. Third, for pleasurable performance; since habit makes perfect activity congenial.

680   Disputations, *de Virtutibus in Communi*, 1

II. INTELLECTUAL VIRTUE

852. A virtue is a habit ensuring good performance. Now a habit sets a man to good activity in two manners or modes: first by providing the aptness, second the right use. By the first mode, a man has the ability of speaking correctly by his habit of grammatical knowledge, but this does not guarantee that he will speak aright, for a grammarian can be uncouth and commit solecisms in his speech; so also with the other sciences and arts. By the second mode, a habit not merely provides the faculty of acting well, but also ensures the right use of this power; thus justice makes the will prompt to deal fairly, and also sees to it that this intention is carried through into execution.

Just as we can speak without hedging only of a complete thing as real and good, so by this latter type of habit alone is a man said to be good without qualification; because virtue is that which makes its possessor good and likewise renders his deeds good; consequently these latter habits alone can be called good without reserve. The former are not virtues simply so called, for they do not ensure that they will be used aright; because he is a good scientist or a good artist a man is not esteemed a good man without reserve; he is good in a relative sense, namely, a good grammarian or a good blacksmith as the case may be.

The mind can be the subject of virtue in this relative sense, as regards both the theoretical and the practical reasons, without any question of goodwill entering in. Thus science, wisdom, and understanding, as well as art, are termed intellectual virtues by Aristotle.[1]

548, 971   *Summa Theologica*, 1a–2ae. lvi. 3

853. Prudence excepted, intellectual virtue can exist without moral virtue.

27   *Summa Theologica*, 1a–2ae. lviii. 5

854. When Thales went out of his house to gaze at the stars he fell into a ditch; to his complaints a little old woman replied, 'Oh Thales, how can you hope to see things in the heavens when you miss what is under your feet?' Then also recall Anaxagoras, rich and noble, yet leaving his estate to devote himself to natural science: he was called negligent because he did not bother about politics. Once somebody said to him, 'Where is your care for your country?' He replied, with a gesture to the sky, 'That is my love.' Prudence is about human goods, concerning which one must take counsel, for they can be otherwise; but wisdom is about good things better than men, things necessary and divine.

Commentary, *VI Ethics, lect.* 6

855. Art is the right idea of things to be made; their goodness does not depend on the disposition of the human appetite, but on the fact that the workmanship is sound. The merit of an artist is judged by the quality of his work; his state of will is irrelevant. Here art is

[1] *Ethics*, $1139^{b}15$.

like the theoretical habits of mind, which are concerned with what things are in themselves, not with our reactions to them. Pleasant humour or spleen make no difference to a mathematical demonstration. Art is a virtue in the same sense; it does not ensure the right use of a thing, for this is proper to moral virtue.

977   *Summa Theologica*, 1a–2ae. lvii. 3

856. Goodwill is required for a man to use his art aright, and this is induced by moral virtue.

Summa Theologica, 1a–2ae. lvii. 5, *ad* 2

857. When artificial things cannot be used without sin then the artist sins by making them, for example idols or superstitious objects. If they can be used either well or ill, swords, arrows, and suchlike, then the craft is not necessarily sinful. As regards feminine ornaments that preserve decency, or even perhaps are extravagant in order to please men, the manufacturers do not sin, unless they go in for harmful absurdities and curiosities.

Summa Theologica, 2a–2ae. clxix. 2, *ad* 4

858. The value of art consists, not in the artist, but in the work of art, for making, which is an action going out into external material, is a perfection, not of the maker, but of the thing made. But the value of prudence is in the doer, who is perfected by his activity, for prudence is the right idea of deeds to be done.

Summa Theologica, 1a–2ae. lvii. 5, *ad* 1

859. A work of art and a moral situation are approached differently. In the former case we are expected to appreciate a particular end; in the latter case we are confronted with the general end of human life as a whole. Fault is a deviation from good purpose. A crime is perpetrated against art when the artist intends to

make a good work but produces a bad one, or intends to make a bad thing but produces a good one. Here the artist is blamed. But to deviate from the common end of human life, as when somebody intends a bad job and succeeds, for instance, in misleading another, then the fault is proper to the doer considered as a man, not as an artist.

27, 611, 971   *Summa Theologica*, 1a–2ae. xxi. 2, *ad* 2

860. A piece of furniture takes after the idea in the mind of the maker rather than after the tool.

Summa Theologica, 3a. lxii. 1

861. Some effects are solely from an external principle, as when the structure of a house is shaped in matter. Others are partly from without and partly from within, for instance health after sickness depends partly on medical art and partly on nature. Art imitates nature in activity, for as nature heals a sick man by altering, checking, and purging his morbid humours, so also does art. Note that art does not act here as a principal cause; it fosters the internal and principal cause, which is nature, strengthening it and ministering instruments used by nature to the intended effect; as when a doctor aids nature by prescribing suitable nourishment and comforts.

1091   *Summa Theologica*, 1a. cxvii. 1

862. Human art is not so powerful as the natural action able to produce a substantial form. Human art cannot go so far as that, for artificial forms are the configurations of accidental wholes. Yet art may apply a proper cause to its proper matter and so effect the alteration of substances, as for instance when heat is used in smelting or distilling.

388   *Summa Theologica*, 3a. lxvi. 4

III. MORAL VIRTUE

863. Loving draws us more to things than knowledge does.

672, 913   *Summa Theologica*, 1a–2ae. xxii. 2

864. Aristotle gives the definition of moral virtue: a habit of choice lying in a mean relative to us and determined by a rational principle.[1] Here there are four notes. First, the genus, touched on when he says that it is a habit. Second, the act of virtue, touched on when he says that it is of choice; habits are defined by acts, and the chief act of virtue is choice. Third, the object or term of the act, touched on when he says that it lies in a mean relative to us; this is important because activity is specified by its object. Fourth, the cause of goodness in virtue, touched on by the clause about its measure by a rational principle; moral virtue is in the appetite according as the latter shares in the life of reason.

Commentary, *II Ethics*, *lect.* 7

865. Well disposed, not only in mind to accept and grasp, but also in will to love and carry out.

Commentary, 1 *ad Corinthios*, *ii*, *lect.* 1

866. The gate to human life hinges on the cardinal virtues. The contemplative life is superhuman, the life of sensual pleasure beastly, but the active life is properly human, and humane activity turns on the practice of the moral virtues.

Disputations, *de Virtutibus Cardinalibus*, 1

867. The moral virtues need not be accompanied by the intellectual virtues of wisdom, science, and art. But

[1] *Ethics*, 1107^{a}1.

they cannot exist without understanding and prudence. For moral virtue is a habit making a good choice. Here two conditions are called for, a good intention of the end, which moral virtue provides by giving us a bias to what is reasonable, and a right taking of means, which implies that the reason takes good counsel, makes the right selection, and commands the correct course, all of which functions attach to prudence and its associate virtues. Moral virtue in consequence requires understanding of principles. As theory works from true premisses so prudence presupposes a true sense of background, for it is the right idea of dealing with a human situation.

27, 977 *Summa Theologica*, 1a–2ae. lviii. 4

868. Prudence concerns the whole of human life and its last end; art deals with a local end.

Summa Theologica, 1a–2ae. lvii. 4, *ad* 3

869. One act cannot cause a habit, nor can many acts, for they are not all simultaneous, and what does not exist does not act. Therefore virtues are not acquired by acts.

I reply, that as many drops of water may hollow a stone, the latest drips profiting by the power of the preceding ones which have appeared to do nothing, so the last act may cause the corresponding act of virtue when the effect of preceding acts be taken into account.

1091 Commentary, *III Sentences*, xxxiii. i. 2. *ii, ad* 4

870. The division of the moral virtues may be traced either by their formal principles or by their subjects. Four cardinal virtues appear when either course is followed.

The formal principle of virtue is reasonable good for the philosopher. This is twofold, essential and applied.

The former lies in the judgements of the reason, and here there is one principal virtue, namely prudence. The order of reason may be applied to what we do, and here there is justice; or to what we feel, and here there are two virtues, temperance when emotions would drive us to do what is unreasonable, and fortitude when they would hold us back.

Division according to the faculties gives the same number. There is the reason itself, holding prudence, and the faculties that are derivatively reasonable, namely the will, which is the subject of justice, and the sensitive appetite, which contains temperance on the concupiscible side, and fortitude on the irascible side.

553, 819   *Summa Theologica*, 1a–2ae. lxi. 2

871. Virtue in the emotional appetites is their habitual conformity with reason.

Summa Theologica, 1a–2ae. lvi. 4

872. These appetites do not obey the nod of reason, but are like free men. On this account they need virtues in order to be well prepared for reasonable activity.

680   *Summa Theologica*, 1a–2ae. lvi. 4, *ad* 3

873. Prudence essentially possesses reasonable good, justice makes it, courage and temperance preserve it.

Summa Theologica, 2a–2ae. cxxiii. 12

874. The chief effective control of human activity is provided by prudence. Virtue springs from man's inner composure, but no less important is his bearing to other people, and here his intercourse is adjusted by justice. His poise when faced with the onset of passion for the pleasures of touch is assured by temperance, and when he would shrink from great perils courage makes him stand intrepid even before the danger of death.

Disputations, *de Virtutibus Cardinalibus*, 1

875. If the titles of virtue stand for their general conditions then they flow into one another: courage is temperate, and temperance is brave, and so with the others.

Disputations, *de Virtutibus Cardinalibus*, 1, *ad* 1

876. Artificial things of different classes have quite disparate principles, and therefore there is no reason why a man should not master one trade and be wholly lacking in another. But the principles of moral objects are so linked together that failure with one will lead to failure with another. Uncontrolled lust will lead to injury, intemperance to a violation of justice, as also in one and the same science a flaw in the principles will invalidate the conclusion. A man is not sufficiently reasonable about one virtue without being reasonable about them all.

852   Disputations, *de Virtutibus Cardinalibus*, 2, *ad* 4

IV. THE VIRTUOUS MEAN

877. Evil comes from tilting the balance when there should be an equilibrium, the bad being either over-weight or underweight. The good of moral virtue lies in the poise of reason. The mean between excess and defect is an equality or conformity.

1008   *Summa Theologica*, 1a–2ae. lxiv. 1

878. The form of goodness in moral virtue derives from the measure of reason; its subject-matter lies in what we do and feel. As regards the former, virtue holds the position of one extreme, namely conformity to reason, while both excess and defect lie at the other extreme of non-conformity. As regards its matter, however, it holds a midway position even-minded among the passions. Hence, Aristotle says that virtue is a mean in respect of its substance, but an extreme with regard to what is best and excellent.[1]

1031   *Summa Theologica*, 1a–2ae. lxiv. 1, *ad* 1

879. The mean and the extremes depend on a variety of circumstances. Nothing prevents one feature in a virtue from being an extreme according to one circumstance and a mean according to another consideration, namely, its conformity with reason. Take magnanimity or magnificence. If we look at the objective size of the projects to which large-minded and splendid characters set themselves we shall praise it as an extreme and a maximum. But if we relate it to other circumstances, then it has the character of a mean, since these virtues are moderated according to the rule of reason, and observe the due conditions of where and when and motive.

Summa Theologica, 1a–2ae. lxiv. 1, *ad* 2

880. Justice deals with operations about external things, wherein the right has to be established absolutely and in itself. Hence, the mean of reason here is the objective mean: justice gives to each man his due, neither more nor less. But the other moral virtues deal with interior passions, wherein what is right cannot be established in the same way, since men vary in their tempers.

1008   *Summa Theologica*, 1a–2ae. lxiv. 2

881. Extravagance and niggardliness, between which moral virtues mediate, must not be taken according to absolute quantities, but in relation to right reason.

Commentary, *III Sentences*, IX. i. 1. *iii*, *ad* 3

882. The size of a virtue depends either on the number of objects to which it extends, after the fashion of dis-

[1] *Ethics*, 1107ᵃ5.

crete quantity, or on the intensity of its activity about an object, after the fashion of continuous quantity.

152   Commentary, *I Sentences*, xvi. ii. 1, *ad* 2

V. VICE

883. The theologian considers sin mainly as an offence against God; the moral philosopher as contrary to reasonableness.

480, 800   *Summa Theologica*, 1a–2ae. lxxi. 6, *ad* 5

884. There is evil, and there is also something from which evil may follow. In the first respect God cannot be feared, since he is goodness itself. In the second respect he may be feared because from him, or with reference to him, some evil may come our way; the evil of punishment respectively and the evil of fault when we are separated from him.

487   *Summa Theologica*, 2a–2ae. xix. 1

885. If a man cleaves to God through fear of punishment it will be servile fear; if through fear of offending him it will be filial fear.

Summa Theologica, 2a–2ae. xix. 2

886. Servile fear is evil owing to its servility. For slavery is opposed to freedom. A slave is one who does not act as the cause of his own actions, but as though moved from without. But he who acts through love sets himself into motion. It is contrary to the very notion of servility to act from love. Consequently servile fear as such is contrary to charity; were servility essential to it it would be intrinsically wrong, even as adultery is intrinsically wrong. Servility, however, is not part of the very essence of servile fear, for the object here is punishment, and it is incidental whether this be regarded as the greatest of all evils, which is the case with a man devoid of charity, or whether it is subordinated to the love of God.

Summa Theologica, 2a–2ae. xix. 4

887. The offence of grave sin proceeds from this, that the will of man is turned away from God by being turned towards some perishable good.

Summa Theologica, 3a. lxxxvi. 2

888. Malice consists in emptiness.

Disputations, III *de Potentia*, 16, *ad* 3

889. There is a double motion in grave sin, a turning away from immutable good and an indulgence in mutable good; the penalty is correspondingly eternal and temporal.

Summa Theologica, 3a. lxxxvi. 4

890. The turning away is common to all grave sins, but by their indulgence they are different from one another, and sometimes hostile.

462   *Summa Theologica*, 3a. lxxxviii. 1

891. It was the opinion of Socrates that every virtue was a kind of knowledge and every sin a kind of ignorance.[1] To some extent he was right, because the will is never attracted by an evil unless in some respect it is perceived as good, and would never take an evil but for some ignorance or error in the reason.

Experience, however, demonstrates that many act against their knowledge. Therefore it is necessary to draw a distinction.[2] For his right conduct man is directed by a twofold knowledge, namely, universal and particular, and a deficiency in either is enough to spoil the rightness of will and deed.

[1] *Ethics*, 1145^{b}25.   [2] *Ethics*, 1146^{b}21.

It is possible for a man to possess correct knowledge, in particular as well as in general, and yet not advert to his knowledge actually; in such a case it is not hard to see how he may act counter to what he does not actually consider. This lack of consideration may happen sometimes through mere lack of attention, or perhaps be caused by some hindrance, as when somebody may be worked up by passion and prevented from considering what he knows in general. This may happen in three ways: by distraction, as already explained; by opposition, because an emotion may conflict with rational judgement; and by physiological change, the result of which may be to fetter the reason, even as in sleep or drunkenness. When passion is very intense a man may lose the use of his reason altogether; many have gone out of their minds through excess of love or anger.

760, 807   *Summa Theologica*, 1a–2ae. lxxvii. 2

892. The argument of the incontinent man has four propositions. On the side of the reason there is, for instance, the general prohibition of the inordinate eating of sweetstuff, commanding, say, that it should not be eaten out of due time. But on the side of desire there is the urge that it is pleasurable. Because concupiscence prevails over reason in the particular case, the situation is judged not by the general law of reason, saying that this is not good enough, but by the general law of concupiscence, saying that anyhow this is sweet. Hence follows his conclusion.

Commentary, *VII Ethics, lect.* 3

893. Sin falls short of the wisdom and prudence that should be in charge of what we do. Therefore a bad man is an ignorant man.

Disputations, xv *de Veritate*, 3, *ad* 2

894. The term *foolishness* conveys the meaning of a certain senselessness in judgement, chiefly in the face of the highest cause, the supreme good and last end. This may be the outcome of congenital disposition, to which no blame attaches, or of such indulgence in worldly concerns that a man is rendered inept at perceiving divine values, and this foolishness is sin.

Summa Theologica, 2a–2ae. xlvi. 2

895. Sin expels love, not by its own force, but because a man voluntarily subjects himself to it.

Disputations, *de Caritate*, 6, *ad* 6

896. Sin acts in virtue of deficient good.

491   *Summa Theologica*, 1a–2ae. xviii. 1, *ad* 1

897. As regards the will, that comes first which is principally intended, and therefore, in those sins whose principal intent is to enjoy some perishable good—intemperance, avarice, and the like—a turning to something precedes the turning away; the latter is not principally intended but happens beside the intention and follows from undisciplined indulgence. But in sins which directly intend to turn away from God—such as infidelity, despair, and the like—the turning away is primary and the turning to other things a later consequence, as is noted in the Epistle to the Ephesians.[1]

VI *Quodlibet*, 16

898. Though nobody is foolish by choice, we may will the things from which foolishness follows.

Summa Theologica, 2a–2ae. xlvi. 2, *ad* 2

899. The worse the vice the better always the opposite virtue.

Commentary, *IV Ethics, lect.* 15

[1] iv. 18.

900. Pride may be taken as an habitual inclination to every manner of sin, or as a general condition in all sins, or as the inordinate desire of one's own private excellence; it is in this last sense that pride is a special sin.

Commentary, *II Sentences*, v. i. 3

901. An inordinate fondness for oneself, and an inordinate conceit.

Commentary, *in Matthaeum, xviii, lect.* 1

902. Well-ordered self-love is right and natural.

Summa Theologica, 1a–2ae. lxxvii. 4, *ad* 1

903. God can be apprehended either in himself or through his effects. By his essence he is very goodness from which nothing can shrink, and therefore it is impossible for a man to see him and hate him. Some of his effects cannot be repugnant to the human will; existence, life, intelligence, these are desired and loved by everybody. But there are other effects which an unruly will may dislike, for instance that sin is forbidden, and punishment inflicted; when God is considered as their author some thereupon may hold him in dislike.

254, 698   *Summa Theologica*, 2a–2ae. xxxiv. 1

904. Vice comes to the body from the soul, and not the other way round.

III *Contra Gentes*, 127

905. Vice cannot entirely destroy the capacity and aptness for grace.

493   Disputations, II *de Malo*, 12

906. The desire for good is more corrupted than is the knowledge of truth.

Summa Theologica, 1a–2ae. cix. 2, *ad* 3

907. To speak of unforgivable sin is to impugn divine power.

Opusc. XIII, *Compendium Theologiae*, 144

908. The order of divine justice does not treat those who are still travellers as though they had arrived. Now to be in an unchangeable state, either of good or of evil, is the end; whereas wayfaring is our present condition, as is evidenced by the mutability of body and soul. Divine justice, therefore, does not require that a man after falling into sin should lie there for ever.

488　　　　　　Opusc. XIII, *Compendium Theologiae*, 145

909. It would be foolish indeed to brood over what has already happened as though trying to make it as though it had not happened. A penitent does not do this; his sorrow is disapproval of the past, coupled with the intention of preventing the results.

349　　　　　　*Summa Theologica*, 3a. lxxxv. 1, *ad* 3

910. God alone forgives and absolves from sin by his own authority.

Summa Theologica, 3a. lxxxiv. 3, *ad* 3

911. Object and last end coincide in the case of a theological virtue.[1] This is not the case with the virtue of penitence, whose material is the expiation of a wrong that has been done, and whose purpose is reconciliation with God.

Commentary, *IV Sentences*, XIV. i. 1. *iv*

[1] The distinction between a moral virtue and a theological virtue is this: the former is occupied with the measure of conduct set by the human reason, the latter reaches to God himself.

XVI

Living beyond Reason[1]

912. Love takes up where knowledge leaves off.

92, 673   *Summa Theologica*, 2a–2ae. xxvii. 4, *ad* 1

913. More is required for the perfecting of knowledge than for the perfecting of love. Knowledge is in the reason, whose function is to analyse what are united in reality and to compare and synthesize what are diverse. For a man's knowledge to be complete he must know, therefore, the nature of a thing, its parts and powers and properties one by one. But love is in the appetite, which takes the thing just as it is: enough that the thing is loved on being known. On this account an object can be loved more than it is known.

92, 686, 785, 961   *Summa Theologica*, 1a–2ae. xxvii. 2, *ad* 2

914. In the reason the object is present as a specific likeness; in the will as a principle and term of motion.

iv *Contra Gentes*, 19

915. A thing can be immediately loved though mediately known.

Disputations, *de Caritate*, 2, *ad* 11

1 The moral system is not enclosed by the rules of reasonable living but is open to a mystery beyond. Even in the secular sections grace keeps breaking in, neither demanded nor merited by the principles of nature, but meeting a capacity for friendship which can be caught up into the personal life of God. Here are relationships surpassing the dependence of creatures, and parts of a whole, on the creator and integrator of the universe. The purely reasonable man is a historical fiction. The ideal of rational virtue has rarely been reckoned sufficient. This chapter deals with the frontier between nature and grace, and the texts give some account of the conditions of the *anima naturaliter christiana*.

916. Knowledge is achieved by the thing known being united through its meaning to the knower. But the effect of love is that the thing itself is somehow united to the lover.

Summa Theologica, 1a–2ae. xxviii. 1, *ad* 3

917. Gratitude tries to return more than has been received.

Summa Theologica, 2a–2ae. cvi. 6

I. SUPERHUMAN VIRTUE

918. There are two kinds of virtue, the one is the common sort adjusting man in a reasonable style, the other is rare and called heroic, crowning man to a superhuman degree. When a brave man fears what should be feared he is virtuous; not to fear would be vicious. But when he trusts in divine help and fears nothing in the world, that is superhuman. Virtues with that kind of effect on a man are called divine.

Commentary, in Matthaeum, v, lect. 2

919. Inspiration signifies a movement from without. Recall that there are two sources of motion in man, one within, namely his reason, the other without, and this is God. Anything set in motion must somehow be like the thing that moves it; moreover, the disposition making it easily and happily tractable is itself a perfection. The higher the mover the more perfect should be the proportionate disposition; we notice this requirement when students come to be taught high doctrine. The human virtues are designed to fit a man to conduct himself reasonably in his inward and outward motions. But higher perfections are required to dispose him to be divinely moved.

Even Aristotle[1] notes that those who are moved by divine instinct have no need to take counsel according to the reason; they follow an intimate instinct and are moved by a better principle.

838   *Summa Theologica*, 1a–2ae. lxviii. 1

920. Heroic or divine virtue does not differ from the normal run of virtue except by its more perfect mode of activity, and because it disposes to values higher than those generally accessible. It is virtue above the usual course, called by Plotinus a certain sublime manner of virtue, and attributed to the purified soul.

Summa Theologica, 3a. vii. 2, *ad* 2

921. Prophets do not speak of their own will.

Commentary, *in Psalmos, v.* 7

922. Some come to ampler goods than they ever dreamt of; they are called fortunate. Others fall short of what they have prudently planned and come to a bad end; they are called unfortunate.

Opusc. xviii, *de Sortibus*

923. The visitation of the Lord may be for condemnation, for correction, for consolation.

Commentary, *in Isaiam, xxiv*

924. In the human soul, as in every other creature, a double passive potentiality should be allowed for, one is proportionate to a natural agent, the other is proportionate to the first cause, which can uplift any creature to an actuality higher than can be produced by a natural cause. This capacity is customarily termed the obediential potentiality of a creature.

744   *Summa Theologica*, 3a. xi. 1

[1] In the *Liber de Bona Fortuna*, a favourite medieval compilation from a chapter of the *Eudemian Ethics* (1246^b37–1248^b11) and a chapter of the *Magna Moralia* (1206^b30–1207^b19).

925. Bear in mind the twofold capacity of human nature; the first is according to the order of natural powers, which God always fulfils, giving to each according to natural capacity. The other is prescribed by the order of divine power, at whose beck every creature stands. Here belongs the capacity for grace. God does not necessarily fulfil this capacity in everyone, otherwise he would be able to do with creatures only what he has done, which is false.

Summa Theologica, 3a. i. 3, *ad* 3

926. That a perfection is present in the human mind, too high to be explained by anything less than the supernatural, is man's nobility. Irrational creatures are impotent here. It does not follow that the highest human perfection is gained by natural power, which may indeed reach to what accords with the state of nature, but not to the heroism of the state of grace.

254   Disputations, XII *de Veritate*, 3, *ad* 12

927. Lest so noble a creature should seem to be utterly void of purpose through being unable to obtain his proper end, man has been given the means of rising to the knowledge of God.

IV *Contra Gentes*, I

II. BELIEF AND TRUST

928. Grace does not destroy nature but completes it. Hence the natural reason subserves faith as the natural desire of will is the undercurrent of charity.

85, 110   *Summa Theologica*, 1a. i. 8, *ad* 2

929. As regards the intellect, the assent of faith is a lowly operation, for the intellect does not see what it believes. But as regards the object of the assent, the operation may be most sublime.

The desire is not quieted but rather excited by the knowledge of faith, for everyone desires to see what he believes. Therefore man's happiness does not consist in believing things about God.

III Contra Gentes, 40

930. Wonder is a kind of desire in knowing. It is the cause of delight because it carries the hope of discovery.

66 <div style="text-align: right"><i>Summa Theologica</i>, 1a–2ae. xxxii. 8</div>

931. Wonder is impossible without reason, for it implies a comparing of effect and cause.

Summa Theologica, 3a. v. 4

932. The slenderest acquaintance with high things is more worth having than the most expert information about low things.

Summa Theologica, 1a. i. 5, ad 1

933. There are various kinds of silence; of dullness, of security, of patience, of a quiet heart.

Commentary, in Jeremiam, viii. 7

934. Faith is the foretaste of that knowledge which hereafter will make us happy.

Opusc. xiii, Compendium Theologiae, 2

935. Believers do not lightly believe truths the human reason cannot verify experimentally. *We have not followed cunningly devised fables.*[1]

I Contra Gentes, 6

936. Even in the grading of the sciences the science dealing with the highest truth, namely metaphysics, is the last the student arrives at. Nevertheless, the introductory sciences suppose certain truths which will be

[1] 2 Pet. i. 16.

more fully developed in metaphysics; each science makes suppositions, which the beginner must believe.

59   Opusc. xvi, Exposition, *de Trinitate*, iii. i, *ad* 4

937. The moral virtues do not essentially constitute the contemplative life, but dispose thereto.

739   *Summa Theologica*, 2a–2ae. clxxx. 2

938. Youth is the cause of hope on these three counts, namely, because the object of hope is future, is difficult, and is possible. For the young live in the future and not in the past, they are not lost in memories but full of confidence. Secondly, their warmth of nature, high spirits, and expansive heart embolden them to reach out to difficult projects; therefore are they mettlesome and of good hope. Thirdly, they have not been thwarted in their plans and their lack of experience encourages them to think that where there's a will there's a way. The last two factors, namely good spirits and a certain recklessness, are also at work in people who are drunk.

Summa Theologica, 1a–2ae. xl. 6

939. In the object of hope four notes are struck: that it is good, future, arduous, possible. Hence, respectively, hope differs from fear, joy, simple desire, despair.

Disputations, *de Spe*, 1

940. Hopelessness about eternal life may come either because heaven is not accounted for much, or because it is reckoned impossible to obtain. Spiritual goods do not strike us as very valuable when our affections are sapped by love of bodily pleasures, and especially sexual pleasures. By craving these a man comes to feel distaste for spiritual values. Thus, despair is caused by lust. We are also led to imagine that this noble prize is beyond our reach by an excessive dejection into which we sink and from which we feel we shall never be extricated. Thus spiritual boredom generates despair.

333   *Summa Theologica*, 2a–2ae. xx. 4

941. If anyone despairs of what he is not born for, or what he has no right to, that would be no sin.

Summa Theologica, 2a–2ae. xx. 1, *ad* 3

III. FRIENDSHIP

942. Human justice, which consists in the observance of laws, is consummated in one precept of charity; the fullness of this law is friendship.

Opusc. xiii, *Compendium Theologiae*, 1

943. Between friends there is no need of justice properly so called. They share everything in common. A friend is an *alter ego*, and a man does not have justice towards himself. Let two men be together; justice is not enough, for something more is required, namely friendship.

Commentary, *VIII Ethics*, *lect.* 1

944. Friendship is more permanent when the give and take is equal and identical, for instance, pleasure for pleasure. Since there are different kinds and quantities of pleasure according to the difference of objects, a settled friendship requires, not merely that pleasure should be repaid with pleasure, but that the pleasure should be in the same thing; thus, happiness in play when one delights in the sport of another, and not when, as sometimes in erotic love, a couple are not enjoying the same thing.

204, 1087   Commentary, *VIII Ethics*, *lect.* 4

945. It is of the nature of friendship not to be hidden; otherwise it would only be a kind of well-wishing.

Commentary, *in Joannem, xiii.* 3

946. If we compare loving our friends and loving our enemies, then the first is better as regards its object or term; but as regards the principle, which is the will, then there is the more merit where there is the greater effort.

Commentary, III Sentences, xxx. i. 3

947. You cannot make friends with people whose company and conversation you do not enjoy—with people, for instance, who are harsh, quarrelsome, and addicted to back-biting. Crusty old men may be benevolent in that they wish well and will do good at a pinch, but they are not truly friendly, for they do not share their lives and rejoice together in the company of friends.

1003, 1004   *Commentary, VIII Ethics, lect.* 6

948. Not every love has the quality of friendship. In the first place it is reserved to that love for another which wills his well-being. When what we will is not the other's good for his sake, but the desire of it as it affects us, that is not friendship, but self-regarding love and some sort of concupiscence. Neither does benevolence suffice for friendship; in addition a mutual loving is required, for friend is friend to friend. This interplay of well-wishing is founded on companionship.

775   *Summa Theologica*, 2a–2ae. xxiii. 1

949. To rejoice and to be sad on the same grounds is the sign of sharing.

III *Contra Gentes*, 151

950. Love goes out to another in two ways: one to a substantial good, as when we love a man for himself; the other to an accidental good or quality, as when we love virtue, not as an end in itself, but as making us good. The former movement of love includes the love of friendship, the latter the love of desire.

Opusc. xiv, Exposition, *de Divinis Nominibus*, iv, *lect.* 10

951. Friendship is love simply speaking; desire is love in a qualified sense.

Summa Theologica, 1a–2ae. xxvi. 4

952. Love is a binding force, by which another is joined to me and cherished as myself.

Summa Theologica, 1a. xx. 1, *ad* 3

953. By loving God a man glows to gaze on his beauty.

Summa Theologica, 2a–2ae. clxxx. 1

954. Love works in a circle, for the beloved moves the lover by stamping a likeness, and the lover then goes out to hold the beloved in reality. Who first was the beginning now becomes the end of motion.

92 *Summa Theologica*, 1a–2ae. xxvi. 2

955. The lover is not content with superficial knowledge of the beloved, but strives for intimate discovery and entrance.

Summa Theologica, 1a–2ae. xxviii. 2

IV. THE LIFE OF PERFECTION

956. Three things are necessary for man's well-being, the knowledge of what to believe, of what to desire, of what to do. The first is taught in the Creed, the second in the Lord's prayer, and the third by Law. Of this we intend to treat. We begin by distinguishing four kinds of law.

The first is called the law of nature. It is no other than the light of intelligence set in us by God, showing us what we should do and what avoid. This light and law was given at creation, though many fancy that if they do not keep the law they may be excused through ignorance. *Many say, who shall show us good things?* as though they were doubtful what to do; and the reply is made: *The light of thy countenance is shed upon us, O Lord,*[1] the light, namely, of intelligence.

But on top of this law the devil has sown another, the law of concupiscence.[2] At the beginning the soul of man was subject to God, and so flesh was subject to reason. Since the devil's suggestion withdrew us from our obedience the flesh has become rebellious; we may wish a reasonable decency, but lust pushes us away. *I see another law in my members warring against the law of my mind,* for the Apostle adds, *bringing me into captivity to the law of sin.*[3] The law of concupiscence frequently corrupts the law of nature and the plan of reason.

Nature being in ruins, the law of Scripture now enters to recall man to deeds of virtue away from vice. Two influences are at work here, fear and love. First, fear; a man begins to avoid sin by the prospect of judgement and hell. *The beginning of wisdom is the fear of the Lord.*[4] And again, *The fear of the Lord casts out sin.*[5] Though a man who avoids sin from motives of fear is not righteous, nevertheless righteousness starts here where the Mosaic Law lays its emphasis. Yet its force is not enough, the hand may obey but the mind is not held, and therefore the Gospel Law sets another measure to keep men away from evil and bent on good, namely, the power of love.

There are three main differences between the law of fear and the law of love. First, the subjects of the former are treated like slaves, while those that observe the latter are treated like freemen. He who acts solely from fear is

[1] Ps. iv. 6.   [2] The *lex fomitis* of Peter Lombard.
[3] Rom. vii. 23.   [4] Ecclus. i. 16.   [5] Ecclus. i. 27.

like a slave; he who acts from love is like a freeman or
son. *Where the spirit of the Lord is, there is liberty.*[1]
Second, those who keep the first are promised temporal
goods, *If ye be willing and obedient, ye shall eat the fat
of the land,*[2] whereas for the second heavenly good is
promised; *If thou wilt have eternal life, keep the commandments.*[3] Thirdly, the former is heavy: *Why do you
seek to lay on our necks a yoke which neither we nor our
fathers could bear?*[4] But the latter is easy: *My yoke is
sweet and my burden light.*[5]

1043   Opusc. xxxv, *de Duobus Praeceptis*

957. Charity draws man to God; faith draws divine
things to us.

92   Disputations, vi *de Potentia*, 9, *ad* 6

958. The object of charity is not the common good,
but the highest good.

1107   Disputations, *de Caritate*, 5, *ad* 4

959. By nature we can love God above all things as the
principle and end of all natural goodness. But in charity
he is offered as our joy in a society of friendship.

Summa Theologica, 1a–2ae. cix. 3, *ad* 1

960. God is the objective of the moral virtues in the
sense of being their final cause, but he is the object of
charity more as the formal cause.

111,911   Disputations, *de Caritate*, 5, *ad* 2

961. A man is judged to be unreservedly perfect in the
life of the spirit by what belongs to its very heart,
though his value in special spheres will be decided by
supplementary qualities. He who is without love lacks

[1] 2 Cor. iii. 17.   [2] Isa. i. 19.   [3] Matt. xix. 17.
[4] Acts xv. 10.   [5] Matt. xi. 30.

the living heart of goodness; he should be diagnosed as spiritually dead. *If I have prophecy and know all mysteries, and all knowledge, and have such faith as to move mountains, but if I have not charity, I am nothing.*[1] The blessed apostle John asserts that the whole spiritual life consists in friendship; *we know that we have passed from death to life, because we love the brethren.*[2]

There are two precepts of charity: *Thou shalt love the Lord thy God with thy whole heart and with thy whole soul and with thy whole mind. This is the first and greatest of the commandments. And the second is like to it: thou shalt love thy neighbour as thyself.*[3]

Let us ponder both in turn. Love's measure may be laid either on the beloved or the lover; on the former when loved as much as lovable, on the latter when the love is according to the full power of the lover. By the first measure God is infinitely worthy of love. To love infinitely, however, is beyond the creature's power, and therefore God alone can match his own goodness with his own power of loving.

Yet creatures can fit the second measure of perfect loving; and in two ways. First, with a love so whole that nothing is lacking, for everything they do is actively turned on God. This is not for wayfarers, but for the blessed in heaven, whose love is always in full expression, and is not merely habitual. Secondly, when there is nothing present that cannot be referred to God, at least by virtual intention.[4] This is the perfection of love now commanded us: *Whether you eat or drink, or whatever you do, do all for the glory of God.*[5]

[1] 1 Cor. xiii. 2.   [2] 1 John iii. 14.   [3] Matt. xxii. 37–9.
[4] St. Thomas is referring to one whose state is that of loving God, but who is not explicitly aware of his charity in all his everyday deeds.   [5] 1 Cor. x. 31.

The counsels inviting us to perfection are designed to free us from worldly affections and thereby set the spirit on God by contemplating, loving, doing his will.

Of temporal goods to be given up external goods or riches come first. *If thou wilt be perfect, go and sell all thou hast, and give to the poor, and thou shalt have treasure in heaven, and come follow me.*[1] Next in the list are the people who are joined to us by kinship and affinity. *If anyone comes to me and does not hate father and mother and wife and children, and brothers and sisters, he cannot be my disciple.*[2] Finally, as adding something greater, it is said, *and even his own life.* This also the Lord teaches. *If any man wishes to follow me let him deny himself and take up his cross and follow me.*[3] The observance of this generous denial and loving hate is in part necessary for salvation and in part the complement of perfection.

After the perfection of loving God the perfection of charity with regard to our neighbour remains to be considered. Here also there are degrees of perfection. There is the perfection necessary to salvation, falling under the necessity of precept, and afterwards the further and more abundant perfection falling under counsel.

What is commanded is this, thou shalt love thy neighbour as thyself. There are three qualities here, for the friendship should be true, right, and holy.

When we love our fellows only in so far as they are of use to us they are not truly loved; we are really loving ourselves and using other people as though they were for our convenience. We do not truly love them as ourselves. He who loves another merely for his own profit or pleasure stands convicted of selfishness. *Charity*

[1] Matt. xix. 21.   [2] Luke xiv. 26.   [3] Matt. xvi. 24.

seeketh not her own,[1] but the good of the beloved. Then secondly, the love of another should be fair and right, which means that a greater good must be preferred to a less. The good of soul must hold the first place, then afterwards comes the body, and lastly external possessions. This scale is instinctive in our self-love: who is there who would not rather be deprived of an eye than of the use of the reason, or who will not spend his possessions for the safety of his body? And so, if somebody prefers his neighbour's possessions to his bodily health, or his body to his spiritual good, he does not rightly love his neighbour as himself. Thirdly, it is commanded that the love of our neighbour should be holy, in that it is ordered to God.

327, 708, 1084   Opusc. xxix, *de Perfectione Vitae Spiritualis,*
1–8, 10, 13

962. Special acts of perfection are counselled, but there is not one of them that may not be commanded in a crisis as necessary for salvation.

Summa Theologica, 2a–2ae. cxxiv. 3, *ad* 1

963. Directly and essentially, the perfection of the Christian life consists in charity, primarily in the love of God, derivatively in the love of our neighbour; as is proclaimed in the two main precepts of the divine law. Now because there is a precept given it does not follow that a set amount is fixed, in this sense that a minimum is commanded and a surplus is left over for our option. The very statement rules this out, for love *with thy whole heart* it commands, and *love as thyself.* The end of the law is love, and there is no stinting about ends, but only with means.

[1] 1 Cor. xiii. 5.

Secondarily and instrumentally, perfection is reached through the counsels which, like the ten commandments, are subordinate to love, though in different ways. For the commandments are designed to remove what is contrary to charity and to establish the conditions without which charity cannot exist. The counsels, however, are designed to rule out what may be obstacles to charity.

Summa Theologica, 2a–2ae. clxxxiv. 3

XVII

Reasonable Virtues[1]

964. The word *cardinal* comes from hinge, on which a door opens, according to the saying,[2] *As a door turneth upon its hinges, so doth the slothful upon his bed.* So the cardinal virtues are those on which pivots the entrance into humane living.

Disputations, de Virtutibus Cardinalibus, 1

I. PRUDENCE

965. Prudence furnishes the right plan for immediate conduct.

Summa Theologica, 1a–2ae. lvii. 4

966. Not for its thoughtfulness alone is prudence to be praised, but also for the practical good sense of its application to conduct.

806   *Summa Theologica*, 2a–2ae. xlvii. 1, *ad* 3

[1] Standards are checked by experience. Despite his sense of ideal form, St. Thomas never seriously attempts to deduce facts from pure theory, least of all in his moral science. Without a philosophy there is no principle of enlightenment, yet theory alone cannot grasp individual situations. Hence the function of prudence, a moral virtue because it supposes good intentions and a bent to the good life, an intellectual virtue because it passes a shrewd judgement about means and ends and applies an idea to practice. All the other moral virtues are interconnected in this practical appreciation. Courage and temperance are general qualities that cover a multitude of virtues, yet they are also special virtues with a limited aim. As such they are not habits of will, but habits of the sensitive appetite.

[2] Prov. xxvi. 14. The play is upon the word *cardo*, hinge, socket.

967. A proper application cannot be executed unless these two terms be known, that which is to be applied and that to which it is to be applied. Human conduct is always an affair of particular situations, and therefore the prudent man must appreciate both the general principles of moral science and the singular objects of his activity.

699, 1067   *Summa Theologica*, 2a–2ae. xlvii. 3

968. Applying the right plan for making something pertains to art; prudence deals with matters of counsel when there are several ways of achieving a purpose. When the theoretical reason makes something, an argument for instance, then it proceeds according to fixed and classical methods, which is the rôle of art rather than of prudence. One may envisage a theoretical art, but scarcely a theoretical prudence.

797, 1053   *Summa Theologica*, 2a–2ae. xlvii. 1, *ad* 3

969. The infinity of singulars cannot be comprehended by the human reason. *Our counsels are uncertain.*[1] Nevertheless, they can be grouped and limited according to what usually happens, and this approximation suffices for prudence.

306, 786, 1063   *Summa Theologica*, 2a–2ae. xlvii. 3, *ad* 2

970. Of the two sides to the rational soul, one of which is called the scientific and the other the opinative, prudence strengthens the latter. Opinion is about things that could happen otherwise, and so is prudence.

23   Commentary, *VI Ethics, lect.* 4

971. Habits that ensure a right kind of deed without concern for whether or not it is performed in the right

[1] Wisd. ix. 14.

spirit are not such full virtues as those that ensure the right temper as well; these latter relate to good as formally humane, that is as taken into and quickening the doer, not merely as an objective and impersonal value. Now prudence devises the application of a right plan to conduct and also induces the right frame of mind; hence it is a virtue not only in the sense that the other intellectual habits are virtues, but also as having the character of the moral virtues, among which it is numbered.

852, 855 *Summa Theologica,* 2a–2ae. xlvii. 4

972. Prudence applies principles to particular issues; consequently it does not establish moral purpose, but contrives the means thereto.

Summa Theologica, 2a–2ae. xlvii. 6

973. That we should live according to right reason is presupposed to prudence. But how, and through what means, our conduct may keep the reasonable measure, that is the affair of prudence.

Summa Theologica, 2a–2ae. xlvii. 7

974. Prudence opens the way for the other virtues.

Summa Theologica, 2a–2ae. xlvii. 6, *ad* 3

975. There are three kinds of prudence; solitary prudence directed to one's own benefit;[1] economic or domestic prudence directed to the good of a household or family; and political prudence ordered to the common good of the State.[2]

1082 *Summa Theologica,* 2a–2ae. xlvii. 11

[1] Also known as 'monastic' prudence.
[2] The State, called by St. Thomas the city, the kingdom, or the political community.

976. What to do, the reasons for doing it, and how to do it.

Disputations, xiv *de Veritate*, 4

977. Three stages can be marked in the prudent control of conduct. The first is to take counsel and discuss the question; the second is to judge about the findings in a speculative temper; the third goes farther and is the work of the practical reason, namely to apply counsel and judgement to what must be done here and now. This act is closer to the immediate issue; it is the principal function of the practical reason and, consequently, of prudence. One sign of this is that the psychological perfection of art consists rather in passing a judgement than in carrying it into effect, and therefore one man is esteemed the better artist who deliberately makes an artistic mistake than another whose mistake is involuntary: the former seems at least to have a good judgement, which the latter lacks. But with prudence it is the other way round; a man is more imprudent who deliberately fails, as being deficient in the principal act of prudence, than he whose error is involuntary.

692   *Summa Theologica*, 2a–2ae. xlvii. 8

978. Some faults are manifestly hostile to prudence —impulsiveness, inconsiderateness, inconstancy, also negligence which is against caution. Others are caricatures which abuse the features of prudence—worldly prudence, cunning and slyness, fraud, and over-anxiety.

Summa Theologica, 2a–2ae. liii, Prologue

979. Acts of prudence are concerned solely with matters of moral virtue. But human happiness does not finally consist in the practice of moral virtue, nor consequently in the activity of prudence.

739   iii *Contra Gentes*, 35

II. COURAGE

980. The nearer a man is to God, who is ever constant, the more steadfast he is and the less fickle.

140   III *Contra Gentes*, 62

981. Courage can be taken to mean either a firmness of spirit, and this is a general virtue or rather a condition of every virtue, or a particular firmness in enduring and repulsing threats in situations fraught with conspicuous difficulty, namely in grave perils, and in this sense courage is a special virtue.

Summa Theologica, 2a–2ae. cxxiii. 2

982. Holding steady in danger is more important than taking the offensive.

Summa Theologica, 2a–2ae. cxxiii. 6

983. In the display of courage two characteristics should be considered, the premeditated deliberateness and the habit of discipline; it is the latter that most appears in emergencies.

838   *Summa Theologica*, 2a–2ae. cxxiii. 9

984. Courage includes patience.

Disputations, *de Virtutibus Cardinalibus*, 1, *ad* 14

985. Magnificence consorts with liberality in its material, with courage in its mode.

Commentary, *III Sentences*, xxxiii. iii. 3. *i, ad* 3

986. The rush of anger chokes the free judgement of truth. The virtue of meekness, which controls anger, makes a man master of himself.

Summa Theologica, 2a–2ae. clvii. 4

987. Savagery takes delight in human suffering. Such pleasure is not human, but bestial. Cruelty is rather different: it exceeds due measure in inflicting punishment, and differs from savagery as malevolence does from bestiality.

Summa Theologica, 2a–2ae. clix. 2

III. TEMPERANCE

988. Justice and courage are more immediately related to the common good than temperance is, for justice controls transactions with others, while courage rides the dangers to be undergone for the common good. Temperance moderates merely one's own personal lusts and pleasures. Therefore the others are greater virtues, and prudence and the divine virtues are more potent still.

756   *Summa Theologica*, 2a–2ae. cxli. 8

989. Job begins his profession of innocence by declaring his freedom from the vice of lasciviousness, which involves many others.

Commentary, *in Job, xxxi, lect.* 1

990. Temperance does not abolish all depraved lusts, but the temperate man does not tolerate them as does the intemperate man.

826   Disputations, *de Virtutibus Cardinalibus*, 1, *ad* 6

991. Derangement—when intelligence is obsequious to sensuality.

III *Contra Gentes*, 81

992. Among the perfections of animal nature included in human nature is the sensitive appetite, termed the sensuality. Even this is born to obey the reason, and so is called reasonable by sharing. It takes on the full quality of voluntariness only inasmuch as it is modified by the reason.

677, 826   *Summa Theologica*, 3a. xviii. 2

B 628   z

993. It is compared to the snake for its sting, not its nature.

Summa Theologica, 3a. xviii. 2, *ad* 2

994. The commanded conformity of the human will with the divine will should be interpreted in terms of deliberate will.

694   *Summa Theologica*, 3a. xviii. 5, *ad* 2

995. If a man wills one thing by his reasonable desire and another by his sense-desire, there is no conflict of contraries, unless the latter prevails.

Summa Theologica, 3a. xviii. 6

996. The special object of temperance is healthy pleasure in the sensation of touch. The special form is from the reason, which appoints the measure; the material, however, is from the desires themselves.

551   *Summa Theologica*, 1a–2ae. lxiii. 4

997. What is contrary to the natural order is vicious. Nature provides pleasure in vitally necessary activities, and the natural order requires that a man should enjoy what is required for the well-being of the individual and the race. Were somebody to avoid pleasure so far as to omit what is a natural necessity he would sin, as though resisting the design of nature. This belongs to the vice of unfeelingness.

735   *Summa Theologica*, 2a–2ae. cxlii. 1

998. A man cannot lead a reasonable life if he avoids all pleasure. He who abhors pleasures because they are pleasurable is boorish and ungracious.

225   *Summa Theologica*, 2a–2ae. cxlii. 1, *ad* 2

999. What is honourable is delightful to man, but

what he finds pleasurable is not always honourable, for it may appeal to the senses and not to the reason.

629   *Summa Theologica*, 2a–2ae. cxlv. 3

1000. Intemperance is superfluous concupiscence, and is called childish on three grounds. First, for what intemperance and children alike desire, namely graceless things. Our deeds are beautiful when they are ordered according to reason; as Cicero says, beauty is what is consonant with that excellence in man whereby he differs from other living things.[1] A child does not bother about counsels of moderation; as Aristotle remarks, neither does lust listen to sobriety.[2]

Secondly, both agree in the event. A child is spoilt when left to his own devices: *A horse not broken in becometh stubborn; and a child left to himself becometh headstrong.*[3] Concupiscence grows stronger with gratification; as Augustine says, when lust is served it becomes custom, and when custom is not resisted it becomes necessity.[4]

Thirdly, both require the same remedy, namely, the use of force. *Withold not correction from a child, thou shalt beat him with the rod, and deliver his soul from hell.*[5] So also when lusts are resisted they may be tamed to the due manner of decency.

755   *Summa Theologica*, 2a–2ae. cxlii. 2

1001. Ornament should befit a person's condition and intention. If a woman decks herself out decently according to her rank and station, and comports herself unpretentiously according to the custom of her country, then she will be acting with modesty, the virtue that sets the style for making an entrance and sitting down and indeed for all deportment. This covers also her actions

---

[1] *de Officiis*, 1.   [2] *Ethics*, 1149ª34.   [3] Ecclus. xxx. 8.
[4] *Confessions*, viii. 5.   [5] Prov. xxiii. 13–14.

to please the husband she has or should have, and to keep him away from other women. Otherwise there will be showing off, and some infection of impurity if it panders to lust.

Commentary, in Isaiam, iii

1002. To know and appreciate your own worth is no sin.

Vainglory directly clashes with magnanimity.

Summa Theologica, 2a–2ae. cxxxii. 1

1003. Jokes and plays are words and gestures that are not instructive, but merely seek to give lively pleasure. We should enjoy them. They are governed by the virtue of witty gaiety to which Aristotle refers and which we call pleasantness.[1] A ready-witted man is quick with repartees and turns speech and action to light relief.

Summa Theologica, 2a–2ae. clxviii. 2

1004. It is against reason to be burdensome to others, showing no amusement and acting as a wet blanket. Those without a sense of fun, who never say anything ridiculous, and are cantankerous with those who do, these are vicious, and are called grumpy and rude.

Summa Theologica, 2a–2ae. clxviii. 4

[1] *Ethics*, 1128^{a}1.

XVIII

Justice[1]

1005. A moralist should be more profoundly concerned with friendship than with justice.

330, 332   Commentary, *VIII Ethics, lect.* 1

1006. Justice without mercy is cruelty, mercy without justice goes out into waste.

Commentary, *in Matthaeum, v.* 2

I. THE OBJECTIVE STANDARD

1007. Justice directs our deeds with regard to other people under the aspect of what is owing to them; friendliness under the aspect of what is demanded by pleasantness and courtesy and generosity.

330, 1088   *Summa Theologica,* 2a–2ae. xxiii. 3, *ad* 1

1008. While the other virtues perfect a man's own personal state, justice stands out as rendering another man his due. What is correct in their activity is measured by reference to the doer, but what is correct in justice leaves aside this consideration and is measured by what

[1] Justice implies an equilibrium between different things. The mean of virtue is judged according to an amount set by an external measure, not, as in the other virtues, largely by the disposition of the person engaged. In its narrowest sense justice is between equals and pays what is owing. Yet there are many situations when fairness is demanded though one of these two conditions is absent. The requirements of common decency, if less stiffly defined, are no less imperative than those of strict right. In the service of God, for instance, or of one's country, there is no question of equality; in generosity, cordiality, and candour there is no contract. Hence arise the various virtues, religion being the chief, which are called potential parts of justice.

is owing to another. Justice squarely meets this obligation, for instance a fair wage for work done. A deed is
termed just when it passes this fundamental test, without
reference to the mood in which it is performed, which
reference is the test for the other virtues. Rights are the
special object of justice.

880, 1068   *Summa Theologica*, 2a–2ae. lvii. 1

1009. A right may be another's due on two titles, one
from the very nature of things, this is termed natural
right; the other from agreement, either private or
public, and this is termed positive right.

1050   *Summa Theologica*, 2a–2ae. lvii. 2

1010. By common agreement human wills can establish
a right in those matters where there is no conflict with
natural justice. Wherefore, Aristotle remarks that in
their principle legal rights may be such or otherwise,
but once they are laid down it is different.[1] What is
contrary to natural right cannot be made just by human
will. *Woe to those who make iniquitous laws.*[2]

1053   *Summa Theologica*, 2a–2ae. lvii. 2, *ad* 2

1011. The precise aim of justice is the administration
of external things, not the making of them, for this is
the affair of art.

858   *Summa Theologica*, 2a–2ae. lviii. 3, *ad* 3

1012. Two main reasons why men fall short of justice
—deference to magnates, deference to the mob.

1101   Commentary, *in Job*, xxxiv, *lect.* 2

II. OWNERSHIP

1013. Whether the possession of external things is
natural to man? We proceed thus to this article.

[1] *Ethics*, 1134[b]20.   [2] Isa. x. 1.

It would seem that it is not natural for man to possess external things. For no man should arrogate to himself what belongs to God. Now dominion over all creatures is proper to God; *the earth is the Lord's,* &c.[1] Therefore the possession of external things is not natural to man.

Second objection: in expounding the words of the rich man in the parable, *I will pull down my barns and build greater, and there will I bestow all my fruits ana my goods,*[2] Basil exclaims,[3] Tell me, which are thine? Where did you take them from and bring them intc your life? Now what a man possesses naturally that can he call his own. Therefore man does not naturally possess external things.

Third objection: according to Ambrose,[4] dominion is the name of power. But man has no power over external things, for he can work no change in their natures; therefore the possession of external things is not natural to him.

But on the contrary, it is written: *thou hast subjected all things under his feet.*[5]

My own explanation begins by drawing a distinction between an exterior thing considered in its nature and in its utilization. In its nature as subject to the will of God, whose nod all things obey, it does not fall under human power. But for its utilization, man has natural ownership of external things, because through his reason and will he can employ them for human benefit. They were made on his behalf. We can argue up to this conclusion by Aristotle's reasoning from the principle that the imperfect is always for the more perfect.[6] Moreover, the rationale of this natural ownership is man's intelligence, where the image of God is found,

---

[1] Ps. xxiii. 1 (Vulgate).   [2] Luke xii. 18.
[3] Homily on Luke xii. 18.   [4] *de Fide ad Gratianum,* i. 1.
[5] Ps. viii. 8.   [6] *Politics,* 1254ª20.

as was declared at his creation: *Let us make man in our image and likeness; and let him have dominion over the fishes of the sea*, &c.[1]

Reply to the first objection: God, who has sovereign dominion over all things, has directed some of them to the sustenance of man's body; and on this account man has natural dominion over them as regards the power of using them.

To the second objection: the rich man is reproved for treating external things as belonging to him by their origin and as though he had not received them from another, namely from God.

The third objection argues from external things in their very natures, where admittedly ownership is limited to God alone.

171, 388   *Summa Theologica*, 2a–2ae. lxvi. 1

1014. Whether it is lawful for a man to possess a thing as his own? We proceed thus to this article.

It would seem that private property is not lawful. For whatever is contrary to the natural law is unlawful. Now according to the natural law all things are held in common, and the possession of property is contrary to this community of goods. Therefore it is unlawful for any man to appropriate any external thing to himself.

Secondly, the words of the rich man already quoted are expounded by Basil[2] as follows: the rich who reckon that the common goods they have seized are their own properties are like those who go in advance to the theatre excluding others and appropriating to themselves what is intended for common use. Now it would be unlawful to obstruct others from laying their hands on common goods. Therefore it is unlawful to appropriate to oneself what belongs to the community.

---

[1] Gen. i. 26.   [2] Homily on Luke xii. 18.

Thirdly, Ambrose says,[1] and he is quoted in the Decretals:[2] let no man call his own that which is common. That he is speaking of external things appears from the context. Therefore it seems unlawful for a man to appropriate an external thing to himself.

But on the contrary Augustine writes of the Apostolics, or those who gave themselves that name with extreme arrogance, who did not admit into communion persons who use marriage or possess property of their own, people such as monks and many clerics in the Catholic Church. The reason why these Apostolics were heretics was that they separated themselves from the Church by allowing no hope of salvation to those who enjoyed the use of these things which they themselves went without. Therefore it is erroneous to maintain that it is unlawful for a man to possess property.

In explanation let me declare that two elements enter into human competence in appropriating external things, the administration and the enjoyment. The first is the power to take care of them and manage them, and here it is lawful for one man to possess property: indeed it is necessary for human living and on three grounds. First, because each man is more careful in looking after what is in his own charge than what is common to many or to all; in the latter case each would shirk the work and leave to another that which concerns the community, as we see when there is a great number of servants. Secondly, because human affairs are conducted in a more orderly fashion when each man is charged with taking care of some particular thing himself, whereas there would be confusion if anyone took charge of anything indeterminately. Thirdly, because a more peaceful state is preserved when each man is contented with what

[1] *Sermo lxix*, de tempore.   [2] Dist. xlvii.

is his own. Hence we observe that quarrels arise more frequently among people who share in common and without division of goods.

The second element in human competence concerns the enjoyment of material things. Here man ought to possess them, not as his own, but as common, to the extent of being ready to communicate them to others in their need. Hence St. Paul says: *Charge the rich of this world to give easily, to communicate to others, &c.*[1]

In reply to the first objection, it should be said that community of goods is attributed to the natural law, not in the sense that natural law dictates that all possessions should be in common and that nothing should be possessed as one's own, but in the sense that the division of possessions is not made by natural law but by human agreement, which belongs to positive law. Hence private ownership is not contrary to natural law, but is an addition to it devised by human reason.

To the second objection: a man would not act unfairly if he went beforehand to the theatre in order to prepare the way for others; what is unfair is blocking the enjoyment of others from going. Similarly, a rich man does not act unlawfully if he encloses what was common at the beginning and gives others a share. But he sins if he indiscriminately excludes others from the benefit. Hence Basil says, How can you abound in wealth while another begs, unless it be that you may obtain the merit of good stewardship and he be crowned with the rewards of patience?

To the third objection: Ambrose is referring to ownership as regards enjoyment, wherefore he adds that he who spends too much is a robber.

Summa Theologica, 2a–2ae. lxvi. 2

[1] 1 Tim. vi. 17–18.

1015. The main purpose of restitution is not to mulct him who has too much, but to supply him who has too little.

Summa Theologica, 2a–2ae. lxii. 6, ad 1

1016. To lend money at usury is grave sin, not because it is forbidden, for rather is it forbidden because it is against natural justice. Consider its meaning. The word comes from *usus*: usury puts a price on a money-loan, and sells the use of money that is lent.

Reflect that different things have different uses. In some cases their use involves the consumption of their substance: the proper use of wine is to be drunk, of bread to be eaten, in both cases their substance is consumed. Similarly, the proper use of money is to be expended in return for other things; as Aristotle remarks, coins are minted to serve exchange.[1] There are other things, however, whose use does not involve the consumption of their substance. The use of a house is to serve as a dwelling, and the nature of dwelling does not require that the house should be pulled down; it is incidental whether the building is improved or becomes dilapidated from being dwelt in. So also with clothes and horses. Because such things are not necessarily consumed in their use, the thing itself and the use of it can be separately conveyed or sold. A man may sell a house and remain the tenant, or he can let the house and remain the landlord.

But in the case of things whose use is their consumption, wherever the use is granted so also is the thing itself, and conversely. When someone lends money, therefore, on the understanding that he will receive his money back and in addition demands a charge for the use of it, it is clear that he is selling separately the substance

[1] Politics, 1257ª33.

of the money and the use of it. In consequence he is selling something that does not exist, or he is selling the same thing twice, which is manifestly against the notion of natural justice. Therefore to lend money at usury is a grave kind of sin, and the same holds true with other things whose use is their consumption, such as wine and flour.

Disputations, XIII de Malo, 4

III. WAR AND PEACE

1017. There are three conditions of a just war. First, the authority of the sovereign by whose command the war is to be waged. For it is not the business of the private individual to declare war or to summon the nation. The second condition is that hostilities should begin because of some crime on the part of the enemy. Wherefore Augustine observes that a just war is wont to be described as one that avenges wrongs, when a nation or state has to be punished for refusing to make amends for the injuries done by its people or to restore what has been seized unjustly. The third condition is a rightful intention, the advancement of good or the avoidance of evil. It may happen that a war declared by legitimate authority for a just cause may yet be rendered unlawful through a wicked intention. Hence Augustine declares that the passion of inflicting harm, the cruel thirst for vengeance, a plundering and implacable spirit, the fever of turmoil, the lust of power and suchlike, all these are justly condemned in war.

Summa Theologica, 2a–2ae. xl. 1

1018. If one man be at concord with another because he is coerced by the fear of penalty and not of his own free will, then his condition is not one of peace.

Summa Theologica, 2a–2ae. xxix. 1, *ad* 1

1019. By peace a man is single-minded in himself and of one mind with others.

Commentary, *in II Thessalonicenses, iii, lect.* 2

1020. Peace is opposed to conflict within oneself, as well as to conflict with others outside.

Summa Theologica, 2a–2ae. xxix. 1, *ad* 2

1021. Peace is indirectly the work of justice, which removes the obstacles, but directly it is the work of friendship.

492 *Summa Theologica,* 2a–2ae. xxix. 3, *ad* 3

1022. Peace is not a virtue, but the fruit of virtue.

Summa Theologica, 2a–2ae. xxix. 4

IV. RELIGION

1023. Religion is neither a theological nor an intellectual virtue. It is a moral virtue, a part of justice, exhibiting a measure of conduct, not tested by emotion, but by the fairness of the actions we offer to God. There is not a sheer equality in it, for we cannot offer God what is due to him, but a relative equality is present, proportionate to human power and divine acceptance. There can be extravagance about religion, not by the circumstance of *how much,* but by other circumstances, for instance, if worship be offered to an unbefitting object, or at improper times, or according to other unsuitable circumstances.

1007 *Summa Theologica,* 2a–2ae. lxxxi. 5, *ad* 3

1024. Religion has two kinds of acts: some are proper and immediate, whereby a man elicits what is directed solely to God, thus to adore and to offer sacrifice. Others proceed from other virtues commanded by religion and directed to the reverence of God, thus to visit children and widows in their tribulation, which is an activity elicited by mercy, and to keep oneself unspotted from the world, which is elicited by temperance, but may be dictated by religion.

Summa Theologica, 2a–2ae. lxxxi. 1, *ad* 1

1025. It is one thing to serve God, another to make an offering in recognition of a liability: the former is common to all virtue, the latter is peculiar to religion.

Commentary, *III Sentences*, IX. i. 1. *ii, ad* 2

1026. The prayer of which we speak here is an act of intelligence, not of will.

Summa Theologica, 2a–2ae. lxxxiii. 1

1027. The interpreter of our desire before God.

Summa Theologica, 2a–2ae. lxxxiii. 9

1028. We use language with God, not to manifest our thoughts to him, for he is the searcher of hearts, but to induce reverence in ourselves and others.

Summa Theologica, 2a–2ae. xci. 1

1029. There are three hoary errors on the subject of prayer. Some maintain that human affairs are not ruled by divine providence, and consequently to worship and pray to God is silly. Others maintain that everything happens of necessity, whether from the immutability of providence or from cosmic determinism or from the system of interacting causes; they also rule out the usefulness of prayer. A third group is of the opinion that while human affairs are indeed ruled by providence and are not the result of necessity, nevertheless the disposition of divine providence is variable and can be swayed by petitions and suchlike. All these postulates we have already disproved. In urging the importance of prayer we should neither load the course of human events with necessity nor yet reckon that the dispositions of the divine plan can be changed.

The matter will be made clearer if we consider that divine providence settles not merely what effects shall come about, but also in what manner and from what causes. Human acts should be numbered among the operative factors. Man must needs act, not in order to change the divine dispositions, but in order to execute them according to the order arranged. The situation is very much the same with respect to natural causes. Such is the case with prayer; we do not pray in order to change the divine disposition, but that we may ask for that which God has arranged to be granted.

334   *Summa Theologica,* 2a–2ae. lxxxiii. 2

1030. Religiosity—religion observed beyond measure.
Commentary, *III Sentences,* IX. i. 1. *iii, ad* 3

1031. Every moral virtue lies in a mean between extremes, and two classes of vice correspond to each of them, one by excess, the other by defect. Excess is not taken merely according to quantity, but also to other circumstances; with some virtues, such as magnificence or magnanimity, the contrary vices are excessive, not because they reach to something bigger for in fact they stoop to less, but because they go too far by not attending to persons and conditions. Thus, superstition is a vice against religion by excess, not that it shows more worship than does true religion, but because worship is offered to the wrong objects or at the wrong time or in the wrong manner.

877   *Summa Theologica,* 2a–2ae. xcii. 1

1032. When in worship there is anything unbefitting the glory of God, when it neither helps man to God

nor disciplines inordinate desire, or when it is against
the rubrics and common custom, then it must be dismissed as so much waste and superstition.

Summa Theologica, 2a–2ae. xciii. 2

1033. Much harm is done by asserting or denying
points irrelevant to religious doctrine as though true
religion were committed to them.

Opusc. xxii, *Declaratio xlii Quaestionum ad
Magistrum Ordinis*, Introduction

1034. Hypocrites are rarely so consummate but that
their wickedness is discovered by word or deed. They
may be guarded in their deliberate conduct, but sudden
emergencies and frustrations find them out. So also
their true colours are revealed when they are thwarted,
and when they have obtained what they desire.

Commentary, *in Matthaeum, vii, lect.* 2

XIX

Law[1]

1035. Law is not right exactly, but the norm of right.

1007   *Summa Theologica*, 2a–2ae. lvii. 1, *ad* 2

1036. As the leading purpose of human law is to bring about the friendship of men among themselves, so divine law is chiefly intended to establish men in friendship with God.

942   *Summa Theologica*, 1a–2ae. xcix. 2

[1] Mind is the primary authority, and so the first emphasis is on the reasonableness of law. It is not a dictate of desire enjoying the might to take advantage of opportunity, but an intelligent plan directing human activity to happiness. No precept has any binding force except in the measure that the eternal ideas in the mind of God are reflected. Yet though the ultimate motive is to lead to personal happiness, the immediate object of public law is to establish the general conditions which make the good life possible. Law is for the common good, and when the common good is taken as the community we meet another emphasis; the need of economy in the making of human laws. These pragmatic and approximate dispositions, less august and searching than the divine and natural precepts, to which they are related less as the deductions of legal science than as the inventions of political art, are designed for what happens in the majority of cases. Though binding in conscience, they are bounded by the field of official justice and public peace. The consequences are that legality in its narrow sense needs to be supplemented by other virtues, and especially to be enlivened by the special virtue of equity. A long and detailed period in the *Summa Theologica* is devoted to the Mosaic legislation; it is a prelude to the study of the Gospel law of love, which bursts out all the fresher and freer for the sustained burden of the older law.

I. CONCEPT OF LAW

1037. The definition of law—an ordinance of reason made for the common good by the public personage who has charge of the community, and promulgated—can be gathered from the four following paragraphs.

Summa Theologica, 1a–2ae. xc. 4

1038. First of all, law is a defined measure or rule by which we are led to act or withheld from acting. The rule and measure of human activity is the reason, the first principle of human activity, whose function it is to direct means to ends. In every class the first principle is the rule and measure of all else. Consequently law is something pertaining to the reason. Though reason itself receives its impulse from the will, for the reason issues its commands about means because the end is willed, nevertheless, the willing of what is commanded must be regulated by the reason to be endowed with the strength of law: this reasonableness must be read into the dictum that the will of the prince has the force of law;[1] otherwise would it be lawlessness rather than law.

700, 775, 801   *Summa Theologica,* 1a–2ae. xc. 1, *c. & ad* 3

1039. Secondly, as the reason is the first principle of human acts so also, within the reason, one interest works as the principle to others, and to this chief and main interest law must be referred. The first principle of the practical reason is our ultimate end, or happiness; law is chiefly concerned with planning for this. Since each part is for its whole as imperfect for perfect, and one individual is part of the perfect community, law is engaged mainly with the scheme of common happiness.

---

[1] The *Lex Regia*, usually so quoted in its truncated form, as a defence of absolute sovereignty.

Therefore Aristotle mentions both happiness and the political group when he says that those laws are called just which produce and preserve happiness and its particulars for the body politic.[1] For the State is the perfect community.[2] Every law is ordered to the common good, and a precept has the force of law only when it serves this community benefit.[3]

725, 1107   *Summa Theologica*, 1a–2ae. xc. 2

1040. To direct affairs for the common good is reserved to the whole people or to its vicegerent. So too the power to enact laws belongs either to the whole people or to the public authority who is the guardian of the community.

1017, 1097   *Summa Theologica*, 1a 2ae. xc. 3

1041. To lay an obligation a law must be applied to the men who have to be regulated, and this means that it must be brought to their knowledge by promulgation.

Summa Theologica, 1a–2ae. xc. 4

1042. No one is obliged to obey a precept unless he be reasonably informed about it.

812, 813   Disputations, xvii *de Veritate*, 3

1043. Divine providence extends to all things. Yet a special rule applies where intelligent creatures are involved. For they excel all others in the perfection of their nature and the dignity of their end: they are masters of their activity and act freely, while others are more acted on than acting. They reach to their destiny by their own proper activity, that is by knowing and

[1] *Ethics*, 1129^{b}17.

[2] Perfect, i.e. self-contained. *Politics*, 1252^{a}5.

[3] A command of the head of a family group, or of the superior of an association within the political community, is not technically a law.

loving God, whereas other creatures show only some traces of this likeness. Now in any undertaking the procedure varies according to the purpose intended and the situation that has to be met, as the method of art varies according to the end proposed and the material employed. Consequently there is one kind of order for rational creatures under divine providence and another for irrational creatures.

To begin with, rational creatures are governed for their own benefit, whereas other creatures are governed for the sake of men. Men are principals, not merely instruments. It is true that parts are for the whole, not the whole for the parts. But rational creatures have an affinity to the whole, for, in a sense, each is all. They are not made for anyone's utility.

Providence directs rational creatures for the welfare and growth of the individual person, not just for the advantage of the race. Many activities flourish that cannot be accounted for by the general urge of nature, as is evidenced by the fact that human inclinations are not the same for all, but are various in different individuals. Actions have a personal value, and are not merely from and for human nature.

To crown his natural appetites man is given a directive for his personal acts, and this we call law. Law is the reason and rule of activity, and therefore is reserved to those who can know the reason of what they do.

The intent of the divine law given to man is to lead him to God. The will cleaves to another either from love or from fear. But there is a great difference between these motives. In the case of fear the first consideration is not the loved object itself but something else, namely, the evil that would impend but for its presence. In the case of love the union is sought for the very sake of the beloved. What is for its own sake is more primary than what is for an outside reason. Hence, love is our strongest union with God, and this above all is intended by the divine law.

The entire purpose of the lawgiver is that man may love God.

334, 956, 1095, 1123   III *Contra Gentes*, 111–16

II. ETERNAL AND NATURAL LAW[1]

1044. The idea existing in God as the principle of the universe and lying behind the governance of things has the force of law. Because naught in the divine reason is conceived in time, for the plan *was set up from eternity, and of old before the earth was made*,[2] therefore is it called the eternal law.

160, 239, 956   *Summa Theologica*, 1a–2ae. xci. 1

---

[1] Eternal law is the source and exemplar of all derivative law, which may be divided as follows:
{ natural law;
{ positive law.
Natural law descends from the primary precepts to conclusions more or less cogent and admitted according to their closeness to moral first principles. Some of these conclusions are approximately equated with the *jus gentium* of Roman jurisprudence, though their legal condition verges into that of positive law. Positive law can be divided according to the person of the legislator into:
{ divine positive law, e.g. the law of Moses;
{ human law, which may be subdivided:
      { canon law;
      { civil law.
Precepts of the natural law may be backed by positive enactment. The supernatural laws of grace respect the above division; their mode is predominantly that of the natural laws, though their object and purpose surpass the range of the human reason. Ecclesiastical law may include civil law dealing with church matters.
[2] Prov. viii. 23.

1045. Some have believed that all justice is arbitrary and not in the nature of things, and have consequently judged injustice accordingly.

Commentary, in Romanos, v, lect. 4

1046. All plans of inferior government should be modelled on the eternal law, since it is the prototype. Hence Augustine says that in temporal law there is nothing just and lawful save what man has drawn from the eternal law.[1]

153, 1096   *Summa Theologica,* 1a–2ae. xciii. 3

1047. Since law is a rule and a measure, it can be in a person in two ways: either as in the ruler and measurer or as in the ruled and measured. All things subject to divine providence are ruled and measured by the eternal law, and consequently it is clear that somehow they share in the eternal law, for under its influence they have their propensities to their appropriate activities and ends. Among all the rest, rational creatures most superbly come under divine providence, by adopting the plan and providing for themselves and for others. Thus they share in the eternal reason and responsibly pursue their proper affairs and purposes. This communication of the eternal law to rational creatures is called the natural law. The natural light of the reason, by which we discern what is right and wrong, is naught else but the impression on us of divine light.

344, 360, 1095   *Summa Theologica,* 1a–2ae. xci. 2

1048. Natural right is contained in the eternal law primarily, and in the natural judicial faculty of human reason secondarily.

803   *Summa Theologica,* 1a–2ae. lxxi. 6, *ad* 4

[1] *de Libero Arbitrio,* i. 6.

1049. The precepts of the natural law are to the practical reason what the first principles of science are to the theoretical reason.

806 *Summa Theologica,* 1a–2ae. xciv. 2

1050. Natural right is what is fitting and commensurate to man's very nature. This may come about in two ways. First, without deliberate adjustment, as male is adapted to female for generation and parent to child for comfort in the very nature of things.[1] Secondly, by a judgement of the consequences. Take ownership for example: in the abstract there is no reason why a field should belong to this man rather than to that man; but if you consider its development and peaceful exploitation, then a piece of property may well be allocated to one rather than to another. To apprehend a thing absolutely and apart from its implications is not peculiar to man; to some degree it is present in animals as well. Taken in this sense, natural right is common to us and the other animals. But for the ordinary and rational human decencies more factors have to be allowed for. To appreciate a situation with an eye to how things will work out in practice is proper to the human reason. Natural rights may be dictated from a judgement of the consequences. The ensuing regulations may not require special legislation, for they are established by the evidence of their reasonableness.

1013, 1014 *Summa Theologica,* 2a–2ae. lvii. 3, *c.* & *ad* 3

III. POSITIVE LAW

1051. Law is a dictate of the practical reason, whose processes are similar to those of the theoretical reason. Both proceed from principles to conclusions. In the

---

[1] Ulpian, *Institutes,* D. i. 1. 2–3.

theoretical reason the conclusions of the different sciences, which are not naturally self-evident but discovered by effort, are based on first principles. Similarly the practical reason proceeds to make concrete the precepts of the natural law, which are like general and indemonstrable principles. These decisions are called human laws, so long as they fulfil the four conditions essential to law.

1037   *Summa Theologica*, 1a–2ae. xci. 3

1052. All laws derive from the eternal law to the extent that they share in right reason.

    61, 62, 63   *Summa Theologica*, 1a–2ae. xciii. 3

1053. Note that a regulation may be derived from the natural law in two ways, either as a conclusion or as a particular application. In the first case the process is similar to that of a demonstrative science, in the second case to that of art, as when common forms are given a particular shape; for example, when an architect builds a house in a special style. So some precepts are inferred from the natural law as conclusions, thus *thou shalt not kill* comes from *thou shalt not harm*. But others relate to the natural law as determinate embodiments; for though it may declare that criminals should be punished, the natural law does not settle the character of the penalty.

Both processes are at work in human law. Laws that are declared as conclusions have their force from the natural law as well as from enactment. But laws that are decreed as applied decisions have their force from human legislation.[1]

    24, 105, 855, 968   *Summa Theologica*, 1a–2ae. xcv .2

[1] According to this distinction, the jurist and statesman have a field of action that is not a department of moral science.

1054. A written code contains but does not institute natural right, where the force comes from nature, not from legality. Positive law contains and institutes a written code, giving it the weight of authority.

Summa Theologica, 2a–2ae. lx. 5

1055. In divine as in human law, some things are commanded because they are good, or forbidden because they are evil. Others again are good because they are commanded, or evil because forbidden.

Summa Theologica, 2a–2ae. lvii. 2, *ad* 3

1056. A human act that is faulty and a sinful kind of act is wrong under any circumstances whatsoever. An act of vice, forbidden by a negative precept, is never to be committed by anyone. By contrast, in an act of virtue, which is commanded by an affirmative precept, many factors have to conspire to make it right, and so what falls under an affirmative precept need not be complied with persistently and in every case, but only when the due conditions of persons, time, place, and situation demand its observance.[1]

793   Disputations, *de Correctione Fraterna*, 1

1057. Human law is imposed on a crowd of men most of whom are not perfect in virtue. Therefore it does not forbid all vices, from which the virtuous keep themselves, but only the graver ones which the majority can avoid, and chiefly those that are damaging to others and on prevention of which depends social stability.

Summa Theologica, 1a–2ae. xcvi. 2

1058. Human law cannot forbid all and everything that is against virtue: it is enough that it forbids deeds

---

[1] For example, a man must never be murdering, but is not always bound to be keeping holy the sabbath day.

against community life; the remainder it tolerates almost as if they were licit, not indeed because they are approved, but because they are not punished.

Summa Theologica, 2a–2ae. lxxvii. 1, *ad* 1

1059. Every act of every virtue is not commanded by human law, but only those that can be enjoined for the sake of the public good.

1107   *Summa Theologica*, 1a–2ae. xcvi. 3

1060. The immediate end of human law is men's own utility.

1099   *Summa Theologica*, 1a–2ae. xcv. 3

1061. In this life there is no punishment for punishment's sake. The time of last judgement has not yet come. The value of human penalties is medicinal and in so far as they promote public security or the cure of the criminal.

485   *Summa Theologica*, 2a–2ae. lxviii. 1

1062. Nobody can be excommunicated except for grave sin, which is an act. Now usually an act is not done by the whole community, but by particular persons acting for themselves. Therefore persons belonging to a community may be excommunicated, but not the community itself. Even in those cases when an act is performed by a whole group, as for instance when several men haul at a boat which nobody by himself is able to shift, it is not likely that a whole community can so consent in evil but that some dissent. It is not God's way, who is judge of all the earth, *to slay the righteous with the wicked*.[1] And so the Church, which should model its judgements accordingly, has cautiously

---

[1] Gen. xviii. 25.

enough made the statute[1] that a whole community should not be excommunicated, lest when gathering up the tares the wheat also be rooted up with them.[2]

302, 1081   Commentary, *IV Sentences*, xviii. ii. 3. *ii*

1063. The practical reason deals with activities in singular and contingent situations. Unlike the theoretical reason it does not determine necessary truths. Consequently human laws cannot have the unerring quality of scientifically demonstrated conclusions. Not every rule need possess final infallibility and certainty; as much as is possible in its class is enough.

29, 965   *Summa Theologica*, 1a–2ae. xci. 3, *ad* 3

1064. Aristotle remarks that the same precision is not to be sought in every topic.[3] In contingent matters that certitude suffices which is true in the majority of cases, though now and then it may fall short.

55   *Summa Theologica*, 1a–2ae. xcvi. 1, *ad* 3

1065. Human authority can legislate only where it can judge. It cannot judge about man's inner motions which are hidden, but only about external behaviour which is manifest. Nevertheless, the good life requires rightness in both. Therefore human law, which cannot adequately encourage or restrain our internal activity, needs to be supplemented by a divine law which can.

Summa Theologica, 1a–2ae. xci. 4

1066. Human laws are proportioned to the common good, which is built up from many personalities, businesses, and occasions. Law must regard them all. Moreover, the well-being of the community is secured

[1] A reference to the ruling of Pope Innocent IV in 1246 that the supreme punishment for corporate delict, or so-called collective guilt, was henceforth illegal.

[2] Matt. xiii. 29.   [3] *Ethics*, 1094[b]13.

by this manifold activity, not for a short time, but over a stretch of centuries through a succession of citizens. Therefore human law makes general regulations rather than particular precepts.

Summa Theologica, 1a–2ae. xcvi. 1

IV. EQUITY

1067. Wisdom differs from mere science in looking at things from a greater height. The same holds true in practical matters. Sometimes a decision has to be taken that cannot follow the common rules of procedure; the situation then has to be appreciated beyond the contriving of conventional prudence. Consequently a higher judging virtue is called for, that kind of prudence called *gnome*, or the ability of seeing through things.

1, 65, 794   *Summa Theologica*, 2a–2ae. li. 4

1068. Laws are laid down for human acts dealing with singular and contingent matters which can have infinite variations. To make a rule to fit every case is impossible. Legislators have to attend to what happens in the majority of cases and should frame their laws accordingly. In some cases the observance of these enactments would upset the balance of justice and be against the common good intended by the law. For example, the law commands that deposits should be returned, but this, though just in most cases, may sometimes be damaging, as when a weapon is returned to a raging maniac. To follow the law as it stands would be wrong; to leave it aside and follow what is demanded by fairness and the common benefit will then be right. To such issues is directed the special virtue of *epieikeia*, which we call equity.[1]

Summa Theologica, 2a–2ae. cxx. 1

[1] *Ethics*, 1137ª31.

1069. The human mind may flatly declare a general truth on matters admitting no exception. But this is not possible in contingent matters. Here there is a usual standard, but in some cases it is not verified. Human deeds, about which laws are passed, belong to this class. Now since the law-maker must deal in general terms, because of the impossibility of comprehending all particular instances, and since his general ruling cannot square with every case, he takes what happens in the great majority of cases, well aware that his directive will fail in some instances. A zoologist says that the human hand has four fingers and a thumb, and yet he recognizes that a freak may display fewer or more.

Commentary, *V Ethics, lect.* 16

1070. When the disciples picked ears of corn on the sabbath they were excused from breaking the law by necessity of hunger. Nor did David transgress the law when he took the loaves it was illegal for him to eat.[1]

Summa Theologica, 3a. xl. 4, *ad* 3

1071. What equity departs from is the letter of the law, not from plain justice. Equity should not be contrasted with just severity, which is a stickler for the letter of the law when that is demanded, not otherwise, for then stiffness would be vicious.

Summa Theologica, 2a–2ae. cxx. 1, *ad* 1

1072. The judgement that the letter of the law is not to be followed in certain given circumstances is not a criticism of the law, but an appreciation of a particular situation that has cropped up.

Summa Theologica, 2a–2ae. cxx. 1, *ad* 2

---

[1] Positive, or disciplinary, laws do not bind when virtue would suffer from their observance.

1073. In matters of doubt there is room for legal interpretation. Yet here it is illegal to depart from the letter of the law without consulting the decision of sovereign authority in the state. Some issues, however, require instant action, not interpretation.

Summa Theologica, 2a–2ae. cxx. 1, *ad* 3

1074. Equity is a kind of justice. A universal nature can be predicated of any one of its specific kinds, though the field is narrowed.[1] Yet there are two manners of essential predication. A general nature may be predicated with the same meaning of different types, thus *animal* of *horse* and *bull*. Or it may be predicated of different realities with a difference of primary and secondary sense, thus *being* of *substance* and *accident*.

Equity is authentic justice, and possesses the character of justice in a more primary sense than does legalistic justice.[2] Legal-mindedness should be directed by equity, which provides a higher rule for human activity.

270, 280   *Summa Theologica*, 2a–2ae. cxx. 2

[1] Thus the full essential meaning, but not the full extent, of *animal* is contained in *horse*.

[2] Equity, in other words, is here taken not as a department of justice, but as the peak of justice.

XX

Community and Society[1]

1075. Solitude is like poverty, an instrument for perfection, not its essence.

To embark on a solitary life without proper training beforehand is very risky.

963 *Summa Theologica*, 2a–2ae. clxxxviii. 8

[1] Under the influence of the civil lawyers, State sovereignty was becoming stylized apart from the people; at the same time the canonists and 'Augustinist' theologians were tending to shift all allegiance to the ecclesiastical authority. Both secularists and clericals are enveloped by the position St. Thomas takes up; though he has little to say about the relations of the *Sacerdotium* and *Imperium*, and never considers the Church and the State as separate and competing organizations. In the conflicts between the spiritual and temporal powers, broken shadows are cast from the more fundamental debate, between the life of a person knowing no bounds and his regulation by the needs of his group. On one side he departs from the traditional doctrine that political subordination is an arrangement forced on men because of their sinfulness; together with the naturalism of Aristotle, he recovered the political temper of loyalty to the present city; the State is no mere conventional makeshift, but a natural fulfilment, the object, not just the occasion, of virtue. On the other side he insists on the rights of conscience and on the relationship of men as persons to God, the universal good transcending the collectivity, without intervention from anything less however large. Though nothing like a programme is offered, two lines of approach may be sketched to the question of the claims of the common good as against any private good. Corresponding to the conception of the universe after the fashion of an organic whole, the political community is taken as a collective group demanding at need the sacrifice of parts. Corresponding to the conception of an association after the fashion of a partnership, the political society is taken in the suppler and more distributive terms of a union of friendship, based on possession by knowledge rather than by physical appropriation. The former calls for the surrender of private inclination and is

1076. The effects of love should be shown as well as felt.

945   Commentary, *ad Romanos, xii, lect.* 2

1077. Despite the company of angels and blessed souls, God would be alone and solitary were there not a plurality of persons in the divine nature. Dwelling with things of a different nature is no remedy for exile. Notwithstanding the plants and beasts in a garden, a man can be lonely there. .

196, 198   *Summa Theologica,* 1a. xxxi. 3, *ad* 1

I. POLITICAL SCIENCE

1078. Aristotle teaches that art imitates nature on these grounds, that as origins are related to one another so correspondingly are their activities and results.[1] Now the origin of works of art is the human mind, the image and issue of the divine mind which is the origin of natural things. Therefore the processes of art should imitate the processes of nature, and works of art the works of nature. A pupil who would learn should watch how his instructor sets about making something, so that in his turn he may work with the same skill. So should the human mind be enlightened by the divine mind when it sets about making things, so should it study natural processes so that it may be in agreement with them. Hence Aristotle remarks that if art could make

swayed by might and coercive law; the latter is already passing beyond the precepts to their purpose and enjoying an intercourse where gain is unaccompanied by loss. Social and civilized groups are mixtures of these two types. Law is reason controlling force in order to reach beyond justice, and the political group should combine respect for the non-rational conditions of community with an attempt to enlarge the field of freedom and agreement.

[1] *Physics,* 194ª21.

natural things it would act like nature, and conversely, if nature could make artificial things it would act like art.[1]

Nature, however, does not finish off works of art but merely prepares the elements and after a fashion offers exemplars for the artist to match. Art for its part, while able to appreciate the works of nature, is unable to produce them. Concerning natural things the mind is contemplative, concerning artificial things it is productive as well. Science is theoretical with the former, practical and operative with the latter, without, however, violating the claims of nature.

Now natural processes develop from simple to compound things, so much so that the highly developed organism is the completion, integration, and purpose of the elements. Such indeed is the case with any whole in comparison with its parts. Similarly in building up from simple components, the practical reason starts from rudimentary and works to rounded-off realities. The human reason has at its disposal, not merely the means of human life, but also how lives should be lived when ruled by reason. Consequently the scientific genetic method applies alike when the reason would construct a ship from timbers or a house from stone and when it would organize a single community from many individuals.

There are different degrees and arrangements in community-groups, but the final and most perfect is the political fellowship which provides all that is needful for civilized life. As men are more important than the means they use, so also is the political group superior to any other grouping the human reason can know about or constitute.

Four features stand out in Aristotle's political

[1] Ibid. 199ª12.

thought; its necessity, workmanship, dignity, and method. First, its necessity. Full human wisdom, in other words philosophy, requires that a scientific statement should be attempted about anything the reason can touch. Now that kind of group called the city or State is a topic for reasoned judgement. Therefore the integrity of philosophy demands the exposition of a political doctrine and the science of citizenship.

Secondly, its workmanship. Practical science differs from theoretical science in that it is meant to work. Now political science should be classed among the practical sciences because the political community is a group which the reason shapes as well as discusses. The practical influence of the reason may be exercised in two channels; either by productive action passing into external material, and this is mainly the affair of the mechanical arts such as metal-founding or ship-building, or by immanent activity such as counselling or choosing, and this is the concern of moral science. Political science comes under moral science, for it is engaged with the ordered relationship of men among themselves, and with the morality of doing rather than the mechanics of production.

Thirdly, we may enlarge on its dignity and standing by comparison with the other practical sciences. The political community is the sovereign construction of the reason; all other groupings are subservient. The mechanical arts are busied with utilities subordinate to human lives. The higher and nobler the subject-matter, the more overriding its interest. So political science must needs be the chief and governing practical interest, since it is occupied with the most final and complete value within the present world. Therefore Aristotle notes that politics rounds off the philosophy of human nature.[1]

[1] *Ethics*, 1181^{b}15.

Fourthly, the method and system of political science. Any theoretical science reaches its conclusions about the behaviour of wholes by studying their elements and principles. The same procedure is followed by political science which studies the principles and elements in the community in order to explain the reaction of the whole group to the various influences at work. Moreover, because it is a practical science, it shows how each part may be developed within the whole.

612   Commentary, *I Politics, lect.* 1

1079. Political ideals will vary according to men's views on human destiny. Those who are persuaded that the purpose of life is pleasure, or power, or honour, will reckon that State best arranged in which they can live comfortably, or acquire great wealth, or achieve great power and lord it over many. Others who think that the crowning good of virtue is the purpose of our present life will want an arrangement under which men can live virtuously and peaceably together. In short, political judgement will be settled by the sort of life a man expects and proposes to lead by living in community.

63   Commentary, *II Politics, lect.* 1

1080. Always remember that political science is supreme, not unconditionally, but in relation to the other practical sciences which deal with human matters and whose purposes are social. For theology, which considers the final end of the entire universe, is of all sciences the most important.

28, 33   Commentary, *I Ethics, lect.* 2

II. THE NATURAL COMMUNITY

1081. Man is a social animal, having many wants he cannot supply for himself. He is born into a group by nature. By living with others he is helped to the good life. And this on two heads.

First, as regards necessities without which life cannot be lived, he is supported by the domestic group. He depends on his parents for his birth, feeding, upbringing. Each member of the family helps the others.

Secondly, as regards the conveniences without which life cannot be lived well, he is helped by the civil group, both for material benefit, for the State provides public services beyond the means of one household, and for moral advantage, thus public authority can check young criminals when paternal warnings go unheeded.

Bear in mind that family and civil groups are unities, not because they are single organisms, but because they are composed of different substances arranged in order; consequently there is a proper activity for a part of such a whole, and this is not a group-activity; a soldier may have interests that are no part of army life and discipline. Conversely the group as a whole manifests operations which are not proper to any of its members, for instance the tactical conduct of an army in battle or the general handling of a ship.

For there are other wholes which are closer unities. The parts are continuous, compacted together, or combining to constitute one nature, and the result is one thing simply speaking, or one substance. In such cases no part is active without the whole being engaged. Movements of parts and of wholes involve one another, and consequently they should be discussed by one and the same science.

In treating of artificial wholes the same department of science does not deal with the whole as well as with the parts. On this account moral science is divided into three sections: the first is individual and takes the activity of one man as directed to his own personal end;

the second, termed economic, takes the functional purpose of the family; and the third, termed political, takes the operations of the civilian group.

533, 1062   Commentary, *I Ethics, lect.* 1

1082. Well-adjusted home and social relationships are indispensable for the proper welfare of each singular person. Nevertheless, domestic and political prudence do not supply the want of personal prudence.

965   Commentary, *VI Ethics, lect.* 7

1083. To be a social and political animal[1] living in a crowd is even more natural to man than to the other animals. His inherited needs declare this dependence. Nature provides food for other animals, covering, weapons of defence, teeth and claws, or at least swiftness of flight. But with man it is different; instead he is endowed with his reason by which he can contrive these aids. Yet to see to all of them is beyond any one man's power; alone he cannot dispatch the business of living. Consequently that he should dwell in association with many is according to his nature.

Furthermore, other animals have an inborn ingenuity with regard to what is beneficial or harmful; a sheep instinctively recognizes that a wolf is a menace, and other animals similarly take advantage of medicinal herbs and other things needful to life. But man's inbred knowledge about these matters is limited to general principles; he has to take pains to work from them to the provision of his needs in each and every case. One solitary man cannot discover everything for himself. He must combine in a team, so that one may help another and different men be reasonably engaged in different jobs, one in medicine, another in this, another in that.

[1] Note the addition of *social* to Aristotle's *political*.

This is made plain by the fact that it is peculiar to man to use language, through which he can adequately disclose his thoughts to another. Other animals may express their common emotions to one another, a dog by barking and other animals by appropriate signs. But man is more communicative, even more so than the gregarious animals, such as storks, ants, and bees. With this in mind, Solomon says: *It is better that two should be together than solitary; for they gain by their mutual companionship.*[1]

626   Opusc. XI, 1 *de Regimine Principum ad Regem Cypri*, 1

1084. The greater the friendship the more permanent it should be. The greatest friendship is that between man and wife; they are coupled not only by physical intercourse, which even among animals conduces to a certain sweet friendship, but also for the sharing of domestic life. In sign whereof is it declared: *a man should leave father and mother for the sake of his wife.*[2]

961   III *Contra Gentes*, 123

1085. Marriage is called true when it achieves its proper perfection. The perfection of anything is two-fold, primary and secondary. The first consists in a thing's form, which constitutes it as a thing of a definite kind. The second consists in the activity through which in some manner it reaches its end. The form of marriage lies in an inseparable union of minds by which either is unalterably plighted to serve the other loyally. The end of marriage is the begetting and rearing of children.

Summa Theologica, 3a. xxix. 2

1086. Promiscuity is contrary to human nature. Intimacy should be reserved to one man with one

[1] Eccles. iv. 9.   [2] Gen. ii. 24.

particular woman, with whom he remains, not briefly, but for a long period, or even for good: this is called matrimony.

Summa Theologica, 2a–2ae. cliv. 2

1087. Friendship demands a certain equality. While a child's right to a father rules out one woman having many husbands at the same time, it is in the name of liberal friendship that one man is not allowed to have many wives. The relationship would otherwise be servile. This is borne out by experience, for when custom allows polygamy wives are treated like servants.

943   III *Contra Gentes*, 123

1088. When we talk about what is right and just we suppose commensurateness to another. But *another* has two senses. First, to mean someone who is simply other, as being altogether distinct; this appears between two independent citizens though both are under the common ruler of the State, and here justice may enter in an unqualified sense.[1] Secondly, to mean someone who is not completely other, for in a sense two people merge into one another; thus in human affairs a child belongs to his father as being somehow a part of his father[2] and a slave belongs to his master as being his instrument and not a principal.[3] Since there is no independence in these cases unqualified justice does not enter, but a special sort of justice, called respectively the *paternal* and the *dominative*.

Though wife is joined to husband and is compared to his own body,[4] she is, nevertheless, more independent of him than child of parents or slave of master. She is taken into the living companionship of marriage. The idea of justice is stronger between husband and wife than

[1] *Ethics*, 1134ª27.   [2] Ibid. 1161ᵇ23.
[3] *Politics*, 1253ᵇ33.   [4] *Eph.* v. 28.

between parents and child, or between master and slave.[1] All the same the rights involved belong rather to domestic fairness than to political justice, because both are caught up in the common life of the household.

Summa Theologica, 2a–2ae. lvii. 4

1089. Aristotle recognized a twofold political justice, natural and legal.[2] This corresponds to the division between natural and civil rights made by the Roman jurists. A complication, however, comes in when the term *civil* is given the same meaning as *political*. For then what Aristotle discusses as a general heading, divided into what is natural and what is conventional, is restricted by the jurists to one department, for they treat civil law as a part of positive law.[3]

It is well to notice that the term *political* or *civil* is rather differently employed by philosophers and by lawyers. Whereas the former go to social usage, and take the politically or civilly just as being that which in fact the citizens enjoy, whether it be established by nature in the mind or instituted by legislation, the latter seek its legal titles, and take it as being that which the city has enacted for its own government.[4]

Commentary, V Ethics, lect. 12

III. EDUCATION

1090. A teacher must not be pictured as pouring his knowledge into the learner, as though particles of the same knowledge could pass from one subject to another.

646   *Disputations*, xi *de Veritate*, 1, *ad* 6

---

[1] *Ethics*, 1134ᵇ15.   [2] *Ethics*, 1134ᵇ19.
[3] *Positive*, i.e. as contrasted with *natural*, not with *negative*.
[4] St. Thomas notes that, when he wrote, *jus* was the lawyer's term, *justum* the moralist's.

1091. The same difference of opinion is acute on three connected points, namely on the bringing forth of forms into being, on the acquisition of the virtues, and on the learning of knowledge.

Some say that the forms of sensible things come completely from outside, that is from a separate substance or form: this they call the giver of forms or active intellect, adding that all lesser factors help merely to prepare the material for the reception of a form. According to Avicenna, the virtuous habits are not of our own making, though we can remove the obstacles to them; likewise scientific knowledge is caused by an intelligence above us, and intelligible forms flow into our mind from this universal intellect.

Others profess the diametrically opposite doctrine that forms are innate and do not come from outside, though an external cause may well serve to release them. They hold that natural forms are latent in matter, and that an efficient cause works merely to bring them into the open. So also with virtuous habits: these, they say, are innate, and the exercise of good deeds is like rubbing away the rust covering the shine of the metal. Some also teach that the soul possesses the science of everything at its creation, and that teaching serves to remind the mind to attend to and recall the things it already knows. Learning, in their estimation, is naught else but remembering.

Neither opinion, however, is well-founded. The first cuts out proximate causes by attributing inferior effects exclusively to the first cause. It spoils the fabric of the universe spun on the connexion of causes. The first cause of its noble goodness makes other things, not only to be, but also to be causes. The second opinion is similarly unseemly, since an obstacle-removing cause amounts to no more than an accidental cause. If lower

causes served merely to unveil knowledge they would
be no better than that.

Therefore the middle and Aristotelean way is to be
preferred. Natural forms pre-exist in matter, not
actually, as the first opinion holds, but potentially.
From matter they are educed into actuality by an
extrinsic proximate cause, not by the first cause alone,
as the second opinion holds. Likewise, virtuous habits
pre-exist, not as achieved qualities of character, but as
instinctive propensities. These are the beginnings of
virtue, brought afterwards to completion by appropriate activities. It is the same with the acquisition of
knowledge: the early conceptions of the mind are like
seeds before they are cultivated. They are known
directly in the light of the active intellect through meanings abstracted from sense-objects, whether they be
simple concepts, such as being, unity, and so forth, or
whether they be judgements, such as first principles—
knowledge is planted in these seeds of meaning.
When it is raised from the knowledge of these general
truths to the actual knowledge of particular truths
(formerly known potentially and as it were in
general) then the mind is said to acquire scientific
knowledge.

Remark, however, that to natural things pre-exist-
ence may be credited in two ways: first, in the active
power of the subject, when the intrinsic principle
suffices to produce a complete actuality, as when a sick
man is restored to health by the natural forces within
him; secondly, in passive potentiality, when intrinsic
principles alone are not sufficient to bring about the
result. In the first case the extrinsic cause acts as a help,
supplying the facilities for the process to issue into act;
thus a doctor is a midwife to nature, strengthening it
and applying medicines which nature uses as instru-

ments. In the second case the extrinsic cause is the principal factor.

Now science pre-exists in the student potentially, not purely passively, but actively; otherwise a man could not acquire science on his own. As a man may be healed in two ways, either by the operation of nature alone or by that assisted by medicine, so also there is a double way of acquiring knowledge: one, when the natural reason by itself arrives at the knowledge of a truth hitherto unknown, this is called discovery; the other, when another person furnishes help, this is called discipline.

In processes where there is a mingling of art and nature, art operates in the same manner and through the same means as nature does. Nature supplies heat to warm someone suffering from cold, and so does medical art; whence art is said to imitate nature. The procedure is copied in the acquisition of scientific knowledge: in leading a pupil to discover truths a teacher follows the same method that a man would adopt in finding things out for himself. The procedure is to apply certain accepted general truths to a determinate subject, thence to particular conclusions and from them to others. Accordingly, one person is said to teach another in that he expounds his own processes of reasoning by signs, which serve as instruments for the natural reasoning of the student to arrive at conclusions previously unknown. As a doctor is said to cause health in a sick man through the operation of nature, so a teacher is said to cause science in another through the operation of the learner's natural reason. In this sense one man can be another's teacher and master.

If he proposes statements that are not developed from self-evident principles, or if he fails to make the connexion clear, he does not cause scientific knowledge, but opinion, or perhaps faith. Even so his exposition, such as it is, is based on innate principles, for it takes for granted that conclusions demonstrated from principles can be held with certainty, that contraries are to be rejected, while other topics may be left open.

500, 516, 548,   *Disputations*, XI *de Veritate*, 1
649, 650, 838

1092. An argument is not much use when it makes many suppositions.

25   II *Contra Gentes*, 38

IV. THE POLITICAL COMMUNITY

1093. If by nature men are to live together, then the group they form must needs be ruled. With many individuals each seeking what suits himself, the mass would disintegrate were there not one power within it caring for the common good. Any organism would disintegrate were there no unifying force working for the common good of all the members. Solomon says, *Where there is no governor, the people shall be scattered*,[1] and with good warrant, for private and common pull different ways. People fall apart by their private interests and come together by their common interests. Of diverse things there are diverse causes. A ruling cause therefore is required, standing apart from interests of private gain, to act for the common good of the many.

The purpose proper to a group of freemen is different from that of a group of slaves, for a freeman is his own master while a slave belongs to another. Therefore, if a group of freemen be directed by the ruler to the common good, the government will be fair and right, worthy of freemen. But if the aim be not the common

[1] Prov. xi. 14.

good, but the private benefit of the ruler, then the government will be unfair and crooked.[1] *Woe to shepherds who feed themselves*, that is, those who seek their own advantage. *Should not the sheep be fed by the shepherd?*[2]

There are three types of deviation from fair government, corresponding to the ruling class that is out to secure its own private interests. If the government is run by one man then he is called a tyrant, a word having the sense of unregulated mastery in its derivation, for a tyrant bears down by sheer force and does not guide in accordance with law; hence in antiquity a man of might was called a tyrant. If it is in the hands of a few then the régime is called an oligarchy, when several men, taking advantage of their wealth, oppress the people like a tyrant multiplied. If power is wielded by the common masses at the expense of men of property then the régime is called a democracy, when the majority amounts to a tyrant writ large.

A fair constitution is similarly graded. When the administration is conducted by the whole community, and chiefly by those ready to defend the commonwealth, the régime is called by the general name of polity. If the administration is in the hands of a few but right-minded magnates, the régime is called an aristocracy, the rule of the best, and these therefore receive the title of nobles. If the government is one man's responsibility, then he is properly named king. *And David my servant shall be king over them; and they shall have one shepherd.*[3] Hence it is essential to kingship that one man should be sovereign and that he should be a good shepherd,

---

[1] The argument turns on the difference between a slave, who is a utility, and a freeman, who is not a means to anyone's advantage.

[2] Ezek. xxxiv. 2.   [3] Ezek. xxxvii. 24.

seeking the common good of the people and not his own private profit.[1]

338, 680, 1109   Opusc. XI, 1 *de Regimine Principum*, 1

1094. Two points should be observed concerning the healthy constitution of a state or nation. One is that all should play a responsible part in the governing: this ensures peace, and the arrangement is liked and maintained by all. The other concerns the type of government; on this head the best arrangement for a state or government is for one to be placed in command, presiding by authority over all, while under him are others with administrative powers, yet for the rulers to belong to all because they are elected by and from all. Such is the best polity, well combined from the different strains of monarchy, since there is one at the head; of aristocracy, since many are given responsibility; and of democracy, since the rulers are chosen from and by the people.

1012   *Summa Theologica*, 1a–2ae. cv. 1

1095. Lordship may be taken in two senses: either as the opposite of slavery—and then a lord means somebody to whom another is subject as a slave; or by and large with reference to subjects of any kind—and then any

[1] These three classical types of political constitution, together with their three caricatures, are not dwelt on by St. Thomas. So long as the government is set on the common good, which of the three tolerable types is emphasized will depend on historical circumstances. He himself prefers a constitution well blent of all three. Elsewhere he notes that the mere numbers of the governing class do not settle the type of constitution. An aristocracy is not necessarily an oligarchy, still less a plutocracy; a democracy not necessarily the majority rule of a working class unable to enjoy leisure, still less the rule of the mob. Though he approves of *status popularis*, the word *democracy* still keeps the ugly sense it had for Plato. *Populus*, it should be noted, is not *plebs*, but includes all citizens of the commonwealth.

man who has the office of ruling and directing freemen may be called a lord. In the state of innocence one man could have been another's master in the latter sense, but not in the former.

The root of the matter is that a slave differs from a freeman because, as Aristotle says,[1] a freeman exists for himself, whereas a slave exists for another's sake. A slave-owner is one who disposes of other people for his own advantage entirely. Since each man desires his own proper benefit and feels it a grievous situation to abandon to another what belongs to himself, such domination inevitably implies hardship for the subject, and therefore would not have been present between man and man had there been no lapse into sin.

But a freeman may have a ruler over him when he is directed for his own good or for the common good. Such dominion would have existed apart from sin, and for two reasons. First, because man is instinctively a social animal, and even in a state of innocence men would have lived sociably together. When many people are involved, one man should preside to watch over the common good, for many as such exert themselves for different things, whereas one keeps a single end in view. Hence Aristotle says[2] that when many work with a common purpose we always find a unified command at the head. Secondly, pre-eminent gifts of intelligence and character would be embarrassing unless they were serviceable for others, according to St. Peter, *as every man hath received grace, ministering the same one to another*.[3] And St. Augustine speaks about the commanders, who are indeed the servants of those they seem to command, ruling not in ambition, but as bound by careful duty; not in domineering, but in nourishing

[1] *Metaphysics*, 982b26.   [2] *Politics*, 1254a28.
[3] 1 Pet. iv. 10.

pity. Thus hath nature's order prescribed, and man by God was thus created.[1]

1043   *Summa Theologica*, 1a. xcvi. 4

1096. Obedience is commanded within the limits of due observance. The duty develops according to the gradation of authorities which have power, not only over temporalities, but also spiritually over the conscience. St. Paul says,[2] *let every soul be subject unto the higher powers, for there is no power but of God.* Therefore a Christian should obey power that is from God, but not otherwise.

Power may not stem from God for two reasons: it may be defective either in its origins or in its exercise.

Concerning the first, the defect may lie either in the personal unworthiness of the man or in some flaw in the manner of obtaining high position—violence, bribery, or some other illicit practice. The former is no bar to the possession of legitimate authority; and because the very form of office is from God, who also causes the duty of obedience, it follows that subjects are bound to obey such a ruler, though as a man he is a good-for-nothing. The latter, however, is a bar, for a man who has snatched power by violence is no true superior or lord, and whoever has the ability may rightly reject him, unless perhaps the power has been subsequently legitimized by the consent of subjects or by higher authority.

The abuse of power may take two directions. Either the ruler imposes what is contrary to the purpose for which authority is instituted, for instance if he dictates vices contrary to the virtues authority is supposed to promote and sustain. In that event, not merely is a man not bound to obey, he is also bound not to obey, following

[1] *De Civitate Dei*, xix. 14–15.   [2] Rom. xiii. 1.

the martyrs, who suffered death rather than carry out the wicked decrees of tyrants. Or the ruler may make demands where his warrant does not run, for instance in exacting tributes to which he has no title, or something of the sort. In such cases a subject is not bound to obey, neither is he bound not to obey.[1]

538   Commentary, *II Sentences*, XLIV, ii. 2

1097. There can be two conditions of peoples. One is that of a free people, able to frame laws for itself. Here the consent of the people to an observance, manifested by custom, is of greater force than the authority of the prince, who does not possess the power of framing laws except in so far as he is the public authority representing the people, for though no particular person can enact laws the whole people can. The other condition is that of a people who do not enjoy the unfettered power of making their own laws or of abrogating the laws of a higher ruler. Nevertheless, even here prevailing custom obtains the force of law so long as it is permitted, and therefore approved, by those whose business it is to legislate.

Summa Theologica, 1a 2ae. xcvii. 3, *ad* 3

1098. By nature all men are equal in liberty, but not in other endowments. One man is not subordinate to another as though he were a utility. Therefore, in a state of integrity there would have been no overlord

---

[1] St. Thomas has little to say on the legal title to sovereignty. It may be noted however that his sympathies did not seem to lie with those lawyers who held that the people had irrevocably transferred their powers to the prince. He gives no support to the doctrine of the Divine Right of Kings. He is clearly opposed to political absolutism. Yet his ideal of the constitutional and representative monarch, together with his respect for order and well-distributed responsibility and property, may be read, too easily for the historian, in terms of democratic liberalism.

ship of domination such as would have abolished the liberty of subjects, but only an authority of administration without prejudice to liberty.

454   Commentary, *II Sentences*, xliv. i. 3, *ad* 1

1099. Laws are passed to ensure the smooth running of the commonwealth. Unrestricted rights are not allowed in any civil constitution. Even in a democratic state, where the whole people exercise power, rights are not absolute but relative, though from the equal liberty of all subjects under the law the state may be described as predominantly egalitarian. The statutes passed by a democracy may be just, not because they reach pure and perfect justice, but because they fit the purpose of the régime.

1057   Commentary, *V Ethics, lect.* 2

1100. There is no unfairness in dealing unequally with equal persons apart from what is strictly their due.

Disputations, iii *de Potentia*, 16, *ad* 19

1101. The disregard of the common good is greater under an oligarchy than under a democracy, where, after all, the welfare of the majority has been attempted. But sorriest of all is a tyranny where the advantage of one man is sought. As the rule of a king is best, so the rule of a tyrant is worst.

Security is banished and everything is uncertain when people are cut off from law and depend on the will, I would even say the greed, of another. A tyrant oppresses the bodies of his subjects, but, what is more damnable, he threatens their spiritual growth, for he is set on his own power, not their progress. He is suspicious of any dignity they may possess that will prejudice his own iniquitous domination. A tyrant is more fearful of good men than of bad men, for he dreads their strange virtue.

Fearful lest they grow strong and so stout of heart as no longer to brook his wicked despotism, but resolve in companionship to enjoy the fruits of peace, a tyrant is constrained to destroy good men's confidence in one another, lest they band together to throw off his yoke. Therefore he sows discord among them, and encourages dissensions and litigation. He forbids celebrations that make for good fellowship, weddings and feastings and suchlike that are wont to promote familiarity and mutual loyalty.

When they are brought up under such a régime of fear men inevitably degenerate. They become mean-spirited and averse from many and strenuous feats.

Opusc. XI, 1 de Regimine Principum, 3

1102. The man to be elected should be the best man for the task, not necessarily the person with the finest character, or the most full of charity.

VIII Quodlibet, 6

1103. It may happen that a man who is less devout or learned may serve the common good better because of his energy or capacity for taking pains or something of the sort.

Summa Theologica, 2a–2ae. lxiii. 2

1104. In fostering the well-being of the whole, which is more important than that of a part, a prudent governor can well neglect a particular fault affecting one section of the community.

459   III <i>Contra Gentes</i>, 71

1105. You have asked where your duty lies concerning the wealth that may, or may not, have come into your possession from the illegal extortions of your officials.

This is the plain answer: if it has reached your hands then you must restore it to the persons concerned if you can, otherwise you must give it to good causes or spend it for the common benefit. If it has not reached you, even if the people who have been victimized are unknown to you, you must compel your officials to make equivalent restitution, lest they make a profit from injustice.[1] Furthermore, they are to be gravely punished, so that others will be deterred from such practices for the future: as Solomon says, *smite a scorner, and the simple will beware*.[2]

Opusc. XIII, *de Regimine Judaeorum ad ducissam Brabantiae*[3]

1106. Note the various kinds of permission. First, lawful concession, as when the prior allows you to visit your parents. Second, dispensation, when he permits you to eat flesh-meat. Third, toleration, when the lesser of two evils is permitted lest a worse supervene. Fourth, indulgence, when something is permitted though the contrary is better, as when the Apostle allowed second marriage. Fifth, forbearance, as when God permits evil so that he may bring forth good.

Commentary, *in Matthaeum, v, lect.* 9

V. THE COMMON GOOD

1107. The proper effect of law is to make its subjects good, either simply speaking or in a relative sense. If the law's essential purpose is the true good, namely, the common good ruled by divine justice, it will follow that those who observe it will be good men. But if the purpose is merely the lawmaker's own profit or pleasure

---

[1] In other worlds, personal justice should govern the conduct of a man in office.

[2] Prov. xix. 25.

[3] Alix of Burgundy, wife of Henry III, Duke of Brabant.

or is repugnant to divine justice, then the effect of the enactment will not be to make men to be simply good, but to be good in a certain kind of way, namely, subservient to the régime. Such goodness can be found in thoroughly bad men: thus we may refer to a good thief, meaning an expert robber.

777, 1039, 1059   *Summa Theologica*, 1a–2ae. xcii. 1

1108. The common good of the state and the singular good of the person do not differ merely as many and one, for there is a formal difference.

Summa Theologica, 2a–2ae. lviii. 7, *ad* 2

1109. An individual who is governed for the sake of the species is not governed because of any inherent worth. But human persons come under divine providence in their own right, for the activities of rational creatures alone are divinely directed for the sake of the individual as well as of the species.

171   iii *Contra Gentes*, 113

1110. By sinning, a man falls back from the level of reason, and to that extent loses the dignity of a human person free within and existing in his own right. He falls into the slavish condition of the beasts, so that he can be disposed of and treated as a utility. Thus the scriptures express it: *man, when he was in honour, did not understand; he hath been compared to senseless beasts, and made like them;*[1] and again, *the fool shall serve the wise.*[2] Hence, though it is intrinsically wicked to kill a man who has kept his worth, nevertheless it may be right to put a criminal out of the way, as it is to kill an animal. Indeed, an evil man is worse than a brute and more harmful, as Aristotle says.[3]

474   *Summa Theologica*, 2a–2ae. lxiv. 2, *ad* 3

[1] Ps. xlviii. 21.   [2] Prov. xi. 29.
[3] *Ethics*, 1150ª7 ; *Politics*, 1253ª.

IIII. A man is not subordinate to the community in all that he is and by all that he has; hence it does not follow that every act should be recompensed by the body politic. But all that a man is and can be must be ordered to God, and therefore every act, whether good or bad, is meritorious or otherwise in his sight.

285   *Summa Theologica*, 1a–2ae. xxi. 4, *ad* 3

III2. In human affairs there is the common good, the well-being of the state or nation; there is also a human good which does not lie in the community, but is personal to each man in himself; not, however, that it is privately profitable to the exclusion of others.

457   III *Contra Gentes*, 80

III3. The common good is more important than private good when both are in the same class, but there may be a nobler private good of a different kind. Thus dedicated virginity is preferred to bodily fruitfulness.

958   *Summa Theologica*, 2a–2ae. clii. 4, *ad* 3

III4. Holy writ describes the company of the faithful sometimes as a household and sometimes as a city, between which there is a double difference: members of a household have intercourse in private matters and are guided by a father; citizens share in public transactions and are ruled by the head of the state.

Commentary, *ad Ephesios*, *ii*, *lect*. 6

III5. Two conditions are implied in a collective term: a plurality of subjects and a corporative unity, as when we speak of *a people*. In the first sense, the term *trinity of persons* is like other collective terms, but not in the second sense.

1062   *Summa Theologica*, 1a. xxxi. 1, *ad* 2

1116. When the part and the whole are in a certain sense identical, the part may to that extent claim what belongs to the whole.

Summa Theologica, 2a–2ae. lxi. 1, *ad* 2

1117. You may meet with a thing that is perfect in two ways. First, by the perfection of its own being, belonging to it according to its proper nature. Since, however, the specific being of one thing is distinct from that of another, the more committed a thing is to being itself the less it will have of sheer perfection, a share of which is displayed in things of quite different natures. Indeed, the perfection of any one thing considered in isolation is an imperfection, for one thing is merely one part of the entire integrity of the universe arising from the assembling together of many singular perfections.

But to offset this limitation there is a second mode of perfection in creatures, according to which an excellence proper to one thing may show itself in another. This is the glory of a thing that can know, to the extent that it knows. For a thing is known inasmuch as it has come home to the knower; whence Aristotle says[1] that the soul is potentially everything and it is what it is by becoming all things. So it is possible for the perfection of the whole world to exist in one thing. Such is the fullness the soul may achieve. According to philosophers, the entire system of the cosmos, complete with all its causes, may be delineated in the soul. This, they maintain, is the last end of man. We, however, set it in the vision of God, for, as Gregory remarks, for those who see him who sees everything, what is there they do not see?

585   Disputations, ii *de Veritate*, 2

[1] *de Anima*, 429ª19, ᵇ30 430ª15.

1118. Among substances the individual merits a special name, and so is termed *hypostasis, suppositum,* or *first substance.* Particular individuals have a still more special and perfect existence in rational substances who are masters of their own activity and act of themselves, unlike other things which are acted upon. Therefore singular rational substances receive the special name of *persons.*

437   *Summa Theologica,* 1a. xxix. 1

1119. Person signifies what is noblest in the whole of nature.

Summa Theologica, 1a. xxix. 2

1120. Personality means completeness, not necessarily particularity in a common nature.

Commentary, *I Sentences,* xxiii. i. 2, *ad* 4

1121. No possession is joyous without a companion.

944   Commentary, *I ad Corinthios, x, lect.* 5

1122. Beauty establishes the integrity of things in themselves, and also their communication in the whole, each in its own style, not with uniformity. The higher are shared and the lower are ennobled by this intercourse.

220   Opusc. xiv, Exposition, *de Divinis Nominibus,* iv, *lect.* 6

1123. Since all good things lead to eternal felicity as to their last end, and this is the special object of charity, it follows that charity embraces in itself all human loves, those alone excepted that are supported on sin. So that love for relations and fellow-citizens and companions voyaging together or for anybody, however associated, can be from charity and worthy of heaven.

Disputations, *de Caritate,* 7

1124. Finally, we must show that men can come to the kingdom, otherwise in vain would they hope and pray. It is possible because of the divine promise: *Fear not, little flock,* said the Lord, *for it is your Father's good pleasure to give you a kingdom.*[1] And the divine pleasure is well able to do what it disposes. *My counsel shall stand, and I will do all my pleasure.*[2] And again, *Who hath resisted his will?*[3]

Opusc. XI, *Compendium Theologiae* (II), 10

[1] Luke xii. 32.   [2] Isa. xlvi. 10.   [3] Rom. ix.

INDEX

(Numbers refer to quotations)

abstract terms, 265, 266, 435, 450, 463, 598, 710.

abstraction, 28, 559, 597, 598, 616, 642, 645, 647, 651, 652, 653.

— three degrees of, 28, 55, 56.

accidental, 436, 468, 470, 487.

— cause, 1091.

— change, 59.

— difference, 48, 559.

— form, 580.

— whole, 533, 1081.

accidents, 48, 54.

action, 113, 134, 344, 401, 487, 588.

activity, 289, 356, 578, 579.

actuality, 122, 239, 390, 432, 433, 434, 579, 593, 639, 1091.

affective knowledge, 92, 93, 94.

Alexander of Aphrodisias, 91.

Al Ghazali, 423.

allegory, 73, 516.

Amaury de Bènes, 191.

Ambrose, St., 1013, 1014.

analogical terms, 153, 215, 270, 279, 436.

analogy, 73, 151, 153, 172, 181, 189, 215, 270, 279, 280, 281, 429, 516, 655, 697, 1074.

Anaxagoras, 59, 432.

angels, 436, 504, 505, 506, 507, 627, 639.

animals, 497, 499, 533, 540, 621, 622, 628, 629, 659, 682, 703, 837, 1083.

annihilation, 407, 408, 409, 410, 488.

Anselm, St., 99, 427.

Anselmic argument, 99.

anthropomorphism, 273.

appearance, 595.

appetite, 318 sqq., 472, 668 sqq.

— natural, 213, 318, 670, 671; *see* natural desire.

— rational, 318, 670, 671, 683, 684.

— sensitive, 318, 670, 671, 824, 871, 872, 992, 996.

apprehension, simple, 56, 605, 606, 609.

aristocracy, 1093, 1094.

Aristotle, 126, 132, 137, 387, 436, 462, 520, 532, 533, 558, 559, 627, 642, 648, 650, 729, 760, 852, 878, 1013, 1014, 1078.

Aristoteleanism, 558, 826, 1091.

art, 23, 61, 117, 304, 314, 316, 318, 339, 363, 373, 383, 455, 565, 611, 784, 838, 852, 855, 856, 857, 858, 859, 860, 861, 862, 868, 876, 977, 1015, 1053, 1078, 1091.

article in *Summa Theologica*, structure of, 99, 462, 1013, 1014.

Augustine, St., 88, 161, 305, 387, 427, 462, 474, 496, 515, 516, 650, 662, 730,